JEREMY CORBYN
and the
STRANGE REBIRTH
of
LABOUR ENGLAND

JEREMY CORBYN
and the
STRANGE REBIRTH
of
LABOUR ENGLAND

FRANCIS BECKETT   MARK SEDDON

Biteback Publishing

First published in Great Britain in 2018 by
Biteback Publishing Ltd
Westminster Tower
3 Albert Embankment
London SE1 7SP
Copyright © Francis Beckett and Mark Seddon 2018

ISBN 978-1-78590-400-4

10 9 8 7 6 5 4 3 2 1

A CIP catalogue record for this book is available from the British Library.

Set in Adobe Caslon Pro

Printed and bound in Great Britain by
CPI Group (UK) Ltd, Croydon CR0 4YY

CONTENTS

ACKNOWLEDGEMENTS

The authors would like to thank in particular: Iain Dale, Martin Rowson and Matt Lyus, without whom this book may not have been possible. Nor would it have been without the support and enthusiasm of the tightly knit and dedicated Biteback team: James Stephens, Olivia Beattie, Bernadette Marron and Padraig Farrell. We should also like to thank the following for their advice, wisdom, general good nature, and indulgence: Clare Short, Jon Lansman, Peter Stefanovic, Emily Thornberry MP, Chris Kaufman, Jay Chavda, Stefan Stern, Grahame Morris MP, Ian Williams, Richard Kozul-Wright, John Cryer MP, Dan Carden MP, Jonathan Arkush, Baroness Dianne Hayter, Jeff Gold and the Working Families Party, the Democratic Socialists of America and the late, great, Rodney Bickerstaffe. And not forgetting, of course, Jon Wrobel and the wonderful staff of the Gay Hussar restaurant in Soho, London, closed for the present, but also set, we hope, for a rebirth.

INTRODUCTION

This started out as a book called *The Strange Death of Labour England*.

We were going to describe the inexorable process, which began in 1979 and continued through the Thatcher and Blair years, of dismantling the England we were brought up in, and replacing it with something much harsher, nastier and crueller; the England our children are going to have to live in because it is what the baby boomer generation have dumped on them. It was conceived over lunch in that most loved of Rabelaisian Labour canteens, the Gay Hussar Hungarian restaurant in London's Soho.

That was the book we intended to write right up to 10 p.m. on 8 June 2017. Like most people, we had begun to assume Labour's experiment with left-wing leadership would end that day in crushing defeat. This was despite the astonishing signals we were beginning to pick up on the ground, during the campaign. Yes, even seasoned optimists such as us were being ground down by the modern-day political curse; the pundits, their polls and their predictions.

Prime Minister Theresa May's gamble of calling an unnecessary general election when she thought Labour was weak and divided and headed by a leader unpopular with his MPs and the mass media looked like it was paying off with a massively increased majority. She had even kicked off her campaign in Labour Halifax. And Labour, we thought, would react to defeat by plunging rightwards. It would look for a Tony Blair lookalike to lead it, and give up all hope of reviving Labour England. It would probably look, we felt, towards David Miliband, who was clearly, once again, looking at himself.

It was a book born out of unrelieved gloom. But the very next morning, during an excited telephone call, we changed not just the title of our book, but our vision of the future. Labour England would be reborn, but it would look very different. Not the strange death, but the strange rebirth.

The title was a tribute to George Dangerfield's 1935 classic *The Strange Death of Liberal England*, and, just as Dangerfield did not mean just the Liberal Party, we didn't mean just the Labour Party.

We meant the Labour England that created, sustained and empowered the Labour Party and Labour governments; that made the country more caring, more instinctively irreverent and egalitarian, less class-ridden.

Labour England made the country what it was where we begin in 1978. The accepted narrative of this time was that this was an era of the Winter of Discontent, of unacceptable trade union power, of inflation and general mismanagement. But there is another narrative that better reflects both the truth and the Labour England of that time.

Britain had never been more equal as a society; the gap between rich and poor, never as narrow. Working-class families had jobs, often unionised jobs, which paid moderately well. Council housing was plentiful, family cars and holidays affordable. Young people actually got a chance to be creative if they wanted to before getting a job or going to college. People were, by and large, happier. They were more secure. They had a clearer idea about what was right and what was wrong.

Labour England was fundamentally a decent place. There was little time for the vulgar, idle rich, and there was respect for our public services and our public servants. Rather than make huge losses, as is the accepted narrative, the nationalised industries usually made pre-tax profits, which were ploughed back into them, and they belonged to us – the people. There was a powerful attachment to a welfare state and health service that cared for people from cradle to grave. Labour governments and the Labour Party would not have existed without Labour England and, if they had existed, they would have been powerless.

Labour England was many things.

It was the National Health Service, Labour's greatest and proudest creation. So powerful and deep was its reach into the nation's psyche that even Margaret Thatcher wouldn't dare to destroy it.

It was the trade unions. A substantial section of the workforce were members of trade unions that fought for their interests at work, achieved great advances in health and safety conditions at work, and much else besides.

It was adult education, where those without material advantages were taught politics and the humanities: the local adult education institutes, university extramural departments, the Workers' Educational Association, Morley College, the places immortalised in Lee Hall's play *The Pitmen Painters*. In the 1970s, every university worth its salt had an extramural department. Today they all have business studies departments instead.

It was second-chance education. It was Birkbeck College, London, and the polytechnics, and a few of the universities, and Ruskin College, and, famously, the City Lit in central London. The City Lit is still there, but most of the people who used to go there forty years ago could not afford it today. Ruskin College was a route out of mindless routine work for thousands of trade union members, who went there sponsored by their unions; and Ruskin is just now closing its trade union courses.

It was Harold Wilson's new Open University.

It was universities where students received grants based upon their parental income and didn't pay tuition fees. Universities that encouraged mature students, that rejoiced in the arts, that had, at their heart, the idea that education was important for the sake of it, and not just for advancing up a career ladder.

It was community schooling. The idea of free comprehensive education for all, championed by the National Union of Teachers and Anthony Crosland, was that there should be a good local primary and secondary school wherever you lived, and communities were cemented by local schools that most children attended, and most parents cared about. Today schools are expected to compete for the brightest and easiest-to-teach pupils.

It was powerful local councils, able to provide a counterbalance to government, able to take decisions on priorities, and on the shape of local education, free of the dead hand of government control imposed in the Thatcher years.

It was council houses and council estates and the communities they housed.

It was local libraries.

And, of course, it was the Labour Party at a local level, fractious, quarrelsome, but alive with self-belief.

Labour England was also that curious meeting of minds, often between self-taught (or educated by life) working-class trade unionists and middle-class liberal intellectuals. You could see that alliance in human form at Labour Party general committee meetings in places like Norwich, Oxford and Bristol. They came together describing themselves often as 'socialists' or sometimes 'social democrats'.

And we do mean Labour England, not Labour Britain. It has its counterpart in Scotland and in Wales. But that is a different story, for a different book, and best written from Scotland and Wales. We mean the place where we, and Jeremy Corbyn, and John McDonnell, recovered from our childhood illnesses in the very earliest NHS hospitals, grew up, and were educated in the lavish, generous style of Labour England.

Though Labour England grows organically, independent of government, it can be helped along by government, and it can be destroyed by government. We thought it had been destroyed for our lifetime by the efforts of the Conservative and New Labour governments, and our task could only be to write its obituary, and hope that our children would have the chance to oversee the creation, not of the Labour England we knew, but of something that did the same job, something better, one day.

And what Jeremy Corbyn showed on 8 June 2017 is that we might, just might, not have to wait that long. If a Labour leader, from what the media called the 'hard' or 'extreme' left of his party, can come so close to victory, can deprive the Conservative Prime Minister of her parliamentary majority, then surely we are close to one of those sea changes that the last Labour Prime Minister of Labour England, Jim Callaghan, described?

Callaghan was reflecting during the 1979 general election. He told his aide, Bernard Donoughue:

> There are times, perhaps once every thirty years, when there is a sea change in politics. It then does not matter what you say or what you do. There is a shift in what the public wants and what it approves of. I suspect that there is now such a sea change – and it is for Mrs Thatcher.

He was right. There were five such sea changes in the twentieth century. First, there was the Liberal landslide of 1906 that brought Henry Campbell-Bannerman, a quiet but determined radical, to Downing Street – producing the first rudimentary welfare state and reforming the House of Lords. Then, in 1931, the nation was terrified by economic collapse and its brief experiment with Labour government, and there was a sea change for the Conservatives.

The third sea change, in 1945, gave Labour's Clement Attlee the chance to create a welfare state and a different sort of society, as soldiers returned once again from the battlefields in search of a more equal country; the fourth, in 1979, gave the equally able and determined Margaret Thatcher the chance to destroy some parts of it and damage the rest. The fifth sea change was in 1997, when Labour was elected by a landslide; but its then leader Tony Blair made rather less use of it than Attlee and others had done.

Worse, Tony Blair set out to traduce much of what those previous Labour governments had done. Notoriously ignorant of both history and sentiment, Blair came to believe his own PR hype. His New Labour experiment was an exercise in 'year zero' politics, because, for him, little worthwhile of note had come before.

We are due the first sea change of the new century, and Corbyn has demonstrated that it may be near. So it doesn't matter if a host of wise pundits tell us that Jeremy Corbyn isn't prime ministerial. We don't need someone prime ministerial. No one is prime ministerial until they become Prime Minister. In 1945, Prime Ministers were thought to be figures of Churchillian magnificence, until the modest, suburban Mr Attlee walked into No 10. In 1964, Prime Ministers were elderly, public-school-educated gentlemen who had fought in the First World War, until a brash, young, state-school-educated Yorkshireman named Harold Wilson took the top job. There is plenty of time for Corbyn to look prime ministerial when he is Prime Minister.

And there's no point in Labour looking for a leader who won't be monstered by the Murdoch and Rothermere press. The media will savage whomever Labour elects, just as Lord Beaverbrook monstered Attlee – unless a Blair-style deal is done with Rupert Murdoch or his monopoly-controlling social media successors, and the price of that would make the election victory not worth having.

Never mind about looking prime ministerial. Labour's leader needs to be like Attlee, someone with the quiet steadfastness of purpose to make the most of the sea change, if it occurs on his or her watch. Someone who can grab the chance while it's there, as Attlee did, and ignore the many siren voices saying that it can't be done.

It doesn't, of course, have to be Corbyn. Corbyn isn't infallible. He has made some bad mistakes and taken some seriously bad advice. We are not Corbynistas, and – as the reader of this book will quickly see – we are far from blind to his faults and are worried about whom he is listening to. But we feel confident that, should a sea change happen while Jeremy Corbyn is leader, he will not waste the chance to change the world. And, if he has gone by then, his legacy will be that Labour has learned the lesson that it does not have to sell all its principles to win.

So this book turned from an obituary for a lost England, to a celebration of an England we suddenly, against the odds, think we dare to hope to see. It will not, of course, be the England that has been lost; and in our Afterword you will find our best guess as to what it might look like.

But it is also an attempt to challenge the narratives about Labour and about Labour governments; about some key events and some key individuals. For over forty years, the agenda, the language, the whole way of looking at things has tended to be shaped by a remarkably small number of pundits, commentators, think tanks and professional politicians. Their world view is, by its very nature, narrow. It has also been dismissive, by and large, of the trade unions or working-class voters who didn't tend to vote the way they should, or listen to the sage advice of those who always know better.

This book is the story of Labour England, starting when it was at the height of its powers in 1978 and Jeremy Corbyn was both a product of it – and one of its most uncompromising defenders.

Corbyn, as a relatively young man in 1978, saw Labour England, not as a finished piece, but as a work in progress, to be improved upon if we only had the imagination and nerve. But this, as it turned out, was a massive miscalculation. There was a sea change to come in 1979, and it was the wrong sea change. It was not time for bold advance, but for stout defence. And the bitterly divided Labour Party was in no condition to defend it due to the machinations of the 1980s; the interminable constitutional wrangles and the open warfare. Corbyn is not exempt from blame for all of this.

That's where our story begins – in 1978.

It ends in 2018, with our best guesses about what will follow.

We both know, like and respect Jeremy Corbyn, and believe he could make a good Prime Minister and achieve some of the things we hope for from a Labour government. But so could lots of people.

We are both the sort of people who feel faintly uncomfortable if we find ourselves, by some mischance, swimming with the current. We are uncomfortable with personality cults, and with intolerance of other people's genuinely held principles and opinions. We were never attracted to the 'democratic centralism' once favoured by communists, and then seamlessly adopted by New Labour, nor the narrow intolerance of many left-wing factions. We're not Corbyn's enemies, although some of his advisers probably think we are, for they come from that strand of socialist thinking which believes that the most dangerous people are not on the right, but those on the left with whom you have differences.

We are critical friends. The left-wing publishing house Verso considered our proposal too ideologically unreliable to take on, and Corbyn's office managed to keep their man away from us while we were writing the book, even though Jeremy managed to poke his face outside his prison for long enough to say that he'd like to talk to us.

But we know who Corbyn is, where he comes from, how he became what he is. We have grown up with him, been where he has been, seen what he has seen. And we want to tell you what it was like, and what it could be like. This book started life as a mournful obituary for a lost world, a better world than the one we currently live in. On 8 June 2017, it turned into an optimistic prophecy.

CHAPTER ONE

IT WAS THE BEST OF TIMES, IT WAS THE WORST OF TIMES

Here is a joke that did the rounds in the late '70s – when trade unions were a power in the land:

> The union's general secretary had had a nasty operation. The president came to visit him in hospital.
>
> 'Morning, general secretary,' he said. 'National executive met yesterday. Wished you a speedy recovery.' He helped himself to a handful of grapes before adding, 'Motion was carried by nine votes to seven with three abstentions.'

The unions were in their pomp. Their power was worth fighting each other for, or at least it seemed to be. All those power struggles in all those smoke-filled rooms, at conferences in Brighton and Blackpool, in the back rooms of the Advisory, Conciliation and Arbitration Service (Acas), they were all for a prize worth having.

Or were they? What was there when the smoke cleared? It had looked like power. It had smelled like power. It had tasted like power. But it wasn't. It was only the appearance of power.

A dreadful drug, that. We could name you half a dozen trade

union leaders who were hooked on the appearance of power in the dog days of Jim Callaghan's government. For the myth that the trade unions were all-powerful suited everyone. It suited the Conservatives and the press. They needed to make everyone frightened of the people they called trade union barons, so they would leave the unions in droves, and the profits could go to shareholders, not employees.

It suited the union leaders, because it made employers frightened of them (and, in at least half a dozen cases we could name, it fed a vanity the size of the Eiffel Tower.)

So, union leaders looked powerful. It is hard to imagine it now, but, in 1979, union leaders were national figures. Jack Jones, Hugh Scanlon, Joe Gormley, Lawrence Daly and Alan Fisher, to name but a few – most people could name them. Newspapers solicited their opinions, if only to then disparage them for the most part. They pronounced magisterially on most subjects, sat on royal commissions and were given peerages when they retired.

At the start of 1978, the Fire Brigades Union called off its first-ever national strike, having won a pay formula that served firefighters well for the next two decades. It seemed to reinforce the idea that unions were powerful and invincible. And yet the power was a myth. Firefighters were in a powerful position because they risked their lives so that we could be safe, and if they withdrew their labour, we felt less safe. There was a sterner test to come.

And that test showed that, with a Labour government in power, with a good case to argue, and when it threw everything it had at the enemy, the unions could be defeated by one rather slimy small businessman who ran a picture processing factory in Brent, north London, called Grunwick.

The businessman was called George Ward, and he had successfully kept trade unions out of his company ever since he founded it, thirteen years earlier. A look inside would have told you why. Most of his workers were Asian women who had first migrated to east Africa from what was then British India, before arriving in Britain when they were expelled, or made unwelcome in Kenya, Uganda and Tanzania.

Without a union, they had little idea how to enforce their rights. Mr Ward is said to have told one worker, 'I can buy a Patel for £15.' Jayaben Desai, who became the de facto strike leader, said, 'Imagine how humiliating it was for us, particularly older women, to be working and to hear the employer saying to a young English girl, "You don't want to come and work here, love, we won't be able to pay the sort of wages which will keep you here."'

Their confidence can hardly have been boosted when, in a widely publicised television interview in January 1978, the Leader of the Opposition, Margaret Thatcher, said, 'People are really rather afraid that this country might be rather swamped by people with a different culture.'

They joined a white collar-trade union called APEX (now part of Unite) and had been on strike for union recognition for two years. Everything in the unions' armoury had been deployed to try to help them. When George Ward wouldn't meet the union, the arbitration service Acas offered to mediate, but Ward said no and fired the 137 strikers. Jayaben Desai was taken to hospital after a management car passed over her foot. Police refused to act, but, just a week later, they arrested a picket for obstruction, and, three days after that, another woman picket was knocked down by a management car.

Roy Grantham, general secretary of APEX, asked Employment Secretary Albert Booth to set up a court of inquiry into the dispute. TUC general secretary Len Murray asked unions to help APEX in any way they could. The Union of Post Office

Workers (UPW) refused to handle Grunwick mail, but withdrew the instruction when threatened with legal action.

The strikers picketed chemist shops, which, in those days, took in pictures and sent them to places like Grunwick to be developed. Fifty-one dismissed strikers took their complaint of unfair dismissal to the industrial tribunal, but the tribunal ruled that it had no jurisdiction in the case.

Three government ministers, Shirley Williams, Fred Mulley and Denis Howell, joined the picket line. A Labour MP, Audrey Wise, was arrested on the picket line. It tells you something that, at what is supposed to be the height of union power, and under a Labour government, all that the government's ministers could do to help was stand hopelessly on the picket line. This is not the behaviour of triumphalist trade unionists shouting, 'We are the masters now.'

None of it worked, so mass pickets began, and it got ugly – and newsworthy. Police arrested eighty-four pickets on the first day of mass picketing. Management paid what it called 'loyal workers' extra and had them driven through the pickets in buses. At vast public expense, police cleared a way for them.

In the summer of 1977, the Yorkshire and Scottish miners joined the picket line. The weapon the press had prepared everyone to fear above anything was on its way to London from Barnsley.

That weapon was called Arthur Scargill, and it was said – by himself in particular – to have single-handedly defeated the government during the 1972 miners' strike, by preventing deliveries to a fuel storage depot in Birmingham. The battle of Saltley Gate, as it became known, led to the local police chief calling for the gates to the depot to be closed to preserve public order, much to the delight of the flying pickets.

This was very much a high-water mark for trade union power, however ephemeral it proved to be. It may even have given rise to a pop group of the same name. Another flavour of that time in popular culture was a band called Strawbs, whose 'Part of the Union' was an instant hit and a favourite for any half-decent send-off for ex-union men and women at funeral services even decades on.

At Saltley, Arthur made a lot of noise, garnered a lot of media attention, was arrested, and was sent back to Yorkshire.

The picket line threw together a young couple, dressed in similar garb, who were later to become rather better known. It wasn't a case of 'love on the dole', more 'love on the picket line'. Harriet Harman and union official Jack Dromey were frequent attenders at the Grunwick picket line. Jack, full bearded and splendidly uncompromising, was photographed holding the megaphone for Arthur.

There was a national day of action against Grunwick. The High Court rejected a challenge by George Ward to an Acas ruling that he should recognise the union. A government report, the Scarman Report, called for union recognition and reinstatement, and Mr Ward told them what they could do with their report.

And that was it. The TUC had thrown everything at it. They had thrown the armoury of negotiation and the law, they had thrown mass pickets, they had thrown public opinion at it – for this really was a group of employees being rottenly treated. They had even thrown Arthur Scargill at it.

But at Grunwick, the unions had lost. Comprehensively and utterly. Even though four members of the strike committee staged a hunger strike outside TUC headquarters, the generals of the movement – the men (they were mostly men) whom the press called union barons, or union bosses, even though they were elected, unlike company bosses such as George Ward, could see nothing for it but surrender.

Anyone who tells you that the trade unions ran the country

until Mrs Thatcher came along to rescue us should remember what happened at Grunwick in 1978, when Britain had a Labour government and Mrs T was no more than a recently elected and untried Leader of the Opposition, undergoing elocution lessons.

Not that this was at all evident to the men who led the unions. They had become self-consciously statesmanlike, and contributed to the myth of their unbridled power by speaking in the cautious, orotund manner of those whose lightest word could sway the fate of nations. They sounded like politicians.

Even the miners, who had ridden to the rescue of the Grunwick workers, were led by Joe Gormley, a comfortable, statesmanlike, middle-of-the-road figure, who hailed from Lancashire.

But Gormley was sixty-one, and could retire any moment, and the nation trembled at the thought that he might be succeeded by one Mick McGahey, the best-known communist in Britain. Gormley, however, like Baldrick in *Blackadder*, had a cunning plan. He intended to delay his retirement until McGahey was too old, under the union's rules, to stand for the job. That would surely dish the left. The union would be bound to fall back on another moderate figure like, er, Joe Gormley.

These matters were followed closely by the newspapers. No self-respecting national newspaper was without its labour and industrial correspondent – the broadsheets like *The Times*, *Guardian* and *Telegraph* had a whole team of them – and they considered themselves the cream of their profession, and often aped the mannerisms of the union leaders whose slightest word they reported.

Labour correspondents were known to turn down a move to covering Parliament. Why would they want to hobnob with some dreary Cabinet minister? They were on 'fancy a pint' terms with the general secretary of the Union of Construction and Allied Trades.

Union leaders were as well known as top politicians, no matter how grey and colourless they might appear. And they didn't come much greyer or more colourless than David Basnett, leader of one of the country's biggest general unions, the General and Municipal Workers' Union (GMWU). A tall, elegant, stately and slightly shy man, Basnett sounded rather like a provincial bank manager. (In those long-dead days there were still banks in the provinces, and banking was still a respectable profession.)

And it was this distinctly un-revolutionary figure who founded Trade Unions for Labour Victory (TULV) in July 1978.

His thinking was this: there had to be a general election no later than 1979. The unions were determined to keep Jim Callaghan's government in power, and they confidently expected that Prime Minister Jim Callaghan was going to call a general election before the end of 1978. Newspapers had been speculating about it for weeks and no denial came from Downing Street. Even more significant – or so the union leaders thought – was the fact that their private soundings had not led to a denial either.

So when the TUC met in Brighton at the beginning of September, Basnett uncoiled his tall frame and launched into the nearest he could get to a rousing speech, which wasn't very near at all. Rousing speeches were not this stiff, conventional, middle-aged man's style, but those who were there awarded him an A for effort.

Having made that effort, Basnett was understandably miffed when Callaghan blew into Brighton, playfully teased the delegates and the press about their expectations of a general election, and said there wasn't going to be one. He even sang a little song, a snatch of an old music hall song:

> There was I, waiting at the church,
> Waiting at the church,
> Waiting at the church.

And added, 'I have promised nobody that I shall be at the altar in October.'

Basnett probably knew the rest of the song, the bits that the Prime Minister did not sing. It would hardly have improved his mood, for it goes like this:

> When I found he'd left me in the lurch,
> Left me in the lurch,
> Left me in the lurch.
> Lor, how it did upset me!
> All at once, he sent me round a note,
> Here's the very note,
> This is what he wrote:
> 'Can't get away to marry you today
> My wife won't let me!'

Callaghan was not the first, and certainly not the last, Prime Minister to have come unstuck over election timing. But it was a pretty strange decision. The Labour government had a wafer-thin majority and had survived on a pact – not a coalition, mind – with the Liberals that had just expired. The polls showed a Labour lead. The unions wanted him to go to the country as soon as possible, before the fragile pact between government and unions, which kept pay claims down, disintegrated.

The danger signs were there, for anyone who wanted to see them. The previous year, a Gallup poll found that 54 per cent of the people thought that Jack Jones, leader of the Transport and General Workers' Union (TGWU), was the most powerful person in Britain, ahead of the Prime Minister. Earlier in the year, Jones, the trade unions' most inspirational figure at that time (and perhaps of any time), retired.

His powerful personality had been the key to holding the

unions uneasily to the pay freeze. Just before his retirement, he had tried to commit the TGWU to another year of wage restraint – and the conference had overturned him.

Chancellor Denis Healey asked Jones's successor, Moss Evans, to have another go. Evans knew his limitations. 'If they did that to Jack Jones, can you imagine what they'd do to me?' he said to Healey.

So, on 26 July, the TUC general council voted to reject the government's 5 per cent pay rise limit and insist on a return to the policy of free collective bargaining.

This, then, was the pre-Thatcher world. It's a world held up to us today as a model of everything we must never be again, and not just because of the mythical stranglehold the trade unions are said to have had on it.

If you fiddle aimlessly with your TV remote one night, you may come across an especially cheap-to-make programme called *It Was Alright in the '70s* in which minor celebrities are played clips from 1970s shows and advertisements. They then put on their most shocked tones to say 'whoa' and 'what?' and 'They thought that was OK?'

In one clip, a pretty young woman in a miniskirt was ogled, and the journalist David Aaronovitch was wheeled on to provide instant genteel horror. (Genteel isn't what the earthy Mr Aaronovitch does best, but he's a trouper and he put on a show.) Then a bit of '70s soft porn came on the screen, and Mr Aaronovitch upped the shock level.

But you know, soft porn is fairly creepy in any decade, and it's still around.

Norman Lamont was on television recently explaining how, as Chancellor, he had rescued the railways, which he said were 'a basket case' in the '70s, by privatising them. Britain's rail system wasn't perfect pre-privatisation, but anyone who was there will tell you that it was a whole load better than it is now.

It needed vast subsidies – it still does. Fares were predictable. If you wanted to go to, say, Exeter, you just looked up the price of a ticket to Exeter. Now it's a lottery. The fare might be a bargain or it might be millionaire territory. It is little comfort, if you are asked to travel to Birmingham for a ludicrous price, to be told that there's a special offer on trains to Exeter.

Trains had enough toilets – these days you're lucky to find one, even luckier if it's working. You could get sleepers to all sorts of places to which you can no longer get sleepers.

Intangible things were better too. It was a kinder society. There is something especially cruel and unfeeling about much of today's public discourse after nearly four decades of neoliberal government.

It is fashionable to deride the '70s. But it was a good time to be alive – and especially to be young – arguably far better than anything we have seen since.

Working-class youngsters could just about afford to live in cities like London. They had enough to get by, to pick up instruments, form bands, set up magazines and be creative.

And that's not just sentiment from superannuated socialists. In 2004, the New Economics Foundation calculated that 1976 was the best year to be alive in Britain. They measured our material standards as well as levels of crime, family breakdown, economic inequality, welfare spending, pollution and the cost of living.

It's been downhill ever since. The last of the glory days of Labour England were in 1978. That winter, it was to meet its greatest trauma since 1931, and nothing would ever be the same again.

It started at Ford. In September, car workers went on strike after the company – which had had a good year, and could afford more – offered them a 5 per cent pay rise in line with government pay policy. In October, the Labour Party conference called for the abolition of the government's pay policy. In November, a strike by members of the Bakers, Food and Allied Workers' Union at Allied Bakeries and Rank Hovis McDougall caused panic buying of bread, and Ford settled for 17 per cent.

In December, Times Newspapers Ltd announced its intention to suspend publication of all its titles, including *The Times*, until agreement was reached with unions over a new industrial relations structure. The papers did not appear again for a year. Briefly the unions looked as though they might be notching up a large-scale victory, but it wasn't a particularly satisfying victory.

The government wanted to impose sanctions on Ford and 220 other companies for their breach of the pay policy, but the House of Commons wouldn't let them.

In January 1979, more lorry drivers' strikes had the government planning for a state of emergency. Moss Evans agreed with ministers a list of emergency supplies which were officially exempt from action, but local shop stewards were not always amenable to instructions from above.

Fifty thousand schoolchildren in Stockport were sent home due to a shortage of central heating fuel after a lightning strike by 2,000 tanker drivers and fuel depot workers in the north-west.

On 10 January, Prime Minister Callaghan returned from an international summit in Guadeloupe and denied there was 'mounting chaos' in Britain, which allowed *The Sun* to run its famous headline; a picture of a smiling Callaghan over a screaming banner that read, 'CRISIS? WHAT CRISIS?'

Callaghan, of course, never said those words or anything like them, but most people thought he had. As it happens, he didn't have a luxurious tan when he flew in from sunny Guadeloupe to a Britain shivering under heavy snow in the harshest winter since 1962/63; but most people thought he had.

Train drivers began a series of 24-hour strikes, and the Royal

College of Nurses asked for nurses' pay to be increased to the same level in real terms as they had had in 1974, which meant a 25 per cent rise. There was a public sector 'day of action' including a 24-hour strike and a march for a £60 minimum wage.

Ambulance drivers and ancillary hospital staff took strike action, to screams of outrage from the press. Waste collectors went on strike, and the Conservative council in Westminster piled its rubbish in the most prominent place possible, which was Leicester Square, and helpfully pointed out to the *Evening Standard* the rats it had attracted.

And then some gravediggers in Liverpool and Manchester went on strike.

Nothing that went before had brought out Fleet Street's finest in quite the same roar of self-righteous fury. 'They won't even let us bury our dead' screamed a *Daily Mail* headline.

Newspaper readers were treated to hair-raising accounts of the horrors they were apparently living through. Corpses would soon be rotting in piles on street corners. There were to be great funeral boats, and dead bodies would be piled onto them and taken out to sea to be chucked over the side. We were helpfully told just how long a heat-sealed bag could keep grandpa and grandma from stinking the place out. Leading Conservative Michael Heseltine told the House of Commons that there were 225 bodies awaiting burial in Liverpool and thirty-eight in Tameside. After a couple of weeks, the gravediggers settled for 14 per cent. Local authority workers, including waste collectors, agreed 11 per cent.

And then, quite quickly, it was all over. Union leaders contributed to the myth of their omnipotence by agreeing a 'concordat' with the government called 'The Economy, the Government, and Trade Union Responsibilities', swiftly christened the St Valentine's Day Concordat. In it, they promised to do all sorts of things they had no power to do.

Locally, the backlog of work was swiftly accomplished, nowhere more so than in the London Borough of Haringey, where lorry drivers demanded a £340-a-week bonus to clear a backlog of work once they returned to their jobs. The claim was put to the Haringey public works committee, whose chair, according to the *Daily Telegraph*, cleared press and public out while it was discussed.

The chair was a councillor who had a day job as an official of the National Union of Public Employees. His name, the *Telegraph* reported, was Corbyn. Jeremy Corbyn. He worked closely with another young union official, Diane Abbott, out of the union's offices in Acton, west London, although media claims, made decades later, suggesting that the pair had taken a motorbike holiday together on the bumpy, cobbled streets of the old East Germany and earned themselves a Stasi file proved wide of the mark. They had in fact gone to France. Oddly enough, the same media failed to print a correction, still less an apology.

Living through the Winter of Discontent was an odd experience. Newspapers and television were blasting out daily tales of the horrors we were experiencing, but as we went about our daily business, things seemed pretty normal. Sure, the streets were a bit messier than usual, but not much more so than after a couple of weeks of Christmas holidays.

Still, it's the England the media saw that has so far made its way into the history books. We feel we suffered, and we feel strengthened by our suffering. Our parents lived through the blitz; we lived through the Winter of Discontent.

So successful was the press at parading the idea of a Winter of Discontent, that elections continued to be fought by the Tories over it well into the 1990s. Nor did it take much on the doorstep to have electors sagely regurgitating the horrors of that time, even though, on questioning, most found it difficult to think of anything in particular that had affected them or anyone they knew. Some had been toddlers at the time. None of this is ever discussed in the international economic context of the time. Western economies, including Britain, had been hit by the OPEC oil price hike of 1973. This had followed in the wake of the Yom Kippur War, as the Saudis in particular flexed their muscles. Inflation was a by-product and wages struggled to keep up. Any government would have struggled, but no Tory government could ever have achieved agreement with the unions over a social contract.

In the short term, the collapse of the social contract did for Jim Callaghan's government, and in the medium term it did for Labour England. And in the long term? As the late Zhou Enlai once said reputedly after being asked about the effects of the French revolution: it's too early to say.

The polling organisation Gallup gave Labour a 5 per cent lead over the Conservatives in November 1978, which turned into a Conservative lead of 7.5 per cent in January 1979, and 20 per cent in February.

On 28 March, the government lost a vote of confidence in the House of Commons by one vote. A Conservative election broadcast was built around the constant repetition of the phrase Callaghan had never used – 'Crisis, what crisis?' – over footage of piles of rubbish, closed factories, picketed hospitals and locked graveyards. The general election was set for 3 May.

CHAPTER TWO

THE FORWARD MARCH
OF LABOUR HALTED

In those long-dead days, Labour's annual conference played a
major part in deciding what was to go into the party's manifesto. So when Callaghan casually dumped the more left-wing
proposals that the conference had demanded, it caused a furore
which would sound odd in today's Labour Party, used as it is
to being treated as a tame canvassing force – at least until the
recent surge in membership under Jeremy Corbyn, when it may
all change again.

Callaghan's manifesto announced its harmlessness with the
title: 'The Labour Way is the Better Way'.

But if Labour did not understand that the 1979 election was
a battle of sharply conflicting ideologies, a battle which pitted
Labour England against Conservative England, Mrs Thatcher
certainly did. At the first Conservative rally of the election campaign at City Hall, Cardiff, she said, 'The slither and slide to the
socialist state is going to be stopped ... halted and turned back.'

She pledged to carry the fight right into 'the castles and strongholds of Labour', condemning the 'ugly apparatus' of 'officious,
jargon-filled, intolerant socialism'. 'We as Conservatives believe
that recovery can only come through the work of individuals ...

For what is the real driving force in society? It's the desire of the individual to do the best for himself and for his family.'

The big picture won, and Labour England lost, but not by the landslide many had predicted. That had to wait until 1983. In 1979, Mrs Thatcher had an overall majority of forty-three seats.

Chancellor Geoffrey Howe's first Budget cut both the standard rate and the top rate of income tax. But VAT went up sharply, from 8 per cent to 15 per cent. Prescription charges were more than doubled, and they were increased again the following year. British Aerospace ceased to be a state corporation.

What was the labour movement going to do? It was obvious, really. It turned on itself, and feasted greedily on its own flesh.

The unions were furious with Callaghan, whom they blamed for the calamities to come. The left were furious with him for ditching the manifesto that they had struggled to get the party to agree to. So the unions made common cause with the left to demand more power for unions and members – and less for MPs.

They told Labour Party officials that requests for increases in union funding would not be welcome until the proposed organisational inquiry into the party, following its election defeat, had been established.

The election of leader and deputy leader would be taken out of the hands of Labour MPs and given to an electoral college in which unions and constituency parties had the main voice. Labour MPs would be subject to a mandatory reselection process before every general election.

The opposition to these changes coalesced around a group called Campaign for Labour Victory. Its pamphlet produced in the autumn called the left's proposals 'naked power politics'. It said Labour's national executive, now controlled by the left, was 'irresponsible' and 'wildly remote' from ordinary Labour voters.

'The Left's preoccupation is in controlling the Labour Party, it is not in achieving government,' it said, and mounted a campaign to wrest control of the NEC from the left.

There was a strange irony in all of this. Trade union leaders had traditionally used their block vote to protect Labour leaders against the left. They had protected Clem Attlee against the Socialist League before the war and against the communists and the Bennites after the war, and had protected Hugh Gaitskell and Harold Wilson against the unilateralists.

The power of the trade union block vote at the Labour Party conference had been used like a vast blunt instrument. When a vote was called, union leaders would stand and hold up a number. That was the number of political-levy-paying members they had, and therefore the number of votes they were casting. The left railed against it, and called it undemocratic.

Now, suddenly, the left went silent on the evils of the block vote, and the right was calling it wickedly undemocratic. Which goes to show that Clement Attlee, the shrewdest of all Labour's leaders, knew what he was talking about when he said, decades earlier, 'Those who rail against the block vote fall silent when it is cast in accordance with their own views.'

It got very nasty, very quickly. The TUC Congress in September debated a motion for mass demonstrations against the government's economic policy. Terry Duffy, the leader of Britain's second-largest union, the AUEW, wanted to oppose it, but his delegation overturned him by eighteen votes to fourteen. So Duffy publicly accused his own delegation of being dominated by communists.

Britain's largest union, the TGWU, supported the proposal. TUC general secretary Len Murray tried to broker a truce in the time-honoured manner, by putting pressure on the small trade union which had proposed the motion – the Furniture, Timber and Allied Trades Union (FTAT) – to withdraw it. FTAT refused. Its motion was narrowly defeated.

It was a preliminary skirmish, rather like the phoney war that began in 1939, fearful only for presaging the horrors to come.

Increasingly, Callaghan looked like a defeated and demoralised leader. A leader who has staked everything on the mantra 'in order to win you must do so and so' cannot easily survive when the party does so and so and he then leads it to defeat.

Callaghan focused firmly on trying to avoid defeat and humiliation at Labour's conference. He tried to persuade the NEC that the conference should not vote on a proposal that the control of the party's election manifesto should pass to the NEC. He failed.

He told the NEC, 'I am deeply disappointed that I clearly have so little influence on the majority of this executive. But the decision will not rest here. You have started a battle which will go on.'

Labour's conference began on 1 October. That very day, the party chairman, Frank Allaun, and its general secretary, Ron Hayward, placed the blame for the party's election defeat on the Labour leadership's failure to back the policy decisions taken at the party conference.

Michael Foot tried to head off the growing confrontation by invoking the labour movement: 'If divisions grow between the political side and the trade union side then our enemies are allowed to triumph.' At the Labour Party conference that autumn, delegates stood and applauded a fiery speech by the left-wing and now ex-Labour MP for Birmingham Selly Oak, Tom Litterick.

He attacked Callaghan, who was still leader of the party, and who had rather revelled in his nickname 'Sunny Jim'. Waving a clutch of policy papers which he claimed Callaghan had vetoed, he quoted a line from a popular television series featuring the late, unlamented paedophile, Jimmy Savile: "'Jim will fix it," they said. Ay, he fixed it. He fixed all of us. He fixed me in particular.' Delegates roared with approval and Tony Benn described it as a 'courageous speech'.

A proposal for changing the method of electing the party leader by opening it up to the entire party was narrowly defeated. But a motion calling for mandatory reselection of sitting Labour MPs was narrowly passed. So was a resolution stating that the NEC (now controlled by the left) should have the final authority over the party's election manifesto.

Just how was all this to work? The devil was to be in the detail. What was to be the exact balance of power between Labour MPs, the trade unions and the ordinary Labour Party members? All of that was left to next time, and the labour movement's navel was to be the focus of its attention for months to come.

The unions, which had helped give birth to the Labour Party in 1906 and were the backbone of what was still called the labour movement, were all facing their own versions of the battle in the party.

Most trade unions had organised left factions. The core of this faction was normally the Socialist Workers Party, which either was or was not a Trotskyite party, depending on which obscure Marxist texts you believed. The faction normally called itself 'rank and file' and claimed to speak for the ordinary members, whose revolutionary zeal was supposed to be being blunted by reactionary leaders.

These factions had their own organisations, their own conferences and their own leaders, which they claimed represented the rank and file. In one of the civil service unions, which produced a magazine called *Red Tape* for its members, the left coalesced round an alternative publication called *Redder Tape*. Left-wing teachers in the National Union of Teachers joined something called Rank-and-File Teacher, while journalists who believed their reactionary leaders were stifling the revolutionary spirit of the average newsroom hack called themselves Journalists' Charter.

These organisations billed themselves as the voice of the rank and file, in opposition to the voice of what they called the 'union bureaucrats', who they believed were holding back the rank and file and preventing mass strikes. When their union held its annual conference, they would hold their own pre-conference conference, so that they could vote in a block for what they considered to be the correct ideological position.

Delegates to the annual TUC Congress would be greeted, as they entered the hall, by dozens of protestors from these organisations shouting, 'TUC get off your knees, call a general strike now.' This chant has proved remarkably resilient. You can still hear it today, if – as with the mating call of near-extinct birds – you know where to look.

Their default position was that union leaders were reactionary timeservers, and that if you wanted something done properly, you must set up an extra committee to do it. So unions became strangled by layer upon layer of committees, all of which required their own bureaucracy.

One former president of the National Union of Journalists (NUJ), in a conscious echo of Stanley Baldwin's famous gibe about newspaper proprietors having 'power without responsibility, the prerogative of the harlot through the ages', said union leaders were left with 'impotence without irresponsibility – the prerogative of the whipping boy through the ages'.

Rank-and-file organisations had an almost mystical belief in the power of strike action, and an instinctive distrust of union leaders. The Socialist Workers Party actually expelled members who applied for jobs with trade unions. On the left flank of the Labour Party, the 'Rank-and-File Mobilising Committee' was born.

So inside each union, left and right were tearing chunks out of each other. At the same time, the largest unions were rushing to take over smaller ones. In the years after 1979, hosts of small craft unions disappeared into the increasingly distended gut of, especially, the TGWU.

In 1978, there were 112 unions affiliated to the TUC. Today, there are forty-nine. It increased the self-importance of the leaders of the big unions, but it helped weaken the unions and the Labour Party. People who felt loyalty to their small craft union could not feel the same loyalty to a big general union, which seemed to them to exist so that its leaders could exercise their political muscle in the Labour Party.

If there was one thing that united left and right in the unions, it was that both sides thought the Labour Party should get its act together.

The right thought the party it had given birth to was rushing off on some Quixotic reforming mission of its own, without consulting the old, wise heads to be found at the top of the trade unions; and they threatened to withhold their money if Labour adopted the left's constitutional changes. The left wondered if the old, stodgy Labour Party was really the vehicle for the revolution they had in mind, and were minded to withhold money until Labour adopted its constitutional changes.

Stuck between the warring factions, all Labour Party treasurer Norman Atkinson could do was plead poverty: 'The party is fast over-spending its income – disastrously so.'

In the midst of all this, it took a remarkable level of groundless optimism for Tony Benn to greet the conference decisions by telling a Tribune rally: 'I think 3 October 1979 will be remembered by every historian of the labour movement because we have made here today very significant advances towards socialism in Britain.'

Callaghan was now starting to sound a little like Hugh Gaitskell in his 'fight, fight and fight again to save the party we love' period. 'I reaffirm, as long as I am leader, the independence of the parliamentary party. At the end of the day, it cannot be subject to any outside influence – that is a fundamental principle of the party,' he told Robin Day on BBC's *Nationwide*.

But no one was listening. That very day, delegates voted to instruct the NEC to look into methods of extending the party's internal democracy to ensure that the party leadership and PLP were more accountable to 'the labour movement'.

It was, despite Tony Benn's euphoria, one of those conferences where nobody wins. Debates had not been about high principle, but about the fine detail of Labour's internal procedures, and this was not a message designed to excite voters, rather the reverse.

About the only relief came in the education debate. The education correspondents were there – in those days specialist correspondents followed policy debates. As they reeled into the bar afterwards, they agreed unanimously with the education correspondent of the *Daily Express*, the theatrical Bruce Kemble. 'We've just heard a future Labour Prime Minister,' said Bruce, raising a celebratory glass to his lips.

The man they had heard, young, romantic, witty, easily the best platform speaker any political party had produced for years, was a short, stocky ginger-haired Welshman, with charm in his voice and fire in his belly.

He was Labour's new education spokesman, and he had attacked the government's 'education genocide' and suggested a Labour government would abolish private schools. Everyone thought him the next Nye Bevan. His name was Neil Kinnock. Michael Foot, who seemed to see him as the son he had never had, would later enthusiastically refer to him as the Welsh Wizard.

'What sickens me', Kinnock told the conference, 'is employers deploring the fall in standards of literacy and numeracy ... Those are the people who were campaigning and spending hundreds of thousands of pounds supporting the Tory Party, begging for, demanding, tax cuts ... You can't have tax cuts and high standards of education.' And he ended the passage with one of those great phrases for which he was soon to be famous: 'They cripple our children and then taunt them for being lame.' (Such soaring oratory would get him into severe trouble now. It occasionally did then.)

Kinnock bravely took himself into the lion's den on occasions. In 1978, he was invited to speak to sixth-formers at one of Britain's most prestigious private schools, Marlborough College in Wiltshire. Typically uncompromising, he promised to abolish the school's charitable status. Marlborough, like Eton and Harrow, was to be a fine comprehensive school. Kinnock believed that his predecessor Shirley Williams's abolition of grammar and direct-grant schools was surely but a stepping stone. Mark Seddon, who was attending a not-quite-so-prestigious public school, had hitched a lift to hear Kinnock make this speech and joined the Labour Party the following day. (His attempt to join three years earlier had been rejected because, at fifteen, he was too young).

Kinnock was already an immensely popular figure at the conference. Two years earlier Kinnock, who has a fine singing voice, brought the house down at the conference revue with his rendering of 'Ol' Man River', about James Callaghan: 'He must know somethin'/But he don't do nothin'.

But that week in Brighton introduced him to a wider audience.

He got the longest standing ovation of the week for what the *Financial Times* called 'a performance in the Bevan tradition – fluent, fervent and forceful'.

Fortunately, the *Financial Times* never managed to penetrate the arcane filing system in the *Tribune* offices in Gray's Inn Road, London. These contained a series of yellowing files with some of the earliest rhetorical flights of fancy by the young Neil Kinnock. These speeches demanded 'workers' control of the commanding heights of the economy'. They were fiercely syndicalist, hugely critical of the behemoths that were the general secretaries and the TUC general council. They would have greatly embarrassed an older Neil Kinnock.

They were contained in a series of filing cabinets overflowing with articles and pictures of those who had been at the forefront of the fight against British colonialism, such as Hastings Banda, Jomo Kenyatta, Cheddi Jagan and Walter Sisulu. The filing system was hugely out of date, even by the 1970s; 'British Guiana' and 'Northern Rhodesia', for instance, having long ago been renamed.

The Bennites managed to ensure that the inquiry into the party's structure would have a majority of left-wing members. Callaghan complained that when he went to his party's NEC, he was 'cross-examined and vilified'. A confidential Campaign for Labour Victory report, sent to members of the shadow Cabinet and Labour MPs, said, 'We are now dealing with the very real likelihood of the destruction of the Labour Party as the broad-based party it has always been … The current crisis can now only be solved for Social Democrats by an effective organisation putting into operation a high-powered campaign.'

The Campaign for Labour Victory was ideologically 'lost', it said, with inadequate financial support and an understaffed organisation. The left was better organised and richer.

CHAPTER THREE

SEEDS OF DESTRUCTION

With Labour fighting its own internal battles, the Conservative government was able to press ahead with its project. In November 1979 it cut a further £3.5 billion of public expenditure, mostly from education, housing, transport, roads and nationalised industries. Within this reduced budget, it could find more money for defence, and had to find more for social security because of rising unemployment.

Just before Christmas it announced the measure which, more than all others, was to destroy Labour England. Nothing was more central to the building of Attlee's New Jerusalem than Nye Bevan's huge council house-building programme, not even Bevan's National Health Service.

Bevan had used local authorities as the engine of his housing policy, and had laid down minimum standards for the homes he built; he saw no reason why the working class should not have comfortable places to live in.

The people who lived in these homes did not own them, and mostly they did not want to. They had spacious and modern houses in which to live and bring up their children, at rents they could afford, something their parents could only have dreamed of. Why should they care about the abstract concept of ownership?

The council house-building programme, giving decent homes

to people who before the war had lived in teeming, squalid slums, was, like the National Health Service, so popular at the time that the Conservative government that replaced Labour in 1951 knew it would be political suicide to undo it. In fact, Housing minister Harold Macmillan embraced the programme: Macmillan managed to build even more houses than Bevan each year, though this was achieved partly by lowering Bevan's standards and building smaller homes. High-rise blocks came later, as the standards declined yet further – though even flats in these blocks were gratefully snapped up by families that had lived for years on crumbling estates which were only demolished in the 1960s.

Council estates were the essence of Labour England. If you were going to destroy Labour England, they had to go, both for themselves and for the fact that they were owned and run by local authorities – another pillar of Labour England.

So, on 20 December, the government published its Housing Bill, which gave five million council tenants the right to buy their homes at discounted prices. The government gave itself power to force sales through against the wishes of the local council. Secretary of State for the Environment Michael Heseltine described it, rightly, as laying the foundations 'for one of the most important social revolutions of this century'. Local councils were prevented from using the receipts from selling off their housing stock, to reinvest in new house-building. Local council house-building soon came to a virtual standstill.

The homeless charity Shelter pointed out the obvious fact that this would 'increase the number of homeless people while decreasing the number of homes available to house them'. Of course, it did. It was followed by the rapid dismantling of rent controls, and those without substantial capital were thrown on the not so tender mercies of private landlords desperate to make a profit from their investment.

The first houses to be bought, naturally, were those built in Bevan's time, before 1950, because they were the best. So council tenants were corralled into the poorest of the council homes before, gradually, they were driven out of those too. By August 1980, less than a year later, Mrs Thatcher was able to present the keys to the owners of the 12,000th council house sold by the Greater London Council and to extend the right to buy to housing association tenants.

The miseries faced by the young today in their increasingly desperate search for somewhere to live are the direct result of this greedy and cynical bit of legislation, passed before most of them were born.

Thatcher's great advantage over Labour was that she was pursuing a vision. It was a cruel vision, but it was a vision. She knew the sort of country she wanted Britain to be. Labour's vision appeared to involve nothing more exciting than passionate expositions of bits of its own constitution. While Conservatives had ringing phrases like 'property-owning democracy', Labour's leaders were shouting, 'Comrades, unite behind the fourth amendment to paragraph 17 (b) (iii) of the party's 1918 constitution.' It didn't have the same ring somehow.

There is a sense in which the battle for the soul of the Labour Party has always been the same one, whether the left was led by James Maxton in the 1920s, Stafford Cripps in the 1930s, Nye Bevan in the 1940s and 1950s, Michael Foot in the 1970s or Tony Benn in the 1980s. But the last year of the 1970s brought a new bitterness and a new intensity, for two reasons. The first was that both sides were prisoners of history. The left remembered how they had been driven out of the party for opposing nuclear disarmament in the '50s, while the right never forgot how they had been mercilessly harried by the Bevanites. Both sides had forgotten Attlee's wise words. Watching Hugh Gaitskell fight his battle for Clause 4 of Labour's constitution, Attlee commented that the 'Labour Party's passion for definition should always be resisted. Hugh excited it. He should have sedated it.' Labour's warring factions could also have tried to remember some equally wise words from Harold Wilson, who once compared the party to a bird because it needed 'both a left wing and a right wing to fly'.

The second reason for the new bitterness and intensity was that the left split. Michael Foot became, unwillingly, part of the centrist establishment. He was outflanked on the left by young men and women who were quite happy to spend their lives in the arid bureaucratic work of manipulating Labour's constitution, in a way that Maxton's and Bevan's supporters would have scorned.

Where Nye Bevan would say contemptuously that what the right wanted as Labour leader was a 'desiccated calculating machine' (he meant Hugh Gaitskell), the new left were happy to become desiccated calculating machines. They positively enjoyed dry committee rooms, where detailed calculations led to inconspicuous but momentous progress. Time spent working out which formulation would be most likely to deliver a left majority, and then justifying it, was never time wasted. Constitutional change was meat and drink to them.

The left's newly emerging calculating machine, the very sharp Jon Lansman (recently reinvented as the moving spirit of Momentum), would argue that this dull work was necessary to shift the party to a radical agenda. The trouble was that, whether true or not, it required the party to do a lot of things that not only failed to capture the public's imagination, but repelled most voters.

Not that Labour wasn't trying to pull itself together, to find a formula which might unite it. It was trying, with all the smooth, silent adeptness of a wounded rhinoceros. The first meeting of its committee of inquiry into its own organisation produced an elaborate, clunking fudge: three co-chairs representing the three partners in the traditional labour movement coalition – and also representing the three emerging factions. The inevitable David Basnett represented the trade unions, and was on the right of the party. Labour MPs, and the emerging soft left, were represented by Michael Foot, and the National Executive and the emerging hard left by Liverpool Walton MP, Eric Heffer.

Meanwhile Lord Underhill, the former national agent of the Labour Party, produced his report on the infiltration of local parties by members of the Trotskyist Militant Tendency. It was a masterpiece of even-handedness and compromise – and it never stood a chance. It criticised the party's NEC for failing to act on 'entryism', but rejected the idea of mass expulsions. You mustn't have a 'witch-hunt', warned Underhill, but you can't go on being tolerant, either. He didn't spell out what the middle way was, perhaps because he couldn't see one.

By June 1982, Lord Underhill's approach had been consigned to the waste bin. Labour's NEC gave Militant three months to disband or conform to the constitutional requirements of a new party register of approved groups. Tony Benn fiercely opposed this and told reporters afterwards, 'I shall die an unregistered socialist.'

Three months later, in an interview on BBC Radio 4's *The World This Weekend*, Michael Foot said that he expected the eight local Labour parties who had chosen Militant-supporting parliamentary candidates to deselect them. They never did, of course, and two of the candidates became MPs the next year.

Meetings of Labour's ruling NEC were bad-tempered and sometimes farcical. At one of them, there was an emotional stand-off between Eric Heffer and Neil Kinnock. Heffer was so infuriated that he stood up and stormed out of the meeting – but instead of heading outside the room, he inadvertently propelled himself into a broom cupboard. Hauling himself away from the clattering brooms and mops, he resumed his seat without saying a word.

Out in the real world, steelworkers went on strike in January 1980, and ministers plotted to cut the benefits of strikers, in the expectation that hardship would force them back to work. They were also working on plans to impose ballots on unions, not just for strike action, but also regular re-elections for top officials, and – much more secretly – on dismantling Britain's steel industry, a rather drastic way of putting an end to strikes in the industry. The steelworkers eventually settled for 16 per cent – they had gone on strike for 20 per cent.

Inflation rose to 21.8 per cent in April 1980, its highest rate in four years. Unemployment topped a million. By June it was 1,467,400, equivalent to 6.2 per cent of the country's workforce, and the next month it was 1,896,634, 7.8 per cent of the workforce. In September it topped the two million mark, and the next year, 1981, it reached three million. Not so long ago most people had assumed that the government of a country with one million unemployed would be doomed to fall.

Tony Benn accused the government of deliberately creating conditions for the destruction of trade union power by stimulating unemployment and legislating to curb union rights. He was, of course, right. Ministers would soon not bother denying it, though it was a couple of years before they would actually boast of it.

Unfortunately, Labour's best efforts (including Benn's) were going mostly into something much closer to home. Labour's commission of inquiry trotted off to Whitehall College in Bishop's Stortford to try to agree on the vital issues of the day: reselection of all MPs; an electoral college for electing the party leader, which had always been the province of Labour MPs; and deciding on who would approve the party's manifesto.

Each one of these was fiercely contested, line by line, and votes tended to be seven to six in favour of the left. There was no consensus, no meeting of minds. So the whole lot was going to have to go to the conference for another acrimonious debate.

The commission had failed. But a statesmanlike David Basnett emerged from the wreckage to tell the world that substantial progress had been made on the party's financial and organisational structure. In the end, though, Basnett had to go back to the day job. He was a professional trade union official; he wanted to hang onto his union's bargaining power, and the Labour Party, created by the unions at the start of the century to bolster their bargaining position, was so helplessly mired in its internal struggle that it could do nothing effective to help.

The idea that the unions had huge, unaccountable power, and that people like Basnett, 'union barons' as newspapers called them, could make and break governments had exerted a powerful hold over the popular imagination.

On 1 August 1980, the government's Employment Act received the royal assent. The Employment Secretary, Jim Prior, was referred to by the press as a 'Tory wet' and the Employment Act was very modest; the real attack on unions was still to come.

The Act prevented anyone from picketing a workplace other than their own; it outlawed most secondary action, that is, sympathy action, designed to put pressure on someone else's employer; it required new closed-shop agreements to be approved by 80 per cent of the eligible workforce in a secret ballot; it protected from dismissal those workers who objected to union membership. The Act also encouraged the use of secret ballots on proposed industrial action and in the election of union officials, by making public funds available to pay for them.

Back in the dugout, three senior Labour figures, Shirley Williams, David Owen and William Rodgers – known, in a parody of the Chinese politics of the time, as the 'Gang of Three' – wrote a letter to *The Guardian* saying that victory for the left in the constitutional and political battles at the forthcoming party conference could justify the creation of a new social democratic party committed to NATO and a mixed economy.

The left-wing Rank-and-File Mobilising Committee replied, 'If the Gang of Three would only stop threatening to leave the party and actually do it, they would spare us all a great deal of trouble. They are out of place in the Labour Party for they are, in all essentials, Conservatives.'

As delegates to the TUC conference at the start of September walked into the sparkling new Brighton conference centre, opened by Prime Minister Callaghan just three years earlier and in another age, they ran the gauntlet of angry protestors with megaphones roaring, 'TUC get off your knees – call a general strike now.'

Union leaders doubted whether they had the power to deliver a general strike. But they also seriously doubted their ability to deliver on Callaghan's call for them to agree a five-year incomes policy.

So they smiled politely and looked statesmanlike, and talked about not ruling out industrial action, and the possibility of doing something illegal. Basnett, dressed in his best suit, talked about how trade unionists might have to go to prison to defend their rights; he sounded less than convincing.

Delegates did, nonetheless, vote for a 'sustained and vigorous campaign of non-cooperation with the government, including, if necessary, industrial action' against the Employment Act. And they balanced it by voting for a joint TUC–Labour Party pre-election plan on pay, prices and anti-inflationary measures. This was not, TGWU leader Moss Evans hastened to reassure everyone, an incomes policy. Precisely what it was, if it was not an incomes policy, Evans did not spell out.

For the left, the hero of the hour was the president of the Yorkshire miners; the man who had delivered victory at Grunwick. Well, almost delivered victory. It seemed like a great defeat for capitalism when Arthur Scargill was elected the youngest member of the TUC general council, promising to fight for 'a socialist policy, and not the tired, worn-out social democratic policy that led to our defeat in 1979'.

The unions have always thought they do the real work of the labour movement. Politicians are grubby chaps who have their occasional uses, a bit like journalists. Scargill was once asked by the playwright John Mortimer why he did not go for a seat in Parliament. Mortimer wrote, 'I was asking King Arthur if he'd care for a post as a corporal. He had been offered four Labour seats, but why should he forsake the reality of union rule for the pallid pretensions of Westminster?'

At the Labour Party's worst moments, it therefore falls to the unions to step in, take over the helm and steady the ship. Ernest Bevin had led the unions in doing just that after 1931, and his successor at the TGWU, Arthur Deakin, had led the rescue mission in the 1950s.

It was more complicated now, because the battles inside the Labour Party were replicated in the unions. The siren voice of Arthur Scargill had its imitators in most unions. But there were still folk at the top of the unions with gravitas, and no one had more gravitas than David Basnett.

So it was Basnett who staged the takeover. He proposed that the unions should oversee how the Labour Party spent its money, effectively reducing the party to what it had once been – the parliamentary voice of the trade unions.

But even in its wounded and impoverished state, the Labour Party this time was having none of it. It had grown up, or thought it had, and no longer wanted or needed the paternal tutelage of union leaders. Callaghan and Benn united to rubbish the plan. 'We must leave the unions in no doubt that although we need their money, they need a Labour government,' said Callaghan.

Labour Party chairman Lady Jeger opened the party conference by warning against 'sectional rigidity' and Balkanisation. 'There must be flexibility for personal views and differences ... The British people will never forgive us if, at this time of crisis, we do not give absolute priority to the fight against the worst government of the century,' she said.

Absolutely, agreed Michael Foot, Jim Callaghan, Denis Healey, Tony Benn, Shirley Williams and David Basnett – and then set about tearing lumps out of each other. In the NEC elections, the left tightened its grip; its majority was now eighteen to eleven.

Francis Beckett remembers arriving late and asking Sally Keeble, then a Labour press officer and later the MP for Northampton North, what had happened so far. 'A lot of men in grey suits have made speeches,' she replied wearily. Most of these speeches invoked what was known at the time as 'This great movement of ours', and known in the pubs where journalists and malcontents lurked as TIGMOO.

The left wanted withdrawal from the common market and NATO, and unilateral nuclear disarmament and nationalisation. But these were mere policies. The real battle was over the party's own constitution. That's what produced all the adrenalin.

The conference voted for mandatory reselection of Labour MPs, but narrowly rejected the idea of giving the NEC power over the party's manifesto. Callaghan fought to the last ditch to keep the leadership in the hands of Labour MPs, and lost.

So that was settled. Except that it wasn't. Who was to have the lion's share of the vote? Should there be three equal portions, for MPs, constituency parties and trade unions? Or an electoral college with half the votes going to the unions, a quarter to Labour MPs and a quarter to the constituencies? Or something else? Nothing could command a majority.

And so, inevitably, came the decision that the whole issue would be debated again at a special conference in January, four months later. Four more months in which the life would be sucked out of Labour politics by the debate on the constitution, much as the life is currently being sucked out of politics by Brexit. Four months in which Labour would have little energy to oppose the government. Four months for frantic and anguished meetings, in which calculations would be made and the disposition of forces agreed, and during all of this time Fleet Street gloated.

When the special conference was convened, at Wembley in January 1981, a classic trade union fix went wrong and handed outright victory to the Bennites, who wanted, and got, 40 per cent of the votes for the unions, with 30 per cent for MPs and 30 per cent for ordinary Labour Party members. It cast the trade unions in the role of arrogant power brokers and lent credibility to the Tory charge that union leaders ran the country under Labour.

By then, Callaghan had resigned. The left were furious, believing he had gone early in order to ensure that his successor was elected by the old system – that is, by Labour MPs alone. He probably did, but his resignation did not achieve the desired result. Michael Foot was elected Labour leader at the age of sixty-seven, beating the front runner and Callaghan's preferred successor Denis Healey by 139 votes to 129.

To many Labour people, Foot's election seemed like a dream come true. They indulged in a brief daydream of a new sort of Prime Minister; a human being who did not have the politician's polish; a leader who was passionate about ideas and determined to turn them into policy; someone who was a writer of distinction, writing not just about politics but also about such people as Lord Byron and H. G. Wells; a leader who could wear a less-than-perfect overcoat at the Cenotaph (and did, to a loud chorus of media condemnation).

The coat in question was actually brand new and made by Jaeger, a gift to Michael from his wife Jill Craigie. The Queen Mother remarked to Foot at the Cenotaph that it was 'a very sensible coat for such an inclement day'. The coat incident might not have become an issue, had it not been for the then Labour MP for Derby South, Walter Johnson, who accused Foot of 'looking like a navvy' while wearing it. The coat continued to hang in a closet at Michael and Jill's home in Hampstead for many years after. Despite the best efforts of Mark Seddon, who wanted to raffle it for funds for *Tribune*, Michael or someone close to him somehow had the item spirited away to the Labour History Museum, where it languishes apparently to this day. In contrast, Ed Miliband's infamous 'Ed-Stone' of chiselled promises was apparently spirited away after the 2015 general election and smashed into smithereens. Its whereabouts remain unknown.

Tony Benn's supporters had persuaded him not to stand for the leadership. To do so, they argued, would be to lend legitimacy to the old process and to the new leader. All that was required was for Labour to have a stand-in leader until a proper leader could be elected under the new system.

So the left never considered Foot – Labour's most left-wing leader since George Lansbury in the 1930s – to have legitimacy. Foot, the veteran Bevanite, spent two unrewarding years fighting against the left. Their hunger for constitutional tinkering within the Labour Party bears an uncanny similarity to the hunger of the Blairites after Blair was elected leader in 1994, when Blair stampeded through seemingly untendentious 'reforms' which stripped policy-making from the grassroots altogether. Oh for a Clem Attlee to say, 'The Labour Party's passion for definition should always be resisted.'

Foot did not establish a trend. Our political leaders over the next quarter of a century were to look more and more like grey-suited purpose-built politicians. The bibliophile leader seemed increasingly an anachronism. His mild-mannered attempts to enforce some kind of shadow Cabinet collective responsibility – like Corbyn, Foot had been a serial rebel – were openly challenged by Tony Benn.

January 1981 saw the split that Foot had hoped to avoid. David Owen, Shirley Williams and Bill Rodgers were joined by Roy Jenkins, who had just completed a four-year term as president of the European Commission and was ready to return to British politics, but not to his old home, the Labour Party. The Gang of Three became the Gang of Four, and they broke away from Labour to found the Social Democratic Party (SDP). Twenty-eight Labour MPs followed them into the new party.

The SDP was to go on to split Labour's vote in the 1983 general election, ensuring the return of the Tories to power. The Gang of Four cited Labour's move to the left at the grassroots as reasons for the deadly fissure. Foot invested a lot of time and energy trying to persuade at least one of them, Shirley Williams, not to defect. She dillied and dallied, and appeared to be on course to step back from the brink, but in the end she threw her lot in with the other three. Short-lived as the SDP may have proved to be, the media bubble that enveloped it at the time ensured that Labour's message was even more muffled than it might have been.

No doubt the Gang of Four's policy differences with the Labour Party mattered to them, but policy now came a bad second to arcane matters relating to Labour's constitution, as the opening sentence of their Limehouse Declaration makes clear:

'The calamitous outcome of the Labour Party Wembley conference demands a new start in British politics. A handful of trade union leaders can now dictate the choice of a future Prime Minister.'

Two months later Tony Benn announced that he would challenge the incumbent, Denis Healey, for the more or less meaningless post of deputy leader of the Labour Party. The Bennites said the new election machinery needed to be 'tested', to which Neil Kinnock responded that this was 'a bit like Christmas morning when a kid's given a watch and starts taking it apart to see how it works'. This was a direct steal from Michael Foot, whose speech involving Keith Joseph, the British economy and a watch, arguably remains one of the greatest pieces of recorded parliamentary oratory.

But arguing against an election was not easy. Jon Lansman would give you a nasty look and say, 'Don't you believe in democracy then?' Lansman and the Campaign for Labour Party Democracy were to play a hugely significant role in pushing for changes aimed at transferring power to the grassroots – a role he was to assume once again three decades on.

Arthur Scargill, now the miners' national president, upped the ante, telling the Scottish miners' gala that anyone who criticised Benn was 'sabotaging not only the candidature of Tony Benn but the principles of socialism which are basic to our movement'.

Since Benn was determined to stand, John Silkin from the soft left also decided to enter the fray, in effect to wreck Benn's campaign. Those who were part of what was starting to be called the soft left – Michael Foot, Neil Kinnock, Robin Cook – encouraged Silkin to stand. They knew there were MPs who did not want to vote for Benn, but would face deselection if they voted for Healey, and Silkin offered them a way out – an anti-Benn left-winger. 'I shall come third,' Silkin told his friends comfortably. 'I hope not to come too bad a third.'

All this set the scene for Labour's dreadful summer in 1981. The three candidates did the rounds of union conferences, and the publicity they attracted ensured that trade unions came to be seen as far more powerful and authoritarian than they really were, with disastrous long-term consequences for them.

The election, billed as an affirmation of grassroots power, was actually the most public demonstration ever of the power of the trade union block vote. It made the unions look like insolent power brokers. When the building trades union UCATT took its decision, the *Sunday Times* reported its decision under the headline: HOW THREE TOP COMMUNISTS SWUNG 200,000 VOTES TO BENN.

The Bennites started to make life hot for Silkin in his Deptford constituency *pour encourager les autres*. And Silkin challenged the Bennites for control of Labour's left-wing weekly magazine, *Tribune*, which had been founded by Aneurin Bevan.

The *Tribune* brouhaha began when loyal Bennite Chris Mullin was chosen as editor. The break from the past twenty years was very sudden. One week in May, the paper broadly supported Foot's leadership, and the next week it opposed it bitterly. The saintliness of Tony Benn was weekly contrasted with the moral turpitude of Michael Foot, and Foot accused Mullin of 'infantile leftism', a specialised but deadly insult, only understood by the few people who knew that Lenin once wrote a pamphlet called 'Left-wing Communism: An Infantile Disorder'.

Silkin led a group of shareholders, including Nye Bevan's widow Jennie Lee, who wanted to use their shares to try to regain control of the paper for the Tribune Group of MPs.

The key figure in all this was, once again, Jon Lansman. He

moved home to Deptford, where he could be a permanent irritant to Silkin, and he took a job as *Tribune*'s business manager. There he arranged a speaking tour of the constituency for Chris Mullin.

The two battles, for *Tribune* and for Deptford, raged with unabated intensity right up to Silkin's sudden and early death in 1987.

Andrew Murray, then the lobby correspondent for the Communist Party newspaper the *Morning Star*, predicted in his column that Mrs Thatcher would be ousted in a Cabinet coup before 1981 was over, and there would be a coalition government consisting of Heathite Tories and the new Social Democratic Party. He also claimed that Labour Party rallies would increasingly tempt people away from their television sets to hear the likes of Tony Benn and Michael Foot speaking, and that Labour's move to the left was irreversible. Let us hope his political instincts are sharper now that he is one of Jeremy Corbyn's closest advisers.

The truth was that Labour England was in a state of civil war. Battles raged in every trade union, and in most of Labour's constituency parties.

In Hemel Hempstead, the Labour MP Robin Corbett had lost his seat to the Conservatives in 1979 and was fighting a pitched battle with the left to be allowed to contest the seat at the next election. The left's candidate was Paul Boateng, chairman of the GLC's police committee. Boateng was never, in fact, an especially left-wing figure, but he was black, and therefore in a position to cast Corbett as a white man holding up the advance of racial equality. Boateng later became a loyal Blairite in government, and latterly Britain's High Commissioner to South Africa and a member of the House of Lords.

By the end of the battle, which Boateng won, such immoderate language had been used by both sides that no Labour candidate stood a chance in Hemel Hempstead. Corbett, meanwhile, got a last-minute nomination for another Tory marginal, Birmingham Erdington.

Come the 1983 election, Corbett's friends from Hemel Hempstead refused to work for Boateng, and travelled up the motorway to canvass for Corbett in Birmingham instead. Corbett, a former journalist with a flair for campaigning, won in Birmingham, while Boateng lost in Hemel Hempstead.

Francis Beckett wrote to congratulate his friend Robin Corbett, suggesting he might feel just a little bit of *Schadenfreude* that he was an MP and Boateng wasn't. Corbett wrote back a four-word letter: 'Me? Gloat? Not half.'

Mark Seddon received a letter from Frank Field MP, who explained why he couldn't bring himself to vote for either Benn or Healey. 'In truth,' he wrote, 'we need the wisdom of King Solomon.'

In the autumn of 1981, Healey narrowly squeaked home; the next election was already probably lost, and the Labour Party was in a state of civil war.

Local Labour parties fell out over all sorts of things: from nuclear disarmament to the precise meaning of obscure passages in Labour's rule book. In Hornsey, members argued over whether to admit veteran Trotskyist Tariq Ali to the party. Both sides saw the vote as a test of ideological purity, and the left won by thirty-three votes to fifteen. The Ealing Southall MP, the late Sidney Bidwell, told Ali to 'go home'. Bidwell's racist jibe earned Tariq Ali more support.

The National Executive Committee said that Labour must not admit Ali, so Barbara Simon, the membership secretary, refused to issue him with a membership card. But the organiser, who was also Ali's key supporter, took a different view. 'He's a member of the party and he'll be issued with a card,' said Jeremy Corbyn.

With Labour preoccupied by such trivia, Prime Minister Thatcher was able to step up the pace in 1981. She gave herself a Cabinet majority for the first time, in part by replacing 'wet' Employment Secretary Jim Prior with the sneering, sharp-toothed Norman Tebbit – 'a wart on a carbuncle' according to Neil Kinnock, while Michael Foot branded him 'a semi-house-trained polecat'. The then popular satirical TV puppet programme, *Spitting Image*, portrayed Tebbit as a bovver boy in boots.

Thatcher also started in earnest on the job of selling off state enterprises: Cable and Wireless, the National Freight Corporation, Britoil, the Docks Board, the channel ferry company Sealink, Amersham International (makers of radioactive chemicals, part of the atomic energy industry), and much more.

CHAPTER FOUR

MELTDOWN

The countdown to armageddon really began with the Bermondsey by-election in February 1982.

Michael Foot's desperately unhappy tenure as Labour's leader was to suffer a further, near-terminal blow in February 1983 with the decision of the party's former Chief Whip Bob Mellish to take a job with the newly established London Docklands Development Corporation, charged with transforming the barren wastelands of both the old Royal Docks in the East End of London and the Surrey Docks in Mellish's deprived south London Bermondsey constituency. Mellish's resignation would force a by-election, the result of which would send tremors throughout the Labour Party and which would be a horrible foretaste of what was to come barely a few months later.

Mellish and his long-time ally and former leader of Southwark Council, John O'Grady, had run this then traditional, predominantly Catholic, working-class seat as something of a private fiefdom. The local party had tired of the heavy hand of old Labour right-wing paternalism and selected a young Australian campaigner, Peter Tatchell, partly on his appeal to revive the iconoclastic radicalism of one of the predecessor MPs for the borough, the still affectionately remembered Dr Alfred Salter. Tatchell also advocated 'extra-parliamentary action' as a way of ensuring a Labour government wouldn't be derailed by all of the usual 'extra-parliamentary' forces that would be arranged against it. But, and with shades of today's media frenzy over 'moderates' being toppled by 'extremists from Momentum', Mellish took to the television interview and appeared, weeping at this 'extremist' takeover of his old manor. Fleet Street's finest immediately took up the cudgels and Tatchell soon found himself experiencing the very worst that could be thrown at him. This was compounded when Michael Foot appeared to get the wrong end of the stick and announced that Tatchell was not 'an endorsed member of the Labour Party, and, so far as I am concerned, never will be endorsed', having been persuaded that the latter's call for 'extra-parliamentary action' was tantamount to revolutionary socialism. Tatchell had in mind more the sort of lively demonstrations Michael had spent his whole life taking part enthusiastically in and had of course been endorsed by the Bermondsey party. The confusion was compounded when the general secretary of the Labour Party confirmed that Tatchell was indeed the official candidate – and by that time the runes were foretold. The row confirmed the Fleet Street caricature of a Militant takeover of the local Labour Party, although Tatchell's own politics were about as far removed from the myopia of the Militant Tendency as it was possible to imagine.

Mark Seddon was an enthusiastic foot soldier in a by-election campaign that was to be marked by its casual brutality and homophobia. One of the first sights he saw was John O'Grady, now in the incarnation of the Real Bermondsey Labour candidate with the support of Bob Mellish, sitting atop the sort of horse and cart once favoured by London's rag-and-bone men, shouting into a megaphone that Tatchell was an 'Australian draft-dodging poof'.

In the early 1980s, the Surrey Docks were largely derelict and the raft of 1930s-era council flats were matched by the corrugated sheeting surrounding demolitions and old Second World War bomb sites. Bermondsey should have been rock-solid Labour, but the party's self-induced shambles were soon exploited by the newly energised Liberals and their candidate, Simon Hughes. The Liberals had no local roots, and usually they were lucky to save their deposit in this old dockers' fiefdom, but Tatchell had been declared beyond the pale and was left to his fate by Labour's front bench and most of the Parliamentary Labour Party. He had bravely declared himself to be gay, an almost unheard-of declaration back then, which opened him up not only for a torrent of abuse, but a deluge of hate mail, arson threats and much else besides.

After one canvassing session, Seddon and a colleague from the Norwich Labour Party returned to Tatchell's council flat on the austere 1930s era Rockingham Estate to be shown a hole that had been drilled into the ceiling of the empty flat above into the candidate's flat below – down which all manner of lavatory waste had been tipped. On another occasion, while getting into a van with fellow canvassers, the shout went out: 'Get the fuck out of the way!' Fortunately the driver managed to put his foot on the accelerator quickly enough to avoid an exploding cooker that had come hurtling from a few floors above. It transpired that the cooker had caught alight and was not being deliberately aimed at a bunch of Labour Party canvassers, but it didn't feel that way at the time.

Tatchell's campaign, despite all of the impediments put in front of it, has a contemporary appeal to it; he promised to save the local St Olave's Hospital from closure, was opposed to the early privatisation of public assets and council house sell-offs of the Tory era, and vowed to get people back to work.

Rumours that the Liberals' candidate, Simon Hughes, was also gay but refusing to condemn the hideous homophobia being hurled at Tatchell rankled at the time – but it would be years before Hughes acknowledged the fact that he was bisexual and of course far too late to be of any recompense to Tatchell, whose monumental defeat at the hands of Hughes and the Liberal Party was one of the greatest by-election disasters ever experienced by the Labour Party. Labour's vote had dropped from 63.6 per cent to 26.1 per cent, with Hughes achieving a just over 9,000 majority over Labour. It amounted to the biggest ever record-ed by-election swing in British political history (44.2 per cent). John O'Grady, a former leader of Southwark Borough Council, representing Real Bermondsey Labour, came third, while the Conservative candidate, Robert Hughes, finished fourth, both losing their deposits. The by-election also saw the first appear-ance of a new party that was to become a familiar fixture on the British political landscape in the coming decades: Screaming Lord Sutch's Official Monster Raving Loony Party fought its first election campaign. Bermondsey was to stay stubbornly in the Hughes camp until 2015, when Labour's Neil Coyne won the seat back. Tatchell was never to stand as a Labour candidate again, although he continued to live in the same flat, in the same estate. Instead he devoted much of his life to gay rights, human rights and a resolute activism frequently ahead of its time. For Michael Foot and the battered and bruised Labour Party, Ber-mondsey was but a terrible foretaste of what was to come.

'How did it happen,' asked the Labour Party press officer who was seconded to the by-election, Monica Foot, after it was all over, 'that a well-meaning, earnest young social worker from the Rockingham estate became a media obsession, with teams of highly paid hacks probing his life and times?'

(In case you're wondering, yes, Monica Foot is one of the Feet – she is the former wife of Michael's nephew, the late left-wing journalist Paul Foot.)

One reason, said Monica, was geographic. 'It was undoubt-edly bad luck that you can get to any part of Bermondsey from Fleet Street and back again in time for lunch.'

But they had something worse to contend with than the unre-strained vitriol of the media. For Bermondsey Labour Party was like every other local Labour Party in 1982, only much more so.

The playwright Steve Gooch lived in Bermondsey, and rang a telephone number he had found for the local Labour Party. The call was answered by an unfriendly male voice, and Steve asked politely if he could please have an application form, as he wished to join the Labour Party.

There was a long silence. At last the voice said, in a voice laden with dark suspicion, 'Are you a friend of Eric?'

Who Eric was, Steve never found out, but it must have been someone in a rival faction to the speaker, who was suspected of recruiting friends as members to be voting fodder for internal power struggles.

And that atmosphere poisoned the campaign. Tatchell sent his leaflets to a printer closely associated with Militant, so La-bour's national agent confiscated them on the eve of the launch. A large committee was set up to run the campaign, and it met for several hours each day, for what Monica Foot calls 'theolog-ical discussion'. (Committee-itis was one of the besetting sins of the Labour movement in the early 1980s.)

Another by-election was due, this time in Darlington – also a seat previously held by Labour, so by convention it was up to Labour to call the by-election. After a disaster like Bermond-sey, a party manager's first instinct is to put the next test off for as long as possible, but Labour's Chief Whip Michael Cocks moved the writ for Darlington to the day after Bermondsey.

Michael Cocks knew what he was doing. Ossie O'Brien was a good candidate: middle-aged, middle of the road, local, a sober, sensible adult education lecturer, but also humorous, clever and quick on his feet.

Monica Foot being understandably exhausted and in need of a holiday, and Labour's other press officers being short on experience of prolonged and unfriendly media exposure, the party sent for the newly liberated Francis Beckett, who had just been made redundant from his job as head of communications at the National Union of Agricultural and Allied Workers.

They found him in Nottingham, where he was putting to bed his very last issue of a trade union magazine. The press conference to launch the campaign had been called for the very next morning and he was required to chair it, so without a change of clothes or a toothbrush, he boarded the Darlington train, and was met at the station by the agent, Terry Johnson, from whom he borrowed a clean shirt for the press conference. Terry being a considerably more substantial man than Francis, the shirt billowed loosely around Francis like a spinnaker as he introduced candidate Ossie O'Brien to the waiting hacks.

Foot sent a member of his shadow Cabinet, Jack Cunningham, to manage the campaign.

'I'm here because Ossie O'Brien is my sort of Labour candidate,' said former Prime Minister Jim Callaghan as he walked through the small front door of the terraced building in the centre of Darlington where Labour had its headquarters, which didn't quite tie in with the image of a united party that Beckett and Cunningham were trying to project.

The Liberals, fresh from their Bermondsey triumph, issued a leaflet saying Michael Foot was unfit to be Prime Minister because he was a unilateralist, and anyway Labour would soon be taken over by the Militant Tendency. The press pack was there in force, hunting the streets for members of the Militant Tendency who might be canvassing for Ossie.

Peter Hitchens of the *Daily Express* came along and wrote a column about how there was an invitation to a Militant meeting pinned to the notice board in Labour headquarters. So much for Labour being united and moderate, he wrote.

'I've taken that bloody Militant notice down,' Johnson told Beckett, early the next morning. 'Well, put it straight back up again,' said Beckett. Hitchens came into the press conference and went straight to the leaflet. Since it was still there, he couldn't file the chortling follow-up piece about how Labour had rushed to take it down.

No famous politician in the land failed to turn up for Darlington. It was Labour's last chance. Foot came, of course, but Labour's star visitor was Neil Kinnock. He stepped smartly off the London train, borrowed £5 from a Labour Party official, and took everyone he found in the nearby party headquarters to the pub. In Darlington, in 1983, you could buy a substantial round of drinks with £5.

In the pub, he did not stop talking for a moment. As a stream of ideas tumbled out of him, each one perfectly wrapped in an evocative phrase, the ageing Labour grandee Barbara Castle listened in uncharacteristic silence, seeming to think that she saw the reincarnation of her dead hero Aneurin Bevan.

Eventually he was dragged out of the pub and across to the biggest hall in town, which seated hundreds and was packed out. He spoke for a full hour, making his audience laugh and cry in turn at his attacks on Margaret Thatcher's government. 'Now, the Cabinet wets – by the way, do you know why they call them that? It's because that's what they do when she shouts at them.'

Then two Labour officials took him to a private room and whispered that they had overheard a plot to get rid of Michael Foot. He buoyed them with his optimism, and for a good five minutes they both believed that soon Foot would be Prime Minister.

Then they went down to the hotel bar where the huge press pack was assembled. There he took them on. This journalist had written a load of rubbish about Footie, that one was so deeply in hock to the Tories that he played 'See the Conquering Heroine Comes' every time Maggie wiped her feet on him. As others left for their beds one by one, his musical Welsh cadences followed them to the hotel lift.

On the train home the next day, Kinnock snagged the houndstooth suit on a protruding hook. No one we know has seen him in a loud suit since then. Seven months later, aged just forty-one, he was leader of his party, and his best years were over.

The de facto leader of the press pack for by-elections in those days was the BBC's Vincent Hanna, who wrote afterwards in *The Journalist*, the NUJ magazine, that on polling day in the media's hotel, the Kings Head,

> the sorrowful face of Francis Beckett, the Labour Party press officer, appears for breakfast. He has had a hard three weeks. He sits trying to keep scrambled egg on his fork and attempts to tell me something but his tongue is still asleep. Francis has handled Ossie O'Brien with some skill, exposing him constantly to the local press, planting articles, issuing stories, fixing picture calls, while carefully controlling access to the nationals. He had the luxury of a candidate who could safely be given his head, except when Peter Hitchens of the Daily Express went on about disarmament. Francis would splutter at him for several minutes and Hitchens would wonder why he never won. I explained that Francis is the best splutterer in the business; he has medals for it.

But when, at mid-morning, Hanna turned up at Labour HQ and asked a grizzled old campaigner what was different about Darlington, he was told, 'It's a feel for the labour movement, a sense of respect for tradition and, above all, it's a real compassion for people. That's why it's so different from Bermondsey and the rantings of the Bennite left, and always will be.' Perhaps he added that Labour was united round Foot, but perhaps he didn't bother.

The labour movement. Labour England. Everyone knew what it meant in those days. What had changed was that the competing factions no longer accepted the other's right to call themselves part of it.

'In the final twenty-four hours,' reported Hanna, 'the SDP reported one Militant in the streets of the town. I saw him myself handing out leaflets and chanting "KTTOJNB" – Kick The Tories Out, Jobs Not Bombs – before being captured and sent to a distant committee room.

'I mentioned this to Francis.

"Oh shit," he says. "Did he say anything?"

"No," I say. "Good," he says. "We are a nice party and don't you forget it," and rushes away.'

Labour won well in Darlington, dulling, if not eliminating, the pain of Bermondsey, but it might have been better had we not, for it was that victory that convinced Mrs Thatcher that she should not wait until she was forced to go to the country in a year's time.

So just two months after Darlington, on 9 May, the Prime Minister announced that the general election would be held on 9 June.

'Right up to that moment I had always had some lingering, wishful hope that she might not actually do it,' wrote Michael Foot in his book *Another Heart and Other Pulses*. 'The resolute approach would have suited her temperament and reputation better. But … the obvious fact that time would give the Labour Party a little longer to bind up its self-inflicted lacerations.'

Perhaps Theresa May borrowed from Margaret Thatcher's decision to call an early election on 9 June 1983 to demonstrate the wisdom of her decision to go to the country well ahead of time, in 2017. May's gamble nearly failed. Thatcher had weathered the muted opposition of her own Tory wets to the massive dose of monetarism administered to Britain's already creaky industrial infrastructure. And she had benefited massively from a crisis that was very much the creation of her own government, in a remote part of the south Atlantic.

The scrapping of a Royal Naval protection vessel, the *Endurance*, charged with ensuring at least the moderate presence of British interest in the barely populated Falkland Islands, had sent a pretty clear message of British non-intent towards its colony to the generals now in charge in Argentina. They were desperately looking for a diversion away from the economic crisis enveloping their own country.

Taking away the islanders' British passports and making them 'citizens of an overseas territory' with limited rights of access to the UK was another own goal by Thatcher's government. Unsurprisingly, the Argentinian leader General Galtieri came to the conclusion that the British couldn't care less about the 'Islas Malvinas', and initially ordered landings and annexed the even more remote and unpopulated former whaling station island of South Georgia.

The dispatch of a military task force to take back the now occupied Falkland Islands was the making of Maggie 'the Iron Lady' Thatcher. Famously she commanded the nation to 'Rejoice at this news' that the ice-bound South Georgia, whose only inhabitants were penguins and a herd of imported Norwegian reindeer, had been recaptured. Many Britons, who weeks before had largely been unaware even of the island's existence, were whipped into fits of self-righteous, patriotic, Argie-bashing fervour by a media that had largely lost any capacity to ask some basic questions about the competence of a government that had lost the islands in the first place.

A similar threat posed by the Argentinians to Britain's remote South Atlantic holdings had taken place in the late 1970s – and while Labour was in office. It had been met by the quiet dispatch of a nuclear Polaris submarine to the waters around the Falkland Islands. Once tipped off, the Argentinians immediately scaled back their bold plans to invade.

Britain's military victory in the Falkland Islands was not a foregone conclusion. It seems doubtful that it could have been achieved without the logistical and intelligence support of the United States – although there had clearly been a pull in the opposite direction by less Anglophile officials in the Pentagon.

Thus, following a military victory that might not have happened without American support, Margaret Thatcher fought the general election by savaging Labour's apparent lack of patriotism (this was despite Michael Foot's support for the retaking of the islands). Thatcher, unlike Theresa May in 2017, was to rout Labour in the 1983 general election.

Labour could no longer, it seemed, count on the automatic loyalty of its supporters. The trade unions were a whole lot weaker and many of those who remained in trade unions had actually voted for the Conservative Party – many for the first time. Part of the attraction was the Tory promise to allow council tenants to buy the properties they rented and for a knockdown price. Another was the promise to sell shares in the nationalised industries such as in British Telecom and other utilities such as gas, electricity and water.

As soon as the election was called, the true spirit of the labour movement in 1983 surfaced. A campaign committee was instantly assembled, and was to meet every morning throughout the campaign at 8 a.m., before the daily press conference. Every interest was represented. They all attended to watch each other suspiciously.

So, average attendance was between thirty and forty. There were not enough seats in the general secretary's office, so they perched on tables and lined up along the walls. One man was there for two days before someone asked who he was. He turned out to be the Special Branch detective assigned to Foot. Foot tried to keep the meeting in order. 'Order, order,' he shouted at regular intervals.

This probably explains why, one dreadful morning after the meeting at Labour's press conference, Labour Party general secretary Jim Mortimer, chairing the press conference from the centre of the platform in the plonking style common at trade union meetings, said, 'At the campaign committee meeting this morning we were all insistent that Michael Foot is the leader of the Labour Party and speaks for the party and we support the manifesto of the party.'

In a long and distinguished trade union career, Mortimer must often have quelled dissent like that. 'Committee says Michael's leader, so let's not have any more of this argy bargy.' Of course, it allowed the press to say that Michael did not have the support of his party.

Much of this information we owe to Jim Innes, co-founder of the *West Highlands Free Press*, a wonderfully noisy and entertaining Scots journalist, broadcaster, Labour Party press officer, with a voice that sounded as though he gargled with gravel. Innes recalled afterwards how he was assigned to look after radio. No one ever discussed the use of radio with him, so he did what he could.

> What it means in practice is that, for example, I go to Denis Healey's people and say, I think he should do such and such a programme. If his diary's got a gap, he may do it. If my powers of persuasion are working, he may do it. If not, he won't. I fight

for Healey's time and my opponents in this fight are the national or regional or constituency agents. It means that I work for the radio stations. The Labour Party just pays my wages.

That sort of freelance activity was common among frustrated staffers. Innes wrote:

Francis Beckett, a freelance brought in for the campaign, decides he'll have to go ahead and win the election on his own. He has a suppressed National Economic Development Council document with a quote from CBI chairman Campbell Fraser to the effect that anyone knowing the truth about our industrial future will take 'the first boat out of the country.

The hierarchy aren't interested. Francis goes direct to Kinnock. Kinnock buys it and they plan a weekend release. When Kinnock produces it, there's a panic when the hacks call to ask why Len Murray went along with keeping the document quiet, but Francis splutters splendidly.

(Everyone seems to have Francis spluttering in 1983. The present authors have no idea why.)

A campaign slogan was quickly enshrined in concrete before anyone could change it, and it read, 'Think positive, act positive, vote Labour.' What no one knows outside a tiny circle is that it was accompanied by the worst campaign song ever written. To a heroic marching tune, it went, in part:

Rebuild Britain, Labour leads the way
To a glorious tomorrow.
Show the Tories Labour's on the way,
To get us out of the mess we're in today.
If you and me believe in democracy,

We're going to put Michael Foot in the league where he belongs.
Think positive, act positive, vote Labour.

The rest is too toe-curlingly embarrassing to write down.

The first six cassettes came to the press office and were distributed in solemn secrecy among the press officers as keepsakes by Jim Innes, with firm instructions to play them to nobody outside.

At bad moments during the campaign, which meant most days, Jim raised spirits in the press office by leading his colleagues round the big central table in a wild dance with the campaign song playing full volume. Outside the press office, no one ever heard it. What happened to the thousands of cassettes which had been ordered, no one knows. It was rumoured that Jim Innes was seen skulking suspiciously close to a nearby skip.

The truth will never now be known, because Jim, to the great regret of his many friends and admirers, died in 2016, aged only sixty-nine.

Michael Foot's wife, Jill Craigie, came into the press office with a scribbled note she had picked up from the floor at St George's Hall in Liverpool. It read, 'If MF talks to any of these drop a picture.' Underneath were the names of leading Liverpool Militants. That was the main business of the election. Footie was in the pockets of Militant. Vote Labour and all sorts of unnamed horrors will befall you and your children. It was slickly done, and Labour had no answer.

The party went down to its worst defeat since 1931. Tony Benn, that master of groundless optimism, hailed '7 million votes for socialism'.

Amid the wreckage, three young men entered Parliament that year of whom the nation was to hear much more. Gordon Brown, thirty-two, the new MP for Dunfermline East, had warned his constituents that there were secret plans to decimate the coal industry.

Tony Blair, the youngest Labour MP at just thirty, had secured a last-minute nomination for Sedgefield and said that when he got to Westminster, he realised he was the luckiest person there.

And in Islington North, 34-year-old Jeremy Corbyn was to spend thirty-two years on Labour's back benches while the other two young men led governments, before being suddenly propelled into the leadership of his party.

The last word belongs to Jim Innes: 'How dare a few hundred members tear the Labour Party asunder for four years and leave millions of Labour voters at the mercy of a Tory government? How dare we arrogantly spend our energies on meaningless manifestoes while those who look to us for help are made redundant?'

CHAPTER FIVE

BACK TO THE '30S WITH MAGGIE

L abour England had at its heart the idea of social, public and co-operative ownership as part of a mixed economy. It shared the same vision as the Scandinavian social democrats or the German and French socialists.

The idea that Labour was committed to public ownership of the corner shop was one ritually trotted out by the Conservatives – who, nonetheless, up until the mid-1970s had little intention of reversing the public ownership of the utilities for instance. Indeed, Edward Heath's government nationalised Rolls-Royce in the early 1970s to save it from possible closure – just as David Cameron's Tory government was to nationalise failing banks that had brought the Anglo-American economies almost to their knees decades later.

But for Margaret Thatcher and her arriviste new Tories, the promise of a new Britain of small shareholders was a powerful one. Glitzy television advertisements urged the public to buy into what they already owned. 'Psst, don't tell Sid!' was the advertising line used to accompany the sell-off of British Gas. 'Buzby', a yellow canary, did the job on British Telecom. No matter that within a dozen or so years the privatised public utilities were largely in the hands of the big corporate shareholders, many of them based overseas.

Even a former Conservative Prime Minister, Harold Macmillan, was to speak out against the sell-off of the 'family silver'. But it would be another thirty-odd years before the grand larceny that had been the sale of often profitable nationalised industries began to be seriously questioned.

On the privatised British railways, for instance, a ticket costs far more than on the nationalised railways in France. Furthermore, some of the organisations being subsidised to run trains over tracks in Britain were nationalised foreign railway companies, such as the French SNCF. When the private operators failed, they were usually rewarded with more franchises and more taxpayers' money.

When the East Coast line returned to public ownership and proved hugely successful and profitable, the government handed it over to the same failing privateers, including the company owned by the subsidy junkie Sir Richard Branson.

Tony Blair and his closest cohorts in New Labour refused to countenance taking back at least some of the utilities into public ownership. Rather the reverse, Peter Mandelson was to cite the ludicrous corner shop claim as he and Blair set about removing any commitment to common ownership in Labour's constitution. Blair would usually excuse himself by saying that it was 'too costly', or in the case of the Post Office, blame the European Union for forcing Britain to outsource its publicly owned companies.

Outsourcing and privatisation were to continue apace as the remnants of the family silver were flogged off. But back in the early 1980s, Labour's praetorian guard, the National Union of Mineworkers (NUM), had to be broken before the real process of breaking up and selling public assets was to begin in real earnest – the National Coal Board being one such target.

The year 1983 had been marked by a small eruption of seemingly unplanned, unrelated events that were in turn to explode into much bigger and profound struggles. These were to determine the future of the declining trade union movement in particular.

The first came on the Ides of March and with the decision of the miners in one of the last remaining pits in the Rhondda Valley, Lewis Merthyr Colliery, to call on their union to come to their aid over plans to shut it on the grounds that it was no longer profitable.

Profitability in coal mines was one of the great industrial bones of contention of the late twentieth century. A mine could go from being profitable to making a loss in fairly quick order if one face stopped being mined while another was under development. The miners' union had long argued that pits should only be shut if exhausted. In Germany, France and the Netherlands, a long-term approach, based on retraining and bringing new industries into areas with a declining coal industry, was the preferred option. Not in Britain, though.

On two occasions in 1984 and in 1992, Tory governments had no compunction whatsoever in shutting down whole swathes of the industry, without any realistic employment prospect for those affected. While doing it, they appeared to take some collective enjoyment in humiliating those they had targeted.

The national leadership of the NUM under Arthur Scargill and his deputy Mick McGahey had long predicted that a hidden Tory plan to run down the coal industry – and Lewis Merthyr – was to be just the beginning of a major pit closure programme.

This was the first whiff of grapeshot in the battle that followed the Tories' victory in the May 1983 general election. In March, Scargill had called for a national strike as a show of solidarity against the threat of pit closures nationally. In a portent of what was to come, he also suggested that strike action could take place without a national ballot of miners being held.

Yet barely a week later, on 8 March, a majority of miners voted to reject a national strike in support of the striking Welsh colliers in a secret pithead ballot. Lewis Merthyr was shut soon afterwards and unlike most of its sister pits whose iconic architecture and headgear was soon to be bulldozed from the landscape, was reinvented as the Rhondda Heritage Park.

On a visit to the park a few years after the convulsive strike of 1984–85, Mark Seddon recognised former south Wales area NUM stalwart Ivor England, now dressed in Victorian collier's gear in his new role as a tourist guide. 'It's bollocks,' said Ivor. 'But it's a job. And most jobs, well they've vanished like an autumn mist from these valleys.'

Would Margaret Thatcher have opted for an early general election had the miners voted for an all-out strike in support of their doomed colleagues in south Wales in March 1983? Would she have risked another general election framed by pictures of striking miners, picket lines and a bitter struggle for the survival of the coalfields and risked an Edward Heath-style debacle?

For when Heath had asked the British electorate, 'Who governs Britain?', in the middle of a national miners' strike over pay in 1974, voters had responded with a fairly definitive answer: 'It's clearly not you!', and sent Harold Wilson back to Downing Street, with Michael Foot as the Employment Secretary to work out a pay deal with Britain's miners.

Britain was a changed place a decade on, but probably not changed enough to produce an entirely different set of circumstances. The Tory government backed off from confrontation in 1981, under the threat of industrial action from the NUM.

Historically, Conservative governments had always avoided confrontation with the miners. Harold Macmillan had once famously warned that as with 'Eton and the Guards', all Tory Prime Ministers should avoid taking on the NUM. Winston

Churchill, when asked in the 1950s whether he had settled with the miners on his terms or theirs, replied, 'On theirs, of course. One must have electric light.'

The appointment of Ian MacGregor, a former American business executive who had been presiding over the shrinking of the British steel industry, to head the publicly owned National Coal Board in March 1983 was to set the scene for much that was to follow.

Industrial convulsions continued. Workers at Ford's giant Halewood plant began a strike over the unfair dismissal of a colleague. Labour's campaign document 'The New Hope for Britain', outlining its strategy for fighting the next general election, proposed an 'emergency programme', to be enacted upon taking office, with increased public investment in transport, housing and social services. A 'national economic assessment' was to be undertaken in co-operation with the trade unions. Also included were proposals to withdraw from the then European Economic Community (EEC) and the establishment of a non-nuclear defence policy by removing nuclear weapons from US and other bases.

The campaign document was to morph into a Labour manifesto, enthusiastically embraced by, among others, the young, upstanding candidate for Sedgefield, Tony Blair. Blair had squeaked into winning the parliamentary nomination on the casting vote of the chairman, Jack Burton. Moreover, this, according to folklore, had been helped by Burton's decision to wave aloft a letter from Michael Foot that waxed enthusiastically over the qualities Blair had demonstrated in fighting the hopeless seat of Beaconsfield in Buckinghamshire a year or so earlier. Blair, despite his later detestation of the Labour left, always had a soft spot for Foot. The manifesto was dubbed 'The longest suicide note in history', by Manchester Gorton MP Gerald Kaufman.

Foot famously and quite uncharacteristically never forgave Kaufman for his outburst, coming as it did in the middle of the general election.

Labour's national campaign is remembered for the general chaos that surrounded it. Shadow Cabinet ministers frequently didn't know where they were supposed to be and sometimes turned up at the wrong venues. And yet the enthusiasm that often met Michael Foot as he travelled the country seemed to suggest that the polls were guilty of underestimating the number of his supporters. Foot's arrival in Norwich coincided with the arrival of footsore participants taking part in the 'People's March for Jobs', who had marched from unemployment-hit towns in the north-east of England to protest the rising level of joblessness and deindustrialisation.

Mark Seddon recalls going to meet the marchers, who were consciously adopting the mantle of the Jarrow hunger marches of the 1930s, as they arrived at the approaches to the city. Foot's natural empathy was well received by them and the image of the day which made it onto the front pages of some of the national press was of the Labour leader, his arms draped around the shoulders of one of the young female marchers who sported a magnificent pink Mohican and multiple nose piercings. Foot then got a rapturous reception in the ancient and packed St Andrew's Hall in the city, as the marchers finally arrived.

But for all of the enthusiasm, the uplifting oratory and the hard work of activists, the campaign was succeeding in motivating existing supporters, but few others. When Michael Foot arrived in Norwich, two Labour MPs represented the city. Yet after the general election, both had been swept away and replaced by Conservatives to the genuine shock and disbelief of virtually everyone who had been there battling it out on the doorsteps.

Margaret Thatcher was returned to office as Prime Minister

with a majority of 144 seats. Labour won the fewest number of seats since the Second World War. Among the prominent parliamentary defeats were those of Shirley Williams, whose Crosby constituency was captured by the Conservatives; Bill Rodgers, whose Stockton North seat was one of only four gained by Labour; and Tony Benn, who lost the newly redrawn Bristol East to the Tory candidate, Jonathan Sayeed.

The party's defeat was so profound and seemingly so final that the Marxist historian Eric Hobsbawm appeared completely vindicated. His 1978 essay 'The Forward March of Labour Halted?' had been roundly castigated when first published, but now looking around at the great raft of largely blue-collar new towns, especially in the south of the country and the Midlands, that had so resolutely turned their backs on the Labour Party, his analysis seemed largely to have been borne out.

Labour's share of the vote fell by 9.3 per cent (despite the result, the Conservative share of the vote also marginally declined by 1.5 per cent) and they only won 662,164 more votes than the SDP – however, due to the first-past-the-post voting system, they finished with 209 seats compared to the SDP–Liberal Alliance's twenty-three.

The only silver lining for Labour's stalwarts was that the SDP had been roundly defeated. The party limped on under the leadership of Dr David Owen, referred to jubilantly by the comrades as 'Dr Death', before disappearing into the nether regions of the Liberal Party.

This new franchise operation began its new existence as the SDP–Liberal Alliance, and is best remembered for its depiction on *Spitting Image*, with Dr Owen and the Liberal leader, David Steel, depicted as puppets (Steel being the pipsqueak ventriloquist's dummy). *Spitting Image* had a huge following, but latter-day TV executives never seemed able to match the wit, guile and courage of their predecessors in pouring scorn on the nation's leaders. Nothing similar has graced Britain's TV screens since.

Not only had any forward march of Labour been halted, it had been thrown into a very sharp reverse, with the Conservatives promising more anti-union legislation and more privatisation, (as well as the abolition of the big Labour-controlled metropolitan authorities including the Greater London Council, thus breaking Labour's municipal powerbases).

Labour's defeat in 1983 was nothing short of catastrophic. Much of the commentariat had been busy writing the party off for years and during the general election, Michael Foot had only really been able to count on the lukewarm support of one national newspaper, the *Daily Mirror*. *The Guardian* had unsurprisingly been an enthusiastic cheerleader for the breakaway SDP. A number of the paper's influential columnists, including the late Hugo Young and Polly Toynbee, were strong supporters.

Labour's former Prime Minister, James Callaghan, who many in the media were now predicting would be the last ever Labour Prime Minister, had sagely said that it would be a mistake to discount the party because it had 'very deep roots'. Arguably those roots enabled the party to begin to throw out a few green shoots again.

By the autumn of that year it was clear that Michael Foot did not want to spend any more time leading the party. His wife, Jill Craigie, who had never been particularly happy about him becoming leader in the first place, was pretty adamant that it was time to call it a day.

On a low bookshelf at Michael and Jill's old home in Pilgrim's Lane, Hampstead, north London, stood an odd-looking china mug with two handles. This, Michael would explain, was a 'love cup' and had been given to him by the wily and mischievous Clive Jenkins, the leader of the white-collar union ASTMS

(Association of Scientific, Technical and Managerial Staff) – a union that Jenkins had largely built from scratch. During the late 1970s and throughout much of the 1980s, wherever there was some kind of serious plot, you could be sure to find that 'Clivey', as he was known, had a hand in it. The cup had two handles to allow it to be shared – but Jenkins hadn't had lovers in mind when he gave it to Michael Foot, rather that one day Foot might share it with his old tormentor, Tony Benn.

Benn irritated Foot enormously. Foot believed that Benn's discovery of democratic socialism, having had an early flirtation with Gaitskellism, was fine, but that it did not entitle him to speak out against collective shadow Cabinet responsibility. And he really, really did not want Benn to challenge Denis Healey for the largely ceremonial position of deputy leader of the party when the party was struggling to survive.

Foot and Benn never really got on or saw eye to eye. Their political differences were in most respects slight, but Foot believed that Benn was often simplistic in his rhetoric and unnecessarily antagonistic. Foot's socialism was very much invested in parliamentary democracy. Benn's socialism, as it developed, owed much more to extra-parliamentary activity, to demonstrations, work-ins, strikes and occupations.

Mark Seddon experienced something of the lasting scratchiness of their relationship, after driving Foot to Durham in 2003 for the annual miners' gala. Guests at what is still called the 'big meeting' are invited to attend a dinner hosted by the Durham Miners' Association on the eve of the gala at the Royal County Hotel in the city centre. Seddon was walking with Foot towards the dining room when Benn appeared and admonished Foot for not wearing a tie and not looking smart enough. 'Really, Michael, you could have made an effort!' Benn expostulated to Foot, who appeared not to have heard him.

It was no surprise to learn that following Labour's 1983 poll disaster, Clive Jenkins was never a million miles from any story around the Labour leadership and specifically who and what might follow. So it was hardly surprising that Jenkins believed that it should fall to him to concentrate minds and force a change on Labour's leadership. Foot may have been reluctant to soldier on, but this solemn duty was still being urged upon him by some.

Jenkins hit upon the bright idea of getting his union conference to nominate Foot for leader – thus obliging Foot to be disobliging for a change and indicate that he didn't want to be nominated. This then opened up the opportunity for Jenkins and his partner in crime, David Basnett of the General, Municipal and Boilermakers Union (GMB), to declare that the young firebrand of the Valleys, Neil Kinnock, should be Labour's new leader.

This also had the advantage of bringing Michael Foot immediately on board. He saw Kinnock not only as a protégé, but also as a reincarnation of his great hero, Aneurin Bevan. 'Neil', Foot would declare, 'is the Welsh wizard! If anyone can get Labour to recover, it is Neil!'

Perhaps Jenkins had another two-handled mug made for Neil Kinnock and Roy Hattersley, the so-called dream ticket that somehow married the Tribunite left with the Croslandite social democratic Labour right in the new leadership of the party.

Hattersley had never shown any inclination to follow the SDP defectors and his social democracy was rooted, genuine and wholly in the Labour tradition. As the party surged ever further to the right under Tony Blair and New Labour, Hattersley would often remark that in maintaining his principles and beliefs, he was now being bypassed and at risk of becoming a dangerous left-winger.

Kinnock's election marked the high-water mark for the Tribunite left of the Labour Party. The Tribune Group of MPs took its name from the weekly newspaper of the same name, which had so long been identified with Aneurin Bevan, Michael Foot, Barbara Castle and a strong internationalist anti-nuclear tradition in the party.

Neil Kinnock had a long association with both the paper and the group. He was a regular writer and contributor and inherited from Michael Foot as a key member of his staff, a former long-standing editor, Dick Clements.

But Kinnock's relationship with the Tribunite wing of the party was to become strained, especially as the miners' strike began to take grip. Years later, he was to tell Jeremy Corbyn's biographer Rosa Prince:

> I've known Jeremy since he was elected in 1983, of course, but I've never had any real acquaintance with him. In the '80s and early '90s he was, as everyone knows, a member of the Campaign Group awkward squad, so we had virtually no contact ... I don't recall either of us seeking a meeting with each other, and we had no political common ground or interests.

This is an extraordinary state of affairs and speaks volumes about the toxic atmosphere inside the Parliamentary Labour Party; for if you talk quietly to either Kinnock or Corbyn, you will find a man who believes passionately in all the things that Labour England and Labour Wales are about.

Corbyn perhaps was inhibited from having anything to do with Kinnock by his mentor, Tony Benn. For his part, Kinnock's attitude will have been influenced by his new chef de cabinet. This was not Dick Clements, whom he inherited from Foot; Clements was soon replaced by a former National Union of Students (NUS) heavyweight, Charles Clarke. And Clarke's view, also quoted by Rosa Prince, is this:

Jeremy would always be seen at the core of every element of rebellion in the party on any issue you were talking about: economics, liberty, international. His politics were the politics of opposition. If he had had his way, we would never have reformed the party in the 1980s, we would never have had a Labour government in 1997.

Clarke was joined at Kinnock's side by Patricia Hewitt, former director of the National Council for Civil Liberties, who became his press officer. One of their boasts was that they would shield Neil from some of the critical (and abusive) mail that he would receive, by the simple expedient of not showing him any of it. But a Labour leader who was only being shown letters heaped with praise could let such notions go to his head.

He was, for those days, very young and inexperienced when he became leader in the wake of Labour's crushing 1983 election defeat, and felt in need of advice. A posse of clever men and women a decade younger than him and politicians of the harsher '70s era became his praetorian guard, including Oxbridge graduates Hewitt, Clarke and Peter Mandelson, who had worked for the British Youth Council. Kinnock says they 'had been student union officers very young, and after that they came and worked for me'. Other Kinnock confidants who had cut their political teeth in student politics included former NUS presidents Jack Straw and Neil Stewart, and former student communist Dr John Reid. Fighting the ultra-left was in their bones. They had fought them in student unions and now they fought them for Kinnock, unrelentingly and obsessively.

They told him he had to acquire gravitas. Hewitt erected a barrier between Kinnock and the lobby journalists, who were used to the old, genial, witty Kinnock. Clarke, says Roy Hattersley, did Kinnock great harm by protecting him when he did not need protecting.

It was a terrible mistake. Clarke told him not to make speeches, because he only needed to make one mistake to lose the next election. But he would not have done that. He knew how not to do that. So Kinnock, this great platform speaker, just stopped using that talent. It was a dreadful waste.

They told him that his personality was all wrong. The noise, the passion, the bons mots, the houndstooth suits, everything that had endeared him to the public before he was elected leader, it all had to go. He started to wrap himself up in grey flannel suits and grey woollen phrases. Brendan Bruce, the Conservative director of communications for part of Kinnock's time as leader, has said, 'Kinnock was badly let down by his image makers in recent years. There were endless things they could have done.'

The quality of the advice he is getting from his private office is very important for any modern opposition leader. Kinnock was getting some very bad advice. It seemed as though his advisers did not trust their man not to bungle if let out without his leash, and perhaps Kinnock started to take himself at their estimate. It was, as we will see, a foretaste of the Corbyn leadership today.

The magic went out of his relationship with journalists. His sure broadcasting touch started to desert him as he began weighing every word and waffling to cover policy divisions. Perhaps, for the first time in his adult life, he felt unsure of himself.

When he became Prime Minister – and at the start of his leadership – most people thought it was a matter of when, not whether, he would be the first person since Ramsay MacDonald in 1924 to run a government without having served in one.

In his heart, he seems to have believed – wrongly – that all these clever Oxbridge folk round him – Clarke, Hewitt, Mandelson – were more intelligent and better qualified than him. So he was, according to Roy Hattersley, far more upset than he should have been when the columnist Hugo Young wrote that Kinnock had 'a pass degree in Industrial Relations from Swansea University on the second try in a bad year'. Comments in Kinnock's papers indicate that he was indeed hurt by Young's snobbish jibe. 'Hugo Young was a friend of mine, and I told him that this was an appalling and stupid thing to write,' says Hattersley. 'Neil could hold his own intellectually with anyone he might need to, as Labour leader or as Prime Minister.' Hattersley does not regard Kinnock as a great intellectual, but he does not believe that you have to be a great intellectual in order to be an effective Prime Minister. History suggests that Hattersley is right.

Oxford is not a prerequisite for becoming Prime Minister; although, since 1945, every leader in Parliament has studied at the prestigious university, excepting Churchill, Callaghan, who gained a Senior Oxford Certificate but could not afford the tuition fees, Major and Brown, who studied at Edinburgh. Perhaps Oxford graduate Hugo Young was still under the impression that an Oxford education was essential.

Unfair attacks, whether from Norman Tebbit and the tabloids on the right, Benn on the left or Hugo Young on the higher intellectual plane, got under Kinnock's skin, which turned out to be thin for a top politician. Denis Healey once said to Hattersley, 'It's all right for us. We've been up to our eyes in shit for years. He's not used to it.'

CHAPTER SIX

BREAKING THE UNIONS

In 1983, Michael Foot's Labour Party may have been roundly defeated, but the trade union movement still believed – or appeared to believe – that it was strong enough to resist what the Tory government had promised during the election campaign and what it was now preparing to legislate for. The first real and acid test of the government's new employment laws came at a small print works in Warrington, in early July, when six workers came out on strike in protest at the use of non-union labour by the owner of the *Stockport Messenger*, Eddie Shah. Shah was soon to become a poster boy for the Thatcherite right of the Tory Party.

The dispute accelerated rapidly and was in effect a dry run for the year-long miners' strike that was to begin the following year. The print workers were highly organised. They were also determined to maintain both collective bargaining rights and the closed shop agreements that ensured that membership of the two main print unions, the National Graphical Association (NGA) and the Society of Graphical and Allied Trades (SOGAT), was a necessary condition of working in print. The big battle over use of the new technology replacing traditional hot metal was to come later.

Of the two, the NGA, with its proud craft traditions, was the most militant and highly organised, with over 130,000 members, and still dominated by the big union chapels that were organised in the dank and dark machine rooms of the big newspaper titles, all still based in Fleet Street, London. One of the most infamous machine rooms was known as the 'black hole of Bouverie Street', which was where the typesetters and compositors wrestled with ageing hot-metal technology to print millions of copies of the *News of the World*.

The debate in the upper echelons of the TUC was increasingly revolving around how best to deal with a Conservative government with a clear mandate and intention to bring in sweeping anti-union laws, including ending the closed shop, and adopting a less confrontational approach. But the leader of the NGA, Joe Wade, saw the *Stockport Messenger* dispute as an existential one for his members.

There followed a series of increasingly fractious recourses to the courts by Eddie Shah, who obtained two injunctions preventing the NGA from trying to pressure suppliers and advertisers from boycotting his newspaper group. As the fines mounted, Wade order his staff not to pay them and said he was prepared to go to prison if necessary.

All of the ingredients seemed to be there for a potential rerun of the imprisonment of the Pentonville Five dockers under Edward Heath's infamous Industrial Relations Act, or of the Grunwick dispute. By 26 November, NGA chapels in Fleet Street had blocked publications of national tiles in solidarity with their fellow members in Warrington. By the end of that month, with the TUC finally giving its support to the NGA, mass picketing began at the *Stockport Messenger* site.

Mark Seddon, along with some other members of his university student union and the Norwich Labour Party, joined two coachloads of NGA members from East Anglia, determined to go to the aid of their fellow members in Warrington.

The coaches arrived in the dark at a scene that was beginning to resemble a medieval battlefield. Lines of police were holding mass pickets back from the perimeter of the print works. On a rough piece of public land not too far from the lorry park where loaded print trucks would emerge from under electric doors, sat the NGA broadcast caravan. Here some of the union's leadership would Tannoy messages of support, advice and instructions to NGA members from across the country.

By the following night, the caravan lay smashed following a raid by baton-wielding police officers determined to destroy the NGA's control vehicle. As the night progressed, the mood on both sides darkened, with sporadic clashes breaking out as pickets surged forward in an attempt to block print trucks laden with copies of the *Stockport Messenger* from leaving the plant. On one occasion one of the electronic doors came crashing down on a truck as it was leaving the plant, causing wild cheering.

As the night progressed, scenes became ever more violent, with arrests and clashes between pickets and police. The following day, seventy protestors were to be hauled before the courts for a variety of offences. But as the night drew on, news filtered down through the mass of protestors that police had stopped six coaches of NUM flying pickets from the South Yorkshire coalfield. The coaches had then been turned back. The union's not-so-secret weapon, Arthur Scargill, did not make it to Warrington.

The action of the police was a taste of things to come. It also helped ensure that there would be no repeat of Saltley Gate or Grunwick.

A combination of police and court action ensured that by the end of the year the print unions were forced through attrition to admit defeat in their round one battle with Eddie Shah. Ironically, after the dispute, Shah gave some of his typesetting business to a small company that had been set up by NGA members.

The NGA, saddled with a court fine of over half a million pounds, pushed the TUC to back it in a planned 24-hour strike of all 133,000 members in a major escalation of the dispute and also as a direct challenge to the government's employment laws. To begin with, the TUC's employment policy and organisation committee voted by nine votes to seven in favour. But this threat to break the law was too much for the TUC general secretary, Len Murray.

Murray, nicknamed 'Madeira' due to his liking for both the aperitif and the island's holidaying reputation, was determined to avoid a full-on confrontation with the re-elected Tory government. The TUC's general council was to vote twenty-nine to twenty-one to back Murray's policy of forbidding the NGA to contravene the Employment Act by supporting strike action. For the leaders of the NGA, it was a bitter disappointment and by December they had effectively admitted defeat. There was little to sugar the pill, although some could point to the irate figure of former Labour MP, turned tabloid Thatcherite, Woodrow Wyatt, whose vigorously anti-union *News of the World* column had been disrupted or 'blacked' on at least one occasion.

Absent from the political and industrial fray since his defeat in Bristol at the general election was the undoubted leader of what was to become known in media circles as the hard left, Tony Benn. Benn's best efforts to move to a safer seat in Bristol immediately before the general election had been stymied by long-standing local and national enemies, including his constituency neighbour and former Chief Whip Michael Cocks, the MP for Bristol South, and union leader John Golding.

Golding, the then leader of the National Communications Union, rejoiced in the soubriquet 'Hammer of the Left' and dedicated himself to ensuring that Benn would remain pinioned in his marginal Bristol South East constituency. Promising union resources for those that might want to organise meetings or any other activities that might ensure that Benn was banished from Parliament and influence, Golding cut a malevolent but effective figure on what should have been known by the same media as Labour's hard right. One prominent member of the NUS, who was known as an effective organiser against Militant, claims that Golding approached him, offering a brown envelope of cash to help in any student Labour activities that could make Benn's return to Westminster more difficult.

But Benn's exile from Parliament was to be short-lived. The decision by a former Labour Cabinet member, Eric Varley, to stand down as the MP for Chesterfield in Derbyshire in order to become chairman of the Coalite Company, based in the same area, cleared the way for a Benn return. The constituency Labour Party leapt at the opportunity to be the one to restore the leader of Labour left and he was duly selected as the party's by-election candidate.

By-elections tended to be much livelier and open to public debate than is the case nowadays and Chesterfield was to prove no exception. Daily press conferences were part and parcel of Labour's campaign, the first famously offering up both Tony Benn and Denis Healey, the two pugilists of the party's bitter deputy leadership campaign, now faking unity for the cameras.

Unfortunately their first appearance together was marred by the sudden collapse, live on camera, of the poles bearing the proud banner of the Chesterfield Labour Party, featuring the famous crooked spire of the town's church. It happened just as Healey was telling everyone what dear friends he and Benn were, and not unnaturally the assembled journalists saw the collapse as a comment upon the truthfulness of what he was saying.

The fact that Tony Benn stood a good chance of being re-turned to Parliament galvanised the media even more than usual, and the BBC's by-election special programme became essential viewing.

As with today's upsurge in political activism on the left, there was no shortage of volunteers from all around the country who converged on Chesterfield and some of the neighbouring mining villages. One was Mark Seddon, who found himself billeted with other activists in a local party member's house in Clay Cross, then a mining and industrial village that achieved deserved fame for hosting one of the very first Co-operative stores, through the auspices of the Clay Cross Pioneer Industrial Society. Its local council refused to implement the Conservatives' 1972 Housing Finance Act, thereby refusing to put up council rents. The Clay Cross rebellion followed in the great tradition of the Poplar Rates Rebellion of 1921, led by George Lansbury, who was later to become Labour leader.

The Clay Cross rebellion also set an example for later attempts by Labour-controlled authorities to stand up for tenants and the low paid; one such council was Lambeth, which, under the leadership of Ted Knight, famously refused to set a local rate in the early 1980s. In Clay Cross, there was huge support for the stand taken by a dozen or so councillors, including Bolsover MP Dennis Skinner's brother David (Dennis had also been a Clay Cross councillor).

For Seddon, a young, impressionable Labour activist, meeting the Skinner clan was an unforgettable experience. Not only was there David, but there was Graham, Gary and their sister, Dawn. The Skinner family had gone on a collective hunger strike in protest at the American bombing campaigns in Vietnam following the Tet Offensive. All of them had in some way contributed to the Clay Cross rebellion and took the punishment when it came in the shape of surcharges and periods of not being allowed to stand for office. David Skinner stood at the corner of one street and pointed to the one house where it was known that someone had 'once voted Tory'. 'No one does that here, and if they did their car would be turned on their roof,' he said half-jokingly. Meanwhile, his older brother Dennis was touring the area, speaking through a Tannoy system that was attached to the top of a car.

In places like Clay Cross, it used to be said, in an often patronising way, that 'you could weigh the votes', or 'a donkey could get in here if it were wearing a red rosette'. The truth was somewhat different.

The metropolitan elite would then – and now – be hard pressed to have even heard of Clay Cross, let alone know where it was. Yet it was at the centre of industrial Britain, its folklore and traditions carved from over a century or more of struggle, whether it be for union rights, the right of women to vote, the privations of the bitter 1926 general strike, during which the mining communities took the lion's share of the battering, or the great industrial convulsions that were to follow, first with nationalisation and then with the long struggle for decent pay and conditions. Clay Cross was home to one of the first co-operatives, a long and deeply enduring movement that still has a political voice in the Co-operative Party, which is itself linked umbilically to Labour.

The Labour Party, as well as the Independent Labour Party, had been at the centre of these battles, so it was hardly surprising that the party's roots ran deep. Tony Benn was of a different caste and class, yet for those communities such as Clay Cross there was never any doubt which side he was on.

Seddon remembers canvassing for Benn, standing on a doorstep, while at the front door, the house owner, a burly-looking man, folded his arms across his chest and looked down, with suspicion: 'Benn, you say! You expect us to support him?' And then with a conspiratorial wink, he winked and volunteered, 'Aye, don't have any worries. Our branch nominated him. We'll all be supporting him here and the whole street as well, I should think.' Much to the disappointment of Labour's hard right, later in March, Benn went on to win the by-election with a majority of just over 6,000, about 1.2 per cent down on the general election result.

Cortonwood Shopping Park near Barnsley advertises its wares online with a young woman in a trendy jumper and woolly hat, hands cupped around a warming latte. The shopping centre itself sits back on top of the site of Cortonwood Colliery, which was the catalyst that sparked the bitter, year-long miners' strike. Cortonwood's stand was to earn it the name 'the Alamo'.

As with much of the once militant South Yorkshire coalfield, there is precious little left to remind anyone of the now vanished industry or the year-long near civil war between the miners and everything that the state could throw at them other than live grenades – and many of whose divisions have still not healed to this day.

The eponymous headgear is long gone in these villages; the odd wheel encased in concrete as a memorial to a lost world. The giant spoil heaps have been landscaped and in many former mining villages, the old terraced houses that still remain have had their chimneys removed. King Coal has been utterly deposed from his throne, and his departure was and still is having major ramifications for a Britain that turned her back on clean coal technology, while continuing to import large, although declining, amounts of coal for power stations that are being closed ahead of time. This invariably led to regular reports of fears or energy shortages in the national media.

These ex-mining communities are still angry almost four decades on. In some areas, UKIP began to replace Labour as a party of choice, although by the 2017 general election, that support appeared to have peaked – for the time being, perhaps. The vote for Brexit was often highest in ex-industrial and ex-mining areas, where people felt they had nothing to lose because nothing could be any worse than what it was and few believed the shock-horror predictions of what Brexit might bring, especially when they came from the same rotten political and business establishment that had long ago consigned their parts of the country to rot.

The Labour governments of the late 1990s and 2000s may have pumped millions into these areas, but regeneration could not replace what had been lost. Low pay and long hours in non-unionised, dead-end jobs were what were on offer, and only if some of the ex-industrial workers were lucky.

For years, many had been urged to apply for incapacity benefit as a means by which the government could massage the unemployment figures. In the former steel town of Redcar, for instance, one ex-steelworker told a journalist in 2017, 'Once we made the best steel in the world. Now we make lattes.' Decades later and despite Labour's revival under Jeremy Corbyn, the demographic still often particularly resistant to their old party are the older, white working class, who have come to see all Westminster politicians as contemptible and the same. When Margaret Thatcher died, effigies of her were burned and a mock funeral procession led by a horse-drawn hearse was held in the streets of Goldthorpe in South Yorkshire. At Easington Colliery in Durham, there wasn't a wake – there was a massive celebration.

In March 1984, the chairman of the then nationalised Coal Board, Ian MacGregor, announced that overcapacity in the industry would be reduced by over 4 million tons and as a result, twenty pits, including and starting with Cortonwood, would be shut. Arthur Scargill had been warning of a 'top secret hit list' of seventy pits threatened with closure. He was derided at the time by government ministers and the media alike. Thirty years after the end of the strike, government papers revealed that there had indeed been a secret government list of seventy-five collieries to be shut over a three-year period, with over 64,000 miners due to be made redundant.

Scargill had been right all along. So had many others who did not share Scargill's political philosophy, and they all came together during the great strike to show us what would be one of the last pictures in our lifetimes of Labour England at its bravest and best.

It is difficult for anyone much younger than forty or who hasn't grown up in one of the old coalfield areas to understand or appreciate the very special bonds of solidarity and support that existed in and among the mining communities. Mining went back generations in very many families. In more generous times, Britain's miners were lauded for helping to 'break the back of the Kaiser's army' (there were a million men working underground at the time of the First World War, huge numbers of whom volunteered for the front).

At other times they were disparaged. Margaret Thatcher had the deep effrontery to accuse them of being 'the enemy within' (the enemy without had been the Argentinians, who had briefly managed to occupy the Falkland Islands due to her government's negligence and incompetence). Miners and their families, it was once said, should be discouraged from having baths in their homes, 'because they would keep coal in them'.

Other unions didn't always reciprocate the miners' legendary solidarity (few picket lines comprising nurses and health workers wouldn't include off-shift miners showing up to give their support). Left all too frequently to fight alone against the private mine owners, before facing off with the Coal Board and the private mine owners all over again after privatisation, their localised 'rag-outs' or strikes were a complete mystery to most who wouldn't have the first idea of the miserable conditions they tended to work in.

Mark Seddon recalls going deep underground and 6 miles out under the sea at Easington Colliery in Durham before the pit closed in 1992. There, miners could still be seen in some places working in thigh-deep freezing water. Further up the coast in Northumberland was Ellington mine or 'Big E'. This was one of the showcase mines and yet the last pit pony was retired from Ellington in 1999. Labour's link with Ellington is maintained to this day by former mineworker, MP and now chair of the Labour Party, Ian Lavery.

Most mothers, of course, would rather their sons worked somewhere less challenging and dangerous, but for the best part of a century other industries had largely been discouraged from setting up in the coalfields, as they might suck labour away from the coal industry.

In the Nottinghamshire coalfield, for instance, there were some other factories, but these were most often than not garment manufacturers and jobs deemed better suited to women.

When the cull of the coalfields came, there were no jobs to follow, just training schemes. The decent, hard-fought-for wage packets were replaced by casual, contracted-out and latterly zero-hour contracts. It wasn't so much the romance of an industry deeply rooted in an essential solidarity around collective safety in what were frequently battlefield conditions at the coal face, it was having a solid job that paid that mattered.

Often geographically isolated and away from the main conurbations, the mining villages supported a very different culture from other parts of the country. Maltby in South Yorkshire was one such mining village that Mark Seddon got to know in the early 1980s – and to which he returned in 2013 to mark the final closure of one of Britain's last deep mines for *The Guardian*.

In Maltby good-natured banter was usually the order of the day and signs that read 'No Swearing' and 'No Spitting' could be spotted in the social clubs. Men were served with pint glasses and women received 'ladies' glasses', which was a source of intense irritation to female outsiders. Local miners – and there were over 2,000 of them at the local pit in the early 1980s – were fiercely loyal in strict order, to the NUM and to the Labour Party. Both institutions ran through Maltby as lettering does in a stick of rock.

The town boasted a large Miners' Welfare Club, very much the centre of social activity, and it supported many other pubs and clubs whose names reflected the different trades and skills of those who worked underground.

The Colliery Industry Social Welfare Organisation, or CISWO as it was known throughout the coalfields, played a hugely important and vital role and one that has barely been acknowledged.

It was a place where you could find allotments, pigeon lofts, and streets named after a succession of Labour leaders: Lansbury Grove, Attlee Close, Gaitskell Close and Hardie Close. The town was self-contained; it was self-sufficient and largely self-policing. A town crier would circle the village on bicycle, ringing a big brass bell if there was news from the pit or locality to broadcast. The town was proud, even if it was grimy. It had purpose.

Maltby Colliery produced coal largely for the local power stations that had been constructed close by the mines and which were fed by what were known as the 'merry-go-round' coal trains that continually moved between the pithead and the power station. It was also being talked of as a 'super-pit', one of the big hitters and one therefore that was unlikely to face closure (it did finally and to sad fanfare in 2013).

And yet the miners of Maltby, alongside Kellingley and the

new, ultra-modern Selby Complex, were all on stand-by for what they knew was an almost inevitable fight to the finish with a newly elected Tory government determined to break the miners' union, sure that the rest of the unions would fall in quick succession once that had happened. That final act began on 6 March with the announcement of the closure of Cortonwood.

The Yorkshire coalfield came to an immediate standstill. So did the south Wales area, with its narrow coal seams and time-limited future. As did the north-east and Scotland – and not forgetting the three militant pits in the Kent coalfield: Snowden, Tilmanstone and Betteshanger. Pickets from this area were famously halted at the Dartford Crossing and turned back by police as they headed to the Nottinghamshire and Midlands coalfields that had kept working.

Hilariously, on one occasion, the police dragnet also stopped and turned back Charles Moore, a Thatcher-supporting columnist on the *Daily Telegraph*.

Moore ('Lord Snooty' as he was nicknamed because of his exaggerated public school mannerisms) protested at this violation of his own rights of free movement. But he never translated this into any defence for the highly questionable practice of the police in one part of the country preventing people from travelling to another part, who were engaged in lawful picketing activities.

Arthur Scargill seized upon the closure of Cortonwood, as he had done the previous year with Lewis Merthyr in south Wales, as proof of the government's hit list. This time, however, he was determined that a national ballot should be avoided because he believed that the Nottinghamshire miners would, come what may, still vote against strike action. On 12 April, after a fractious meeting of the NUM executive, Scargill ruled out a national ballot altogether, having received backing from thirteen members against eight.

This decision, more than any other, including launching a national strike when the coal stocks were at their highest and ahead of spring, was arguably the most momentous and influential of all. It ensured that the Labour Party and the trade unions would be consumed by the arguments around what Scargill called 'ballot-itis' and meant that it would be easier for other union leaders to walk away. We shall never know if the Nottinghamshire miners would have gone along with a national ballot that had voted for industrial action. Had they continued to work in spite of it, their position would likely have been that much weaker.

As pickets fanned out across the country, one local union official seemingly realising the importance of this trial of strength between union and government said, 'If we lose, things will never be the same again.'

The government was to maintain the fiction throughout that it had no role to play and that the dispute was essentially between the union and the National Coal Board, which of course was owned by the government. And yet in the intervening years, plenty of evidence has emerged showing that ministers were intricately involved in both preparing for a strike and managing resources to ensure that the police and army were fully equipped to contain picketing. That is why picket lines erupted into violence as the full panoply of the state was marshalled in order to get handfuls of strikers into idle pits where they were paid to sit around in the cafeterias all day.

The small mining town of Ollerton in north Nottinghamshire soon became the scene of intense picketing, as local miners kept working and large groups of miners' pickets from South Yorkshire tried to block the entrance to the pit yard. The situation became increasingly violent.

The first fatality of that bitter strike came in mid-March. A young striking miner from Wakefield, Davy Jones, was hit fatally by a flying brick during a particularly savage skirmish on the picket line. Jones became the first of three men to be killed during the dispute, including a taxi driver in south Wales, who was hit by missiles dropped from a bridge by striking miners. He had been ferrying in two working miners.

Some of the miners at Ollerton had come from contracting coalfields in Scotland and the north-east in the 1960s, lured with the promise of well-paid, secure jobs and working in large, airy seams. Some of them had also kept that strong attachment to the union and had vivid memories or tales of previous strikes. Determined not to throw their lot in with the local Nottinghamshire 'scabs' or 'blacklegs', a minority came out on strike with the national union and since they formed a majority on the governing board of the Ollerton Miners' Welfare, were able to use this behemoth of a building as a strike centre and, as the screws were tightened further and further, as a soup kitchen.

As the dispute intensified, Ollerton found itself on occasion physically cut off from the rest of the country. The police took it upon themselves to mount roadblocks and stop vehicles from going in or out of the town.

In a car with a small group of supporters from Norwich, Seddon witnessed this likely highly illegal action first-hand, as the car he was travelling in was first flagged down and the driver questioned as to what business he had travelling into the town. When it became clear that none of the occupants actually lived in Ollerton, the police turned it round and forbade entry.

Women played a vital role right from the very beginning. Many of them were from families whose fathers and sons had worked in the industry for generations. The memories of bitter lockouts, the general strike of 1926 and the major contractions of the industry in the 1960s had bred a degree of caution among both men and women. The idea that miners were somehow strike happy and militant for the sake of it, which much of the media seemed to believe, was far from the truth. There was a deep reluctance to engage in confrontation, because the hardship associated with going on strike had permeated deep. In the spring of 1984, huge rallies organised by women from the mining communities took place beginning with the 12th of May Barnsley rally of the WAPC (Women Against Pit Closures), in which over 10,000 women took part. On 14 May a rally in Mansfield, in the heart of the Nottinghamshire coalfield, in support of striking miners, was attended by an estimated 20,000 pitmen and their wives. Although the majority of the protest was peaceful, violence later broke out and sixty arrests were made. Among the speakers addressing the demonstrators were Tony Benn and Dennis Skinner.

The strike proved to be a liberating period for many women, who suddenly found themselves speaking at public events and travelling across the country taking their case to places that they had never been to before. The strike would never have been as solid or as long-lasting without the women of the coalfields. Some went into public life after the strike, becoming councillors and MPs.

The miners' cause also attracted other individuals and groups who had long faced uphill battles for recognition and long campaigns for social justice. Lesbians and Gays Support the Miners brought together people who would otherwise have never met, and probably never had any understanding of each other. The extraordinary story of how one lesbian and gay support group developed powerful and long-lasting links with the Onllwyn miners of the Dulais Valley in south Wales not only led eventually to a celebrated film, *Pride*, but in concrete terms to the south Wales area of the NUM being the first to successfully propose a TUC resolution for equality for gays and lesbians.

In Nottinghamshire and elsewhere in the Midlands, the miners had a reputation for 'moderation'. Jobs seemed more secure for a start. So for the small minority who did go on strike, there were the added hardships of isolation and less help as the year ground on. The Ollerton soup kitchen became a vital and central part of life for the women who ran it, who cooked and ensured that gifts of food as well as clothing and toys were shared fairly among families.

Each week on a Saturday or Sunday, a convoy of vehicles would leave Norwich, whose Labour activists and latterly the City Council had unofficially twinned with the mining town, carrying vital food and other supplies. These had all been collected from across the city and county of Norfolk in the preceding week. Typically cars and vans, some from the University of East Anglia Students Union, would head out west into the flatlands of Lincolnshire, stopping half way at a local road café, before wending their way to the Miners' Welfare Hall, where it would soon be a case of all hands on deck as supplies were unloaded and hot meals cooked.

Striking miners were earmarked different parts of the country both for picketing activities and for the increasingly vital job of fundraising. The small number of striking miners in north Nottinghamshire were allocated East Anglia and, in particular, Norwich. Based in union offices in the Norwich Labour Club, striking miners organised fundraising events, street collections and even a market trader's stall. As the strike intensified and small local ports began to be used for shipments of imported coal, these same striking miners attempted to organise regional picketing activities. Hearing that coal was being imported into the small Essex port of Wivenhoe, the Norwich Trades Council hired a double-decker bus that went careering down to Essex in a valiant attempt to stop the black stuff from being landed.

The bus driver got lost and by the time the motley crew of local trade unionists and students had arrived, any coal that had been expected had already been loaded in.

On another occasion, this time with a group of striking Geordie miners from Westoe and Wearmouth collieries in the Durham coalfield, Seddon recalls joining one of their pickets, this time in the heart of Norwich. A small operation on the River Yare had begun importing coal. Hearing that this could soon become a target, the local Norfolk constabulary had taken to guarding the gates. Miner pickets arrived, and seeing the phalanx of blue uniforms, disported themselves in front of the local police acting out a fierce some Zulu warrior dance routine, replete with blood-curdling chanting. The local police had never seen or experienced anything like this and didn't know how to intervene. The strikers' operation had been a success.

Elsewhere in the country it was of course a very different story. Confrontations were often violent and away from the cameras and at a time when there were no mobile phones or small hand-held videos, things could get out of hand.

For two weeks in August, the east Durham town of Easington Colliery fell under police occupation, as one miner – from a workforce of over 2,000 – went back to work. The scenes of riot police running amok, tearing through houses and backyards in pursuit of young miners dressed in jeans and sneakers also were to feature in the movie *Billy Elliot*. Back then, the colliery looked out over a small patchwork of back-to-back terraces in a village that bore the same name. It was small enough to occupy and control entry to and the police were under firm orders to do whatever it took to get the one strike breaker back into work. Arrests and violence were commonplace.

Mark Seddon recalls going to stay with the family of a Durham miner who had been briefly in Norwich and getting up at the crack of dawn to travel with a small group of strikers to a local hall where the picketing tactics of the day would be planned. The trick was to outfox the police if possible and pick a venue where they could be taken by surprise and be overwhelmed by numbers.

For while the law allowed up to six pickets to peacefully try and persuade strike breakers whether they be local workers or delivery drivers from crossing a picket line, it did not allow for any large-scale physical attempts to stop people or vehicles from accessing a workplace. That morning, it was decided by local strike leaders to focus all picketing activities on the narrow approaches to Dawdon Colliery, another one of the small con-stellation of coastal deep mines whose workings went 6 miles or so deep under the North Sea.

It was a particularly bitter January morning, pitch black with heavy snow forecast. By this time, any semblance of civility be-tween the miners and police had long ago passed. The police, who had somehow anticipated the 'big push' planned at Dawdon, weren't from the county but from London. Across the coalfields and faithfully reported at the top of most BBC news bulletins, were the military-style attempts to get handfuls of strike breakers across picket lines and into work. As numbers trickled back as the year went on, the BBC would typically begin each evening newscast with a report of the daily tally of strike breakers from across the coalfields. News reporting from the biggest set-piece standoff of the strike between thousands of miners and police, including mounted police, at the Orgreave Coking Works in South Yorkshire, would quite accurately be described today as 'fake news'. The BBC deliberately reversed footage of some of the clashes involving pickets throwing missiles and mounted police charging them. The events had been the other way round, but it was to be decades before the BBC finally fessed up.

Ministers believed that a combination of tough measures to break the strike, coupled with helpful media reporting alongside the special court measures being taken to sequester the union's cash, would force strikers to yield. On that morning in Dawdon in January 1985, the good-natured banter from men whose faces were pinched with both cold and having lacked nutritious food for a long time, gave way to silence as two green NCB buses, whose windscreen and windows were covered in metal grills, headed quickly towards the colliery gates. There were no pickets allowed to stand and try and dissuade the driver or the few shadowy figures inside the vehicles, instead, on a signal, striking miners on both sides of the road surged forward, pushing headlong into police lines. The police lines buckled and narrowed, the buses slowed but there was just enough space for them to squeeze through. Emotions were raw; anger there was aplenty on both sides. Some miners claimed that they had been hit and kicked, a few unlucky ones were dragged away and put in the back of police vans. A police charge and conviction would inevitably mean that there would never be a job for a man again after the strike back at the pit.

As the empty green buses pulled out from the yard and now with the cold morning sunshine peeping over the tops of chimneys, hundreds of miners gave vent to their frustrations, running in their wake, throwing snowballs or anything else that came to hand as the buses moved off.

One of the pickets declared that on occasions they had managed to pull one over the police, especially the hated London Met, some of whom would sometimes wave their pay packets at them from the safety of their vans. 'We built a great big fucking snowman around a water hydrant,' one recalled, 'cop's helmet and coat, the lot. As soon as we saw the coppers' vans, we started lobbing stuff from behind the snowman – and then one of the police vans decided to take out our snowman! Well, you can imagine the rest.'

One of the traditions of the north-east was that of 'sea coaling'. Waste from the mines was taken by conveyor lines and tipped into the North Sea, with the small amounts of coal that hadn't been extracted often being washed up on the beaches. Pensioners would usually be seen as the tide departed, wheeling their bikes, carrying heavy sacks and rakes, and filling them with sea coal. During the strike, the sea coal became an important part of simply keeping warm. Elsewhere miners and their families could often be found scrabbling on pit heaps for coal, some risking being entombed in the process. Indeed, on one occasion, that is precisely what happened.

For years after the strike, the Justice for Mineworkers campaign battled for the hundreds left jobless due to arrests, often for minor infractions, but few ever received justice.

One who did was the late Paul Whetton, from Tuxford in Nottinghamshire. The Coal Board was forced to reinstate him after the strike and, as a result, Whetton not unsurprisingly decided that he wanted restitution for all that he and his family had suffered. The Coal Board offered to pay him for the concessionary coal that, as an employee, he had missed out on for over a year. But Paul Whetton would have none of it. 'I told them I wanted the coal, every last bloody cobble of it', and so it came to pass that a large pyramid of the black stuff graced the small front garden of his terraced house and became the talk of the town.

During the strike, some miners would claim that soldiers had been drafted in to boost police numbers. Certainly in some parts of the country, police were photographed without any numbered identification on their uniforms.

On 13 September, the Department of Health and Social Security confirmed that families of striking miners were being refused grants to pay for funerals under supplementary benefit rules. A Yorkshire family was refused a grant to bury their twelve-year-old son because his father was a striking miner.

On 21 September, the largest picketing operation in South Yorkshire since the start of the strike saw clashes between police and pickets at Maltby Colliery. On 9 November, a lone miner, escorted in a police convoy, returned to work at Cortonwood, sparking serious unrest. One arrested at the scene and marched off to a Black Maria was NUM official and local Rother Valley MP Kevin Barron. Elsewhere in the coalfields, the sense of a battle at risk of being lost spurred ever more tense and bitter stand-offs. Rioting in Armthorpe near Doncaster saw police vans being overturned and palls of black smoke rising outside the pit gates. Petrol bombs had been thrown and it was a wonder that no one had been killed.

The predicament for the Labour Party and much of the trade union leadership from the outset was defined by the fateful decision of the NUM not to have a ballot. The actual facts on the ground, namely that the bulk of the union was on strike in most parts of the country, was more than enough to persuade the grassroots of what used to be described as the 'labour movement' to get behind the miners. But the sometimes violent scenes of confrontation, coupled with the fact that most of the Midlands mines worked throughout the strike, not only weakened it but also allowed the Thatcher government to exploit the divisions and develop what was effectively a national police force.

In an interview on Channel 4's *Diverse Reports*, John Alderson, the former chief constable of Devon and Cornwall, argued that owing to the miners' strike, Britain now had 'what amounts to a paramilitary police force under national control'. In October, it was estimated that the cost of policing the dispute was £150 million.

Some trade unions gave a lot of support to the miners, in particular on the railways and at the docks. But the leaders of the steelworkers union, the ISTC, made it clear that there would be no solidarity action from them. The massive engineering union, the AUEW, led by Terry Duffy, was busy trying to negotiate single and no-strike agreements with employers, while electricians' union leader Eric Hammond used the TUC Congress in September to savage the miners' leaders, including Scargill. 'The miners', he said, 'were lions led by donkeys.'

The defeat of the miners at Orgreave Coking Works owes as much to the police action as it does those who continued to work there and the truckers who broke the picket lines. The Labour Party NEC committed to support the miners and Roy Hattersley, Labour's deputy leader, when asked, said that if he were a Nottinghamshire miner, he would be on strike. The prominent Labour backbencher Joan Maynard, who the press used to like to pillory as the 'Member for Leipzig East', or even more unfairly as 'Stalin's granny', was game enough to have one of her rousing speeches set to rap.

But as that extraordinary year dragged on, relations between the NUM and the TUC became more and more strained. As they did with the Labour leader, Neil Kinnock, who represented a south Wales mining seat but who was criticised for not showing enough solidarity with the miners. He was frequently attacked by Scargill and others, because he was prepared to condemn violence, including from striking miners.

In Aberavon in November, the then general secretary of the TUC, Norman Willis, was captured on camera speaking at a mass meeting as a noose was lowered behind him by a striking miner who was angry at Willis's perceived lukewarm support for the strike.

Willis said, 'When I see the hardship, when I see the sacrifice,

I wish I could guarantee you all the support you need … But the TUC is not an army and I'm not a field marshal.' He condemned police violence, but then added, 'Any miner, too, who resorts to violence wounds the miners' case far more than they damage their opponents' resolve.'

And then, as the noose came down over Willis's head, Arthur Scargill sat beside him, impassive, staring straight ahead. Willis the old trade union professional was furious with Scargill. A word from Scargill, he said afterwards, would have been enough to have the noose removed. Scargill did not say that word.

Christmas promised to be a particularly tough time for many of the now besieged mining communities, and as the trickle back to work crushed spirits. Miners in the small north Wales area were the first to return, but elsewhere a ferocious reaction often met the handful of strike breakers desperate enough to break picket lines in the most militant areas. At Cortonwood, where the strike had begun, some 4,000 pickets tried to stop a solitary strike breaker who had the whole panoply of the Coal Board and police on his side.

The Ollerton miners support group in Norwich, in common with many similar groups up and down the country, attempted to put some festive cheer into Christmas for families in the town and also by hosting children in Norwich. Significant amounts of money, food, drink and toys were furnished by local support groups, often organised around local Labour parties or trades councils.

But by the early New Year it was becoming increasingly obvious that the strike was faltering and couldn't be won against such insuperable odds.

On 21 January, a request by Labour MP Jeremy Corbyn for an emergency debate on the miners' strike was rejected by the Speaker, Bernard Weatherill. Just days earlier, Neil Kinnock had criticised a number of left-wing MPs, members of Labour's Campaign Group, after they forced the Speaker to suspend the sitting of the House for twenty minutes in an attempt to persuade the government to provide more time to debate the miners' strike.

Mark Seddon recalls being in the home of striking miner Taff King and his wife, Linda, in Ollerton on 3 March, when the news came through that the strike was ending. Taff looked crestfallen, while a look of utter relief came over Linda's face. Seeing her husband's reaction, she began to cry, but it seemed at the time that these were not tears of sadness.

The defeat of Britain's miners was one of those seminal events that was to reshape industrial relations in Britain, tipping them more and more towards the employer and away from the now deeply weakened trade union movement. Change came very quickly in the coalfields, with the planned run-down speeded up. There was little sign of the new investment and machinery promised by the Energy Secretary, Patrick Walker; instead, the Tories were to begin a process that was to lead to the privatisation of the rump of the coal industry and the ending of Britain's promising commitment to clean coal technology. Huge reserves of coal were capped, vastly expensive machinery was abandoned, trapped underground, and very much as Scargill had predicted, Britain came to rely more and more on cheaper, imported coal, often from countries with poor safety records underground. The mass media that had reported daily on strike-breaking progress in pit villages up and down the country was rarely seen now, occasionally turning up to report yet another closure and demolition.

Neil Kinnock, who had never had much time for Scargill and who felt that the year-long miners' strike had been lost because of Scargill's lack of tactical sense, believed that it had also been a lost and disastrous year for the Labour Party. Increasingly distanced from sections of the left in the Parliamentary Labour Party, Kinnock began a slow process of shifting the party away from some of the policies he and others believed were holding it back.

CHAPTER SEVEN

RETURN OF THE ROBBER BARONS

Following the 2015 general election, Clive Lewis, a Labour MP who successfully gained a seat that he had had little hope of winning according to the pollsters, rose from the green benches and gave what by most accounts was one of the more memorable maiden speeches.

The MP for Norwich South was a former BBC journalist, who had also served as a Territorial Army soldier, completing a tour of Afghanistan. He told a packed chamber that he had recently stood atop the ramparts of the ancient castle that graces the city.

'From the top of Norwich Castle, you can see our city spread out in uneven but concentric circles,' Lewis explained. 'As you move progressively out from the sites of historical importance, you eventually see the advent of nineteenth- and twentieth-century affordable housing. My fear is that future generations will look out from that castle top and ask, "What happened to the social housing of the twenty-first century?" The answer could well be the following: the foresight and wisdom of those spanning a century was squandered. The robber barons were back, he said.

Just as it is now, Norwich City Council was in the mid-1980s in the hands of a by and large thoughtful, left-leaning Labour administration, rooted in a history of municipal socialism that Lewis had alluded to in his speech. By the mid-1980s, with actual Labour governments now a distant memory, Labour's local authority powerbase was the second line of defence against a Tory government now scenting blood having rubbed the miners' noses in it.

Norwich wasn't one of the powerful, left-led metropolitan councils that the Thatcherites now clearly had their eyes upon, but everything it and other authorities like it stood for was anathema to the Conservatives. A special sort of venom came from the new breed of Tory hard-liners who, having gained control of London authorities such as Wandsworth and Westminster, were clearing their boroughs of working-class voters by decanting council house tenants into other parts of London. Their social engineering was designed to achieve the 'yuppification' of parts of inner London, while also ensuring in-built Tory majorities in perpetuity. Their agenda of outsourcing local services came to be codified and legislated on, handing huge public subsidies to their friends in the private sector, while making elected councils and councillors increasingly powerless – and therefore fairly pointless as many electors concluded.

Labour England was best personified by cities like Norwich. The city fathers and mothers had contrived over decades to build some of the most attractive and generous council houses and estates. The city boasted plenty of well-kept parks and other amenities including the city-owned airport. Schools were well maintained; libraries were plentiful, as were municipally owned swimming pools. Local authorities in the 1980s still owned and ran the buses and these were frequent and cheap, even if you could still smoke on the top deck. Signs posted at roadsides on the approaches to the city read, 'Welcome to Norwich. A Fine City'.

This now largely lost world stands as a distinctive metaphor for much that was really good about the post-war years and in particular in that most traduced decade, the 1970s. Increasingly, working-class people from the '60s onwards could afford to go on holiday, buy a new car and get on the housing ladder if they wished. Or they could have a decent council house or flat and pay reasonable rents. University fees were but a distant gleam in a man called Tony Blair's eye. Back then, a grant system ensured that those from the poorest families received the most help.

Social mobility was increasingly taken for granted. In Norwich, the city fathers and mothers took the promise of higher education seriously enough to hand over the municipal golf course to the new University of East Anglia.

Mark Seddon, a student there in the 1980s, recalls taking an octogenarian activist in the National Union of Agricultural and Allied Workers, Arthur Amis, who was dressed in an ancient dark three-piece suit with fob-watch, on a tour of the university. Arthur had started working on the land, plodding behind a horse and plough in the 1920s. He had barely travelled fifteen miles from his native village of Trunch his whole life. His trip to talk to students in Norwich about his life as a union organiser and from a time marked by debilitating insecurity of seasonal employment and tied cottages was an unrivalled revelation to him – particularly the Sainsbury Centre for Visual Arts.

Unsurprisingly, perhaps, Labour's local city leaders saw the Thatcherite promise to sell off council housing stock as a very real threat to keeping often diverse economic communities together. They believed that the best houses would be sold first, that those who remained as council tenants would find themselves ghettoised in some of the blocks thrown up in less generous times. They also believed that being prevented from spending the receipts of heavily discounted council housing stock would lead to a housing shortage.

In all of this, they were to be proved right, as Britain's housing crisis essentially became one of near-permanent shortage and reality. Labour Norwich, under its then mayor, Len Stevenson, took the government to the High Court in a bid to stop it being forced to sell off its precious housing stock. It made many of these arguments forcefully but it didn't prevail. It was the only Labour council to stand up to Margaret Thatcher in this way, once again proving that old city adage about the importance of 'doing different'.

At a more local level still, Labour England was in many ways personified by those who made up the local Labour Party in Norwich and the Trades Council, to which local unions sent delegates. Both the local party and the Trades Council were large and very active during the 1980s and continued to be to varying degrees in the decades that followed. There was a split between town and gown, familiar to those in other Labour university cities such as Bristol, Durham or Oxford, but it wasn't unhealthy.

There was a working-class base to the constituency, with a newer breed of local public service workers, including those who worked at the university and other higher education establishments. The youth wing largely comprised Labour students, some of whom would make the city their permanent home after leaving university. One Labour councillor who had just done that some decades earlier would tell anyone who listened that, 'Norwich was the graveyard for ambition, but who wouldn't give that up to stay in the city?'

There was a small branch of the Labour Party Young Socialists (LPYS), whose leading light was also a supporter in the Trotskyist Militant Tendency. His father was a local NHS worker and shop steward and his mother was also a respected local trade unionist, so the one or two efforts to expel the young firebrand and his followers were always going to be doomed.

Apart from attempting to sell copies of *Militant* at local general committee meetings, the youngsters in the LPYS would spend evenings discussing capitalism and built-in obsolescence, with particular reference to the shock discovery of a light bulb that had been burning continuously in Texas since 1919 or thereabouts.

In truth there was never any heart to chuck out the handful of youngsters who had thrown in their lot with the Militant Tendency in Norwich. They were harmless.

The party raised money locally through a well-organised Tote, with squads of largely pensioners knocking on doors all year round. The Tote, with its regular but small pay-outs, was an interface between the public and the party.

But Norwich Labour could also claim over 2,000 party members, lively local ward parties with regular newsletters and activities. Years later, Tony Blair in his pomp would claim that he would make New Labour a mass membership party. This was largely based upon a not-so-novel recruitment method of sending someone around Trimdon Labour Club in Blair's Sedgefield constituency to sell membership like raffle tickets for a pound a pop. Norwich, usually something of a Labour bell-wether, had both a large and politically active membership long before Blair landed in Sedgefield.

The general committee was typically attended by upwards of ninety delegates from local ward parties and trade unions. In the early 1980s, both local MPs, John Garrett from the Tribunite wing of the party and David Ennals of the traditional Labour right (who would be viewed as suspiciously left-wing nowadays), would deliver their parliamentary reports. Motions would be keenly debated by members and if passed would usually bind the city council or the MPs to do something or other. Meetings took place in a well-appointed Labour club that had been opened by Harold Wilson when Prime Minister.

In addition to the offices, there was a large meeting hall and a popular bar. Periodically, keynote speakers would descend on Norwich, including on one occasion Dennis Skinner, aka the 'Beast of Bolsover', who was surprised to find himself loudly and verbally tackled for not tacking to the left enough by a dungaree-wearing Labour student.

Her name was Caroline Flint, and she went on to become a minister in Tony Blair's government and was about as New Labour as it was possible to be.

Another speaker, John Prescott, came to Norwich a few times, on one occasion being heckled by an ASLEF train driver on paternal rights – not Prescott's, but his. A flustered Prescott turned to Mark Seddon who was sitting nearby and asked if he knew the answer to what was proving to be a difficult question. Sadly Seddon had no idea either, and Prescott's answer failed to placate.

Norwich, in common with other constituency Labour parties, balloted for two candidates to attend the annual Labour Party conference, usually held in either Brighton or Blackpool. The conference in 1985, months on from the final death throes of the bitter miners' strike, came during a period of introspection that the Labour Party drifts into with depressing regularity. Yet earlier in the year in mid-March, a MORI poll had put Labour at 40 per cent, some four points ahead of the Conservatives, who were at 36 per cent. Polls tended to be a little more accurate back then, perhaps because voters were more honest with pollsters and/or it was much easier to poll people on old-fashioned telephone landlines, and yet Labour's lead did nothing to dampen the rush to the barricades between hard left and soft left and Labour's old right wing for good measure upping the ante.

Labour's next big line of defence took the form of the big metropolitan authorities, foremost in their number the Greater London Council. As the government squared up to Labour's last real fiefdoms, such as the Greater London Council, which baited ministers daily with its huge banner counting London's unemployed just across the River Thames from Parliament, the trade unions were about to be plunged into their biggest test against the new anti-union laws. These outlawed secondary picketing, but they also gave new powers to employers to hire and fire at will.

What was to happen in the streets of Wapping in east London was the final emasculation of the remaining industrial power of organised labour. Rupert Murdoch seized his chance in early 1986, demanding that the workforce on his three national titles, *The Times*, the *Sunday Times* and *The Sun*, accept new printing technology on his terms, and accept that 90 per cent of them would lose their jobs in return for enhanced redundancy payments.

Unsurprisingly, Murdoch's own papers and much of the rest of Fleet Street depicted the titanic battle that was to follow as one of modernity versus Luddite dinosaurs. The truth, as ever, was more complicated.

In the early 1980s, most of Britain's newspapers were printed in Fleet Street, on hot metal and with highly skilled workers. These workers aligned themselves according to their trade in respective craft unions, including NATSOPA (the print operatives union) and the gloriously named SLADE (representing lithographic workers) and based in, of course, Caxton House, south London. These were to merge into one powerful union, Sogat 82, led by Brenda Dean. The smaller National Graphical Association (NGA) was hugely powerful.

Work in the machine rooms in the bowels of the old newspaper buildings was hot, noisy and tough. Most of the printers hailed from old printing families in the East End of London – and the bosses were content to let the unions do the recruiting and training, in return for a pre-closed-shop union agreement and relatively high industrial wages.

The new technology would certainly have made the printers' jobs a lot less noisy and hazardous. Indeed it had been operating with union agreement in the provinces for some time, but there was little attempt to sugar the pill. With the threat of mass redundancies hanging over them, both Sogat and the NGA voted by a large margin to strike in January 1986.

Murdoch and his right-hand man, Bill O'Neill, decided on the expedient sacking of 5,500 workers overnight and moving production of his newspapers immediately to a newly constructed plant away from Fleet Street in Wapping. O'Neill, a fellow Australian who had started out in Murdoch's papers as a union organiser, became the chief union basher – his correspondence on how to engineer a strike and then use the new anti-union laws to clean up was famously leaked at the time.

Astonishingly Murdoch's full frontal assault on his Fleet Street labour force was aided and abetted by the electricians' union, the EETPU, led by fierce anti-leftist Eric Hammond.

The new News International distribution plant in Wapping was surrounded by barbed wire and new security cameras while vans relayed specially recruited EETPU members from Southampton and Glasgow across the increasingly bitter picket lines to operate the new direct input technology.

Both the Labour Party and the TUC urged a boycott of the News International titles – the plea on Labour's part being made by a new director of communications, Peter Mandelson.

By early February, the nightly picketing of the plant had grown and on 15 February, mounted police charged well over 5,000 printers and their supporters in what became known as the battle of Wapping. Mark Seddon was with NGA London and Norwich stalwart Dave Gladwell on the night of one of the police charges down narrow, half-derelict cobbled streets. Missiles were thrown by some of the demonstrators and all attempts to close the road were resisted by police with dogs. When the horse charge came, Gladwell whispered to Seddon, 'I should have brought some ball bearings with me!'

With the almost inevitable defeat of the print unions at Wapping, Mrs Thatcher's brave new dawn finally broke. She had seen the Labour Party off (twice) and was about to do so yet again. She had broken the back of organised labour, and would by early 1986 have abolished the Greater London Council and dismembered the metropolitan authorities such as South Yorkshire County Council and Merseyside County Council. She had privatised much of what had been publicly owned, and beaten the National Union of Mineworkers.

Her vision of a home- and share-owning democracy was shared by most of Fleet Street. Championing the idea that 'greed could be good', her government unshackled the City of London in a 'big bang' of deregulated burning red tape. Old notions of achieving greater equality were swiftly abandoned as people were urged to pull themselves up by their bootstraps. To a degree, much of this chimed with the mood in London and the south-east of England in particular and among those who had bought their council houses or invested in some BT or British Gas shares.

Labour's incessant wrangling, its defence of a crumbling status quo, a deeply hostile national media and a mendacious snobbery meant that Neil Kinnock never really stood a chance.

And all of this was nearly ten years since Professor Eric Hobsbawm had written his essay, prophetically titled 'The Forward March of Labour Halted?'

But as the Thatcherites swivelled their guns towards the print unions, the party was to become ever more consumed over the future of the small Trotskyist organisation the Militant Tendency.

CHAPTER EIGHT

MILITANT TENDENCIES

Militant had emerged from the Revolutionary Socialist League, and its guru was the craggy-faced, reclusive Ted Grant, who originally had hailed from South Africa and who rapidly became a media hate figure, although gallingly for the press, Grant kept himself away from the cameras and the headlines.

Militant was just one of the Heinz variety of Trotskyist sects that included the Workers Revolutionary Party (John McDonnell having been a disciple in his youth), the Socialist Workers Party and Socialist Action. This last was rather more thoughtful and less sectarian, and had influence in the GLC, where a number of its supporters congregated around the leadership of Ken Livingstone.

Militant were largely seen by left-wing critics as vaguely worthy but incredibly dull. Others on the left, including Tony Benn, tended to indulge them. Some older party members thought that being on the left was a rite of passage for any self-regarding party activist and tended to think that these same youngsters would 'grow out of it'. Yet even at its height, Militant itself could only claim over 8,000 hardcore true believers.

Sections of the media, aided and abetted by some Labour MPs who should probably have known better, would raise the ghost of the Militant Tendency following the election of Jeremy Corbyn as leader and the rise of the activist-based Momentum. There were some parallels – Momentum seemed to be strongest in some of those areas that had traditionally been strongholds of Militant such as Liverpool, London and Brighton. But most Momentum supporters – and there were around 40,000 of them by mid-2018 – wouldn't know who Leon Trotsky was, let alone about any of his 'transitional demands'. True, some ageing Trotskyites and others gravitated towards Momentum, but in time-honoured Labour tradition, most of its supporters owed more to Methodism than Marx.

Although it had been active and increasing in its largely youthful membership throughout the '70s, from its early base in the Liverpool Walton constituency, Militant by the late 1970s was becoming more influential.

The organisation probably first really registered in public consciousness with the row over the employment of Militant supporter Andy Bevan by the Labour Party Young Socialists (LPYS). Bevan's employment exercised leader James Callaghan, but a series of resolutions put to the NEC demanding action against him and the Tendency failed to pass. Older members re-called another surging, popular youth wing, the Labour League of Youth. It had been shut down in 1954 largely for being far too critical of the party's leadership.

In the late 1970s, James Callaghan tasked Reg Underhill, now Lord Underhill, with investigating the activities of the Militant Tendency. Underhill was a former Labour Party national agent, softly spoken and self-effacing. His report into the organisation was damning, and yet no action was taken. Underhill would later regret that his party had allowed the entryist group to continue to grow.

And so Militant tended to be handled with kid gloves by the

party apparatus, until by the early 1980s its influence in Liverpool in particular and in white-collar unions such as the Civil and Public Servants Association (CPSA) became too loud and influential to ignore.

Yet the idea that many of the young people who were Militant supporters and active in the LYPS were all brainwashed entryists, hell-bent on the destruction of the Labour Party, was wide of the mark – although some at the core of the group certainly were. If you were young and radical and lived in inner-city Liverpool, there was a good chance that you might be repelled by the old rotten borough and emptied-out local Labour fiefdoms. Militant, with its straightforward, understandable if simplistic demands for things such as the nationalisation of the top 200 monopolies, had an appeal.

So did its promise to build thousands of new council homes. LPYS summer schools may have been unimaginably dull for savvy metropolitan student leftists, but for the average working-class youngster – and LPYS was overwhelmingly working-class – a camping holiday, even if it did involve learning some of the works of Leon Trotsky by rote, was time out from those parts of Britain's inner city and industrial heartlands your average middle-class student knew little of.

Militant's growth and the media interest in it ensured that the Labour hierarchy would eventually crank into action.

Labour's left was divided as to what to do about it. Many around Neil Kinnock believed that it was an entryist organisation and fundamentally undemocratic. Labour's remaining right-leaning politicians who hadn't defected to the SDP, such as deputy leader Roy Hattersley and trade union leaders including Eric Hammond of the electricians' union, were happy to throw their weight behind Kinnock.

They saw Militant as a real impediment to winning a general

election. They believed that voters by and large were repelled by the ultra-left – and also that left-wing posturing around such groups did absolutely nothing to advance the possibility of actually achieving power to reverse a Tory agenda that had come seriously close to breaking the back of organised labour.

Others on the hard left, such as Tony Benn, Eric Heffer, Joan Maynard and Jeremy Corbyn, saw Militant in a rather different light. They saw lots of passion and commitment from youngsters that could be channelled in the right direction, but they also saw in attempts to expel Militant's leading lights a possible continuity, which could lead to a far broader attack on Labour's left. What, they would ask, 'would stop Labour's Right from turning on all of us'?

Militant's editorial board – the Tendency printed a weekly paper – had been expelled in 1983 when Michael Foot was still Labour leader and not much progress had been made in the time since in choking the organisation off.

For all of the sound and fury, Militant struggled to make much headway in getting many of their more prominent supporters selected as parliamentary candidates. Some candidate hopefuls, such as Ray Apps in Brighton, had been around for decades and had become part of the furniture. Labour, after all, had always been a very broad church. Apps had become a Labour councillor in Brighton as had his long-time comrade, Rod Fitch, a Militant-supporting Labour candidate in the city's Kemptown constituency.

Apps, a printer by trade and activist in the NATSOPA print union, was a regular fixture at Labour Party conferences in Brighton. When finally the party machine – in the shape of the woman dubbed by Militant as the 'witchfinder general', Joyce Gould – expelled Apps along with six other Militant-supporting councillors, an editorial in *The Times* exclaimed, 'Now Labour conferences are Apps free zones.'

The difficulty for Labour's hierarchy was that some like Apps were, if not actually loved, respected. Few would doubt their motivation, but plenty would dispute their methods.

Yet in Gateshead, across the Scottish central belt and in many other constituencies, Militant were failing to have their candidates selected. At its height, Militant could only ever claim a handful of MPs, including the Liverpool firefighter Terry Fields and Militant veteran Pat Wall, whose selection in Bradford was only confirmed by the NEC once he had promised to relinquish any ties to Militant.

In Coventry, the earnest and well-regarded Dave Nellist took an average worker's wage rather than that of an MP. When the tumbrils came for Nellist, he was given every opportunity to renounce Militant, because there was a genuine reluctance even among some of his bitterest critics to turf out such an obviously hard-working MP. Nellist ultimately refused and joined his fellow comrades out in the cold.

The curious thing about Militant was just how Liverpool-centric the organisation and its supporters often seemed to be, or perhaps wanted to sound. Its leading lights included Derek Hatton, Liverpool City Council's deputy leader – who subsequently became leader after ousting the genial John Hamilton from his role. Other prominent Liverpudlians included local MP Terry Fields and the somehow slightly menacing figure of Tony Mulhearn, who was president of the Liverpool District Labour Party and a former ship's printer and cab driver. Young Militant supporters would often be heard speaking in Liverpool accents, despite possibly never having visited the city. On one occasion, at a Labour student conference, which is where some of the toughest and most unpleasant battles took place, two brothers from opposing factions, Militant and Clause Four, spoke – one in middle-class home counties, the other in broad scouse.

Mark Seddon, who was president of the University of East

Anglia Students' Union in 1984, recalls getting a call from the then president of the National Union of Students, Phil Woolas (Woolas was to go on to serve as a minister in one of Tony Blair's governments, before being obliged to step down from his Oldham seat in 2010, having been found to have been in breach of the Representation of the People Act following a bruising election campaign against the Liberal Democrats).

Woolas was very concerned that Militant were on the verge of winning control of the National Organisation of Labour Students and told Seddon how important it was that his university's Labour club, one of the larger ones in the country, ensured that it had its full complement of delegates. Apart from having attended one of the interminably boring Labour Party Young Socialists meetings on capitalism, built-in obsolescence and the everlasting light bulb in Norwich, Seddon, along with his friends in East Anglia, remained largely innocent of the battles raging around the Trotskyist group at the time.

The fight between what the media would today call the 'left' and the 'moderates' for control of the Labour student body came to a head at the Hull Labour students' conference in 1984. The moderates, who for the most part would describe themselves as supporters of Neil Kinnock, had set up an organisation called Clause Four, named after the clause in Labour's constitution that committed the party to the common ownership of the means of production, distribution and exchange – and which was later to be an early casualty of Tony Blair's mission to modernise the party.

In the first batch of elections, the pro-Militant slate won some positions. The second batch never took place after the party official in charge closed down the conference. This was because the Clause Four group had alleged that one of their members had been thumped by a female Militant supporter, something that wasn't denied at the time.

Then it transpired that more votes had been cast than delegates accredited and Militant declared that they had evidence of how the ballot had been rigged and demanded a roll call vote. They bungled it by accusing the Labour Party official in charge personally, without evidence. He took his chance and closed down the conference.

Years later, Danny Nicol, a delegate from Oxford University, revealed that his delegation had indeed rigged the ballot. They had been given more ballot forms than they had delegates, which accounted for the discrepancy between registered delegates and votes cast.

On their return to Norwich, the East Anglia delegation also discovered that one of their members had been issued with more than one ballot paper, but had forgotten about it and put it in a file. Had he voted early and often, the Clause Four 'victory' over Militant would have been by an even larger margin.

A number of Labour students who had cut their teeth battling the Militant Tendency graduated to become Members of Parliament, including Caroline Flint and John Denham, who was the driving force behind Clause Four and the author of *Paved with Good Intentions: The Politics of Militant*. One of the organisers of the Hull conference was John Mann, who subsequently became the Labour MP for Bassetlaw in Nottinghamshire.

The sheer amount of energy and vitriol poured by both sides into a battle over control of the student body was a revelation.

These battles were being played out elsewhere in Parliament and in local government, especially in Liverpool, the real birthplace of Militant and the powerbase for the organisation. In 1982, Liverpool District Labour Council had adopted the slogan that had been that of George Lansbury's Poplar rebel councillors, 'Better to break the law than break the poor.'

During the early 1980s, there appeared to be parallel events taking place when it came to the Militant Tendency. In London, the national media warned about a takeover of the Labour Party by the militant left and party leaders found themselves being drawn into a series of battles over the group on the National Executive Committee and within the Parliamentary Labour Party. But in Liverpool, Labour's local election vote increased by 40 per cent – 22,000 extra votes. In Broadgreen, Labour's vote increased by 50 per cent and in the June 1983 elections, Militant supporter Terry Fields, standing on the slogan of 'A workers' MP on a workers' wage', had won the seat for Labour.

The Liverpool Labour Party's vote continued to rise: in 1982 Labour got 54,000 votes in the city; in 1983, 77,000 votes; and, in 1984, this increased to over 90,000. In thirty-three of the thirty-four contested seats, Labour's vote increased. Labour held all fourteen seats it was defending and seven seats were won from the Tories.

However, no more than sixteen of the elected councillors were Militant members and the leader of the council, John Hamilton, was very much from the traditional Tribunite wing of the party. The city council had also embarked on a major council-house-building programme, one of the few Labour local authorities to buck the trend. It was to build over 5,000 homes.

However, it was the decision to set an illegal budget in 1985, with the demand that the government made up what the city council said that it had been 'robbed' of – some £30 million after it had been rate-capped – that set the council on a collision course with the Labour leadership. It was also transparently obvious that as a Tory government had no intention of coming to the aid of Militant-run Liverpool or left-wing Lambeth Council, then led by 'red' Ted Knight, councillors soon found themselves running out of money.

The scene was set for one of Neil Kinnock's most memorable conference speeches in the September of that year, when he savaged Militant-controlled Liverpool City Council, which, by that time, had had to lay off large numbers of council workers. Kinnock attacked the 'grotesque chaos of a Labour council, a Labour council, hiring taxis to scuttle round the city handing out redundancy notices to its own workers'. Eric Heffer, who was not a member of the Militant Tendency, but who nonetheless supported the council and was opposed to any expulsions, stormed off the platform of the conference in fury.

To the media, he became the 'Hefferlump'. Heffer was far more complicated, clever and likeable than his media caricature would allow. So was Joan Maynard, the redoubtable Sheffield MP and former organiser for the National Union of Agricultural and Allied Workers.

The battle over Militant was a decisive trial of strength between Neil Kinnock, who was now joined in his battle by what the media would describe as the soft left, and the by now badly bruised soft left.

Shadow Foreign Secretary Denis Healey described the speech as being of 'historic importance', as it had 'shifted the centre of gravity not just of the Labour Party but of the labour movement as a whole decisively'. Bob Parry, Labour MP for Liverpool Riverside, denounced Kinnock as 'the biggest traitor since Ramsay MacDonald'. Parry, nicknamed 'Gulliver' for his propensity to travel largely at the expense of others around the world, was a tall, shambling figure, who would on occasions save money by sleeping in the House of Commons Library overnight to avoid having to pay hotel bills. For some years he used to be accompanied by a scruffy poodle, to which he would occasionally feed scraps of chocolate from his jacket pocket.

Following the conference in November, a meeting of Labour's NEC voted 21–5 to suspend Liverpool's district Labour Party. It also opted to set up an investigation committee to examine claims of malpractice, intimidation and corruption. Neil Kinnock, now in full post-conference throttle, said, 'It is generally recognised that the Militant Tendency is a maggot on the body of the party. We are seeing Militant on the way out and democratic socialism very much on the way in.'

But not everyone rallied to Kinnock from Labour's soft left. David Blunkett, an NEC member and leader of Sheffield City Council, and in those days a rather intolerant left-winger, criticised the decision to expel a local seller of the *Militant* newspaper in Sheffield as taking 'a sledgehammer to crack a nut'. Kinnock accused Tony Benn of suffering from 'mischievous hallucinations' following Benn's comment that 'the party starts here with the expulsion of this man and ends up joining the SDP'.

Polls appeared to show public support for Kinnock's stance, but what they couldn't depict was just what voters really thought of a party that was engaged in endless navel-gazing and internal disputes.

This is a practice well honed by all sides in the Labour Party, which has bedevilled it almost from the beginning. But all of this was before the age of social media, when even the pretence of 'being on the same side' would give way to base name-calling and worse. But what the present authors wonder is how in recent years a party with such noble aims has managed to harbour so many clearly quite malevolent and unpleasant people, and make some of them MPs?

The reckoning for the years of discord and division would come later in 1987 at the general election that Neil Kinnock and the Labour Party were to lose.

Since the late 1970s, Labour England had atrophied and shrunk; its somnolent, wasted body was being picked over by some within the party who clearly saw it simply as a vehicle to advance their sects, whether from the left or right, and by sections of the media, who wanted it pronounced dead altogether.

Clearly something needed to change drastically in the Labour Party, or all that would likely end up holding it together was a combination of the ever loyal trade unions, and an electoral system of first past the post that would allow a party to limp on, providing it could continue to count on the residual loyalties and folk memories of working-class voters in what would euphemistically come to be described as the party's 'heartlands'.

Neil Kinnock's struggle with the Militant Tendency would drag on throughout 1986. The party's monthly NEC meetings would become media spectacles as the intricacies of the party's rule book and legal recommendations and rulings were played out in front of waiting journalists.

Neil Kinnock would use four words for every one actually needed, Eric Heffer would ritually walk out, while Tony Benn would attend to the phalanx of television cameras outside the party's Walworth Road headquarters in south London.

Having been the party's front man with the broadcast media since the late 1950s, Benn knew the importance of presentation and style. He would address his comments not to the TV reporter, but look directly into the camera and talk to the 'people at home'.

We wonder how wise Kinnock and his supporters were to spend so much time trying to uproot and expel a small, yet highly influential Trotskyite sect, enabling the media to report it as Labour's most important story? And what were Tony Benn and others such as Joan Maynard and Eric Heffer doing speaking at Militant-supported conferences, playing to their gallery and giving every impression of endorsing an organisation whose ideology and methods of organisation were anathema to Labour's history and democratic socialist trajectory?

If they didn't support Militant, many of the Tendency's defenders scarcely criticised it, or its methods, which were modelled on what is euphemistically called 'democratic centralism'. They certainly gave more of an impression that they held their own party leadership in less regard than they did Messrs Hatton, Mulhearn and the rest of the Militant cabal. In truth, the battle over Militant was an extension of the battle for the soul of the Labour Party. It wasn't until 1991, when a by-election was triggered in Liverpool Walton following Eric Heffer's death and Militant supporter Lesley Mahmood decided to run against the official Labour Party candidate, Peter Kilfoyle, that Kinnock was finally able to turn the tables on the organisation. Kilfoyle, who had been instrumental in defeating Militant in the city, gained an 18,000 majority over Mahmood.

Labour's old right could never appreciate the depths of disillusion and despair that had developed in the dog days of that last Labour government. The left for its part became split, occurring ironically following the election of two leaders from the Tribunite left of the party, Michael Foot and Neil Kinnock. The new hard left saw surrender and defeat everywhere. It believed that Kinnock had thrown in his lot with right-wing trade union leaders such as Ken Cure of the engineers and Eric Hammond. To an extent it was right, but its actions were pushing Kinnock in that direction.

It feared that the purge of Militant would lead to the purging of other left-leaning groups in the party. Eric Heffer even wrote a book, and its prescience was perhaps demonstrated by the eventual emergence of New Labour – it was titled *Labour's Future: Socialist or SDP Mark 2?*

It also saw hard-fought policy victories, most notably over unilateral nuclear disarmament, severely threatened and undermined. Neil Kinnock had cut his teeth as a supporter of CND, but once leader, his support became more nuanced.

Labour's policy on leaving the EEC, as it was then, was reversed, the promise to close the American bases and send back the nuclear cruise missiles was dropped. Over time, the powerful NEC policy committees, such as the home policy committee, were relegated – a process that was to move into full throttle with the advent of Tony Blair.

Kinnock had no equal as both orator and firebrand, his gradual transformation into a more carefully considered political figure provoked ire on the left. Kinnock had never seen eye to eye with Benn, regarding him as a patrician on a patronising, purist, pseudo-protean mission doomed to failure. It seems doubtful that Kinnock would have even regarded Benn's socialism as something amounting to radical romanticism. Benn for his part saw in Kinnock an essentially lightweight figure and one who would tack to the right not just for the case of short-term expediency, but in order to crush those on the left who had helped build his powerbase. Both in their own way were tragically right and wrong.

Benn never forgave Kinnock. In Benn's last volume of memoirs, written when he was close to death, he could not bring himself to mention Kinnock's name even once without a cruel sneer. He refers to him as 'Neil Kinnock, now sixty five, laughing boy Kinnock'. Kinnock's ready laugh is one of his most attractive traits.

Kinnock was transparently sincere and ferociously eloquent. No one else had so discomfited the Tory attack dog Norman Tebbit. When Tebbit confronted Kinnock on television and twitted him about Labour moving leftwards, Kinnock said, 'Parties do change. If they didn't, we'd still have nice old Ted Heath instead of this gang of barbarians.' Tebbit, like Benn, never forgave him.

The tragedy of Labour then – and now – is the inordinate destructive energy invested by both sides, while those Labour was created to serve stare ahead into a long distance of Tory rule.

When the Tories fall out, they do so in a savage almost

inchoate manner. Nothing can match the depths to which they will plunge. But then just as soon as it started, it is all over.

With Labour, ancient enmities extend, re-emerge and fester. Following the purge of Militant, the party leadership and the left were at loggerheads again over the creation of Labour Party 'black sections'.

Identity politics were fast replacing class politics on the British left. Black sections were mooted and advocated for the potential for black advancement through positive discrimination and to get more ethnic minority councillors and MPs elected. Just as today, when we hear accusations of anti-Semitism, those campaigning for black sections, including Sharon Adkin and Lambeth Council leader Linda Bellos, accused Labour publicly of being 'a racist party' in opposing them.

A National Executive Committee now controlled by Neil Kinnock and his supporters blocked Sharon Adkin's candidacy in Nottingham East after she accused the party of being racist. Was the Labour Party racist? No more than it is anti-Semitic today.

The arguments, as ever, were about how to reach the promised land.

Neil Kinnock and his supporters believed genuinely that having black sections could actually open the party up to attack for a form of organisational apartheid. Sharon Adkin, Linda Bellos and others believed that black sections gave the best opportunity for ethnic minorities to advance politically.

Similar arguments raged around all-women shortlists for parliamentary selections, with outriders such as the late Jo Richardson and Clare Short coming under sustained fire when they argued for positive discrimination and the achievement of equal representation for women. Today, virtually no one disputes the need for positive discrimination for women, or for gay members

and ethnic minority members. If they did, they would probably be suspended from the Labour Party. But back in the late
1980s, it was the much-vilified Labour left leading the charge,
and sometimes not just against the party machine but against
well-paid barristers.

But the national media were more interested, as ever, in taking
Labour's dirty washing and hanging it in the most public places.
London's left soon became an easy caricature, as a young, more
cosmopolitan and more liberated generation, who were more
motivated by identity politics than class, became the loony left.

A rash of stories – sometimes made easier to tell by the antics
of some Labour councillors and activists – began to appear.
Many had absolutely no foundation – such as the claim that
Labour-controlled Haringey Council had banned the nurs-
ery rhyme 'Baa, Baa, Black Sheep', or indeed the mention of
black bin bags, on the grounds that mentioning the word 'black'
could be construed as racist. Never mind, if these were repeated
enough, the damage would be done over time.

But then Labour's hard left would sometimes almost deliberately court media opprobrium, such as when a new Labour-led
administration took power in Ealing and shoved up the local
rates by over 60 per cent. One of the more enthusiastic supporters of this self-defeating policy was a young Labour councillor
called Hilary Benn. Mark Seddon, by then living in Acton,
watched spellbound as Labour support simply melted away in
his street almost overnight.

CHAPTER NINE

THE WILDERNESS YEARS

On 3 January 1988, Margaret Thatcher became the longest-serving Prime Minister of the twentieth century, having occupied 10 Downing Street for eight years and 244 days. Exactly three weeks later, Arthur Scargill was re-elected as president of the NUM by a narrow majority, winning 53.8 per cent of the vote against 46.2 per cent for his challenger (and membership was now in free fall as the pit closure programme struck hard). Seven years earlier, he had won the post with 70.3 per cent of the vote.

The decline in Scargill's fortunes, even in his own bailiwick, mirrored the decline of the NUM itself, and the decline of the NUM was a metaphor for the decline of Labour England.

The Labour Party was powerless to ride to the rescue of Labour England because the 1987 election defeat had brought out Labour's circular firing squad in force. Tony Benn was busy attacking Neil Kinnock, launching a 'campaign for socialism', and telling anyone who would listen, 'I genuinely do not believe the Labour Party's electable if we pursue the present course.' Kinnock was busy attacking Benn, condemning 'self-enthroned revolutionaries' in Labour's ranks.

In March, the Bennite Jeremy Corbyn had an unsuccessful go at wresting the chairmanship of the Greater London Labour

Party from Glenys Thornton, a popular and well-regarded figure on all wings of the party. She is now Baroness Thornton and speaks on Health for Labour in the Lords.

Kinnock was in the blackest of depressions. It took him a good year to recover, and in a sense he has never recovered. The wounds of his long and bitter struggle with the Bennites and of the ferocious media campaign waged against him hit this complex and sensitive man hard, and the ebullience which came naturally to him in 1983 was starting to sound very forced by 1987.

A post-election meeting between Kinnock, his adviser Charles Clarke and Peter Mandelson concluded that Labour must change dramatically. They agreed that Labour's campaign had been brilliant; it was Labour's policy that had let it down. The logic of this required further sweeping policy changes. They would have to accept that the market economy worked best, except in healthcare, education and social services, and they would have to ditch unilateral nuclear disarmament. And they would have to build up the Mandelson myth – the myth of the great communicator. It is that myth upon which Mandelson's luminous career was built.

Actually, communication is one skill Mandelson lacks. His writing is turgid and self-indulgent. As a broadcaster, though articulate, he sounds oily and insincere. 'When we do surveys, Mandelson is always bottom of the poll for trust,' the veteran pollster Bob Worcester once told us.

His skill lies in what most of us know as office politics. Like his famous grandfather Herbert Morrison, he knows the Labour Party inside out and knows how to make it do the things he wants it to do. Like his grandfather, he found that that skill bought you influence, but not love and friendship. He craved love and friendship. This is where Tony Blair came in. The young Sedgefield MP employed his winning charm on Mandelson.

Mandelson, so Labour Party officials of the time tell us, grew to adore Blair. There was an extraordinary personal chemistry between them. Blair called Mandelson 'Pete' – no one else ever did. They would sit and talk for hours, secretively, on their long train journeys to their northern constituencies. And that is why Blair, and not Gordon Brown, became Prime Minister in 1997.

The diagnosis – that the presentation was fine and the problem was the policy – was not supported by Labour's pollsters, MORI. Bob Worcester of MORI had advised Kinnock to be himself – exactly the opposite of the advice he was getting from Mandelson. Mandelson's answer to this was to change the pollsters. Out went Worcester, dismissed – so he always believed – for not telling the leader the things Mandelson wanted the leader to hear. In came marketing and PR people Philip Gould and Deborah Mattinson, and a greater reliance on focus groups rather than quantitative polling.

Now, the problem with focus groups – 'qualitative research' in pollsters' jargon – is that they can be made to mean pretty much anything. Here's an example: Mattinson wrote to Kinnock, 'Top of mind are the "loony" lesbian/gay issues. In fact, however, extremism links to everything else. It's an umbrella for all Labour's negatives: trade unions, mismanagement of the economy (local government experience), defence.'

Benn challenged Kinnock for the leadership, and Eric Heffer and John Prescott both challenged Roy Hattersley for deputy leader. It wasn't a popular decision, even among their friends. David Blunkett said it would be hopeless – and Blunkett in those days was still revered on the hard left of the party. (It was still some years before Blunkett suddenly became Tony Blair's ideological soulmate and the hammer of the left, and Prescott became Blair's deputy, having suddenly discovered that Hattersley wasn't too right-wing after all – he was too left-wing. They must rank as the two fastest conversions since Paul the Apostle wondered idly how far he still had to go to reach Damascus.)

Clare Short, Labour's frontbench spokeswoman for Employment and a member of Benn's Campaign Group, called the challenge a 'waste of everyone's time'. The Campaign Group secretary, Jeremy Corbyn, rejected rumours that the vote in favour of a challenge was 15–7. But Short and five others resigned from the Campaign Group in protest at the decision.

Never mind: the challenge was on, whether Short or Blunkett liked it or not, and that was summer 1988 gone, with voters seeing very little of Labour but Kinnock and Benn sniping at each other.

It meant that when another citadel of Labour England fell, it went almost unnoticed. The Local Government Act's Section 28 prohibited local authorities from 'intentionally promot[ing] homosexuality or publish[ing] material with the intention of promoting homosexuality' and 'promot[ing] the teaching in any maintained school of the acceptability of homosexuality as a pretended family relationship'. Crucially, the local government Act also forced local councils to go out to tender from private companies for contracts.

Despite all the noise and fury, there was never the slightest chance of Kinnock and Hattersley losing the leadership contests; they won overwhelmingly, and by 1990 things were looking up. By-elections were going Labour's way – in March 1990 the party took Mid Staffordshire from the Conservatives by 9,449 votes, overturning a Conservative majority of 14,654.

And Thatcher had gone a step too far, by enacting the poll tax. It abolished the system of rates – taxes paid on the value of your property – and substituted a tax which would be the same however rich or poor you were. It was a drastic way of redistributing wealth from the poor to the rich. Thatcher by then seemed to have thought she was walking on water and could do anything she wanted; but this was one watery step too far.

In central London, 200,000 people marched against it, the polls worsened for the government, and in the local council elections, Labour gained 284 seats, and their projected share of the vote, 44 per cent, was their highest since 1981. The Conservative Party lost 222 seats with their share of the vote falling by 3 per cent to 33 per cent.

Labour managed to turn even this into a set of internal power struggles. Jeremy Corbyn favoured refusing to pay the poll tax, the leadership didn't. Shadow Environment spokesman Bryan Gould called a press conference to produce Labour's alternative, and – so Gould claims – Peter Mandelson sabotaged it by 'forgetting' to invite the press; for Mandelson had decided that Gould was on his way out, and should be helped on his way. The most important thing to happen at the press conference was that Gould's deputy David Blunkett's guide dog was sick on the floor.

Thatcher's Secretary of State for Trade and Industry, and one of her closest allies, Nicholas Ridley, embarrassed her by telling the world that giving up sovereignty to the European Union was as bad as giving it up to Adolf Hitler. In those days that was regarded as a pretty extreme thing to say, and he was forced to resign.

Even a foreign war (Saddam Hussein invaded Kuwait that year) couldn't save the embattled Prime Minister. Millions of words have been written about the nine days in November 1990 between former Chancellor Geoffrey Howe's devastating speech attacking his former boss on 13 November and her final acceptance of defeat on 22 November, and all we need do here is note that by the end of the month, Britain had a new Conservative Prime Minister. His name was John Major, and no one expected him to be there long.

Major scrapped the poll tax, led the nation into war to help drive Saddam Hussein out of Kuwait, and revived the Conservatives' hope that they might just scrape home at the next general election after all. Their advertising took on a certain pugnacity, as well as a magnificent disregard for such inhibiting factors as truth. The first poster of the Major era claimed that Labour's plans would mean tax increases of more than £1,000 for the average voter, and Major called the general election for 9 April.

Labour entered the campaign with a three-point lead in the polls, which somehow, between 24 March and 9 April, turned into an eight-point Conservative lead, enough to give Major an overall parliamentary majority.

For a party that was supposed to have campaigning down to a fine art, Labour managed to run an abysmal campaign in 1992. Whatever the truth about the 1987 loss, there is no doubt about 1992. It was campaign that lost Labour the election, not policy. The men who had told Labour to sell itself like soap flakes let their party down.

Kinnock's minders, who never quite trusted their man to be left alone, wrapped him in cotton wool all the way through, right up to the moment when he was to make his triumphant appearance at a great rally in Sheffield, a few days before polling day. This rally was a great, pompous, glitzy, self-regarding exercise, a massive miscalculation by those who were supposed to be so very good at running elections.

One of the event's planners explained beforehand in a private memorandum:

It will be a TV spectacular. It will be full of music, movement of people, light effects and an audio visual presentation ... Neil Kinnock will arrive by helicopter and the event will climax with his speech from the podium, surrounded by the shadow cabinet ... The closing sequence will be timed to coincide with the opening titles of the main BBC news and the reporter's piece to camera ... Regional groups will be provided by us with US convention style banner … We will see [Neil Kinnock] on the big screen arrive by helicopter on a field adjacent to the arena. While he is travelling by car to the arena, the first of the celebrity endorsements will be shown on the big screen … Neil Kinnock will be announced and will walk the length of the arena, accompanied by the shadow cabinet … As the main BBC News comes on air, we will set off the indoor pyrotechnics, light shows and confetti guns.

It would have been a disaster even if it had all gone according to plan. But it didn't go according to plan. Earlier speakers overran, Kinnock appeared ten minutes late, and 10,000 people in the hall erupted with excitement. Kinnock's repeated cries of 'all right' from the podium went down a treat in the hall, but came across dreadfully on television.

Kinnock blamed himself. In a television documentary, *The Wilderness Years*, screened on BBC 2 in 1995, Kinnock said, 'This roar hit me and for a couple of seconds I responded to it, and all of the years in which I'd attempted to build a fairly reserved, starchy persona – in a few seconds they slipped away.' Who the hell told him that a reserved, starchy persona was better than his flexible, ebullient and sensitive nature?

But the problem was not Kinnock's performance, it was the gaudy triumphalism of the whole affair. And in any case, if the spin doctors had not kept the lid so firmly closed on the real Kinnock, the dam inside him might not have burst on that Sheffield stage.

Shadow Chancellor John Smith and Gordon Brown had hunkered down for the duration of the campaign in offices in Waterloo, far from the madding crowds back in Labour's Walworth Road HQ. Despite some well-aimed guerrilla attacks, most notably at the daily press conferences chaired by

Conservative Party chairman Chris Patten, Brown always seemed to know that this election was not going to be won. He probably knew that it could well be over after the Tories unveiled their first Labour tax bombshell advertisements and party political broadcasts. John Smith's moderate attempt to shift the direct taxation burden back onto the wealthy was coming under withering fire. The trouble was that Labour not only didn't really see this coming, the party then failed to go on the offensive to fight the claims.

The election lost, Kinnock departed with haste and dignity. Two days later *The Sun* ran its triumphant, gloating headline: 'IT'S THE SUN WOT WON IT'.

Conservative chiefs agreed. Lord McAlpine, the former Conservative Party treasurer, said in the *Sunday Telegraph*:

> The heroes of this campaign were Sir David English [editor of the *Daily Mail*], Sir Nicholas Lloyd [editor of the *Daily Express*], Kelvin MacKenzie [editor of *The Sun*] and the other editors of the grander Tory press. Never in the past nine elections have they come out so strongly in favour of the Conservatives. Never has their attack on the Labour Party been so comprehensive … This was how the election was won, and if the politicians, elated in their hour of victory, are tempted to believe otherwise, they are in real trouble next time.

These words have chilled every Labour leader since. They helped dictate Tony Blair's strategy, as we shall see. And they haunt Jeremy Corbyn today; for he must know that if the press were determined to make that sort of effort to stop Neil Kinnock, what might they not do to stop Corbyn? Shadow Chancellor John Smith was overwhelmingly elected to succeed Kinnock, and five months after the election, on 16 September, the idea that our money was safe in the hands of a Conservative government suddenly looked very foolish indeed. Chancellor Norman Lamont spent billions of pounds of Britain's reserves that day buying up sterling in order to stay in the European Exchange Rate Mechanism by preventing the pound from falling below its agreed level. He failed, and Britain crashed out of the ERM.

CHAPTER TEN

THE RISE OF BLAIR

1992–1997

Norman Lamont paid the price for failure, evicted from the Treasury at the first Cabinet reshuffle in May 1993, despite being Major's long-standing friend and ally. He turned down the consolation Cabinet post he was offered at Environment and did his best to put the knife into his old friend with a resignation speech dripping with venom and wounded *amour-propre*: 'The government listens too much to the pollsters and the party managers … As a result, there is too much short-termism, too much reacting to events and not enough shaping of events. We give the impression of being in office but not in power.'

It was no good. Geoffrey Howe he wasn't. The PM hardly noticed.

Well, he wouldn't. Norman Lamont came quite low down on the list of John Major's troubles. The Tories' reputation for economic competence was utterly blown. For Major, the name of the game was survival. He led a chronically divided party, and his Cabinet were constantly at each other's throats over Europe. Each day that he could go to bed still at the head of his party and his government was a triumph and a minor miracle. We have seen nothing like it until Theresa May's premiership.

He probably did not even notice when the organisation that was to haunt his party was born in September 1993. An obscure group of anti-EU campaigners called the Anti-Federalist League, founded and led by an LSE lecturer called Alan Sked, met at the London School of Economics and decided to turn themselves into a political party. They called it the UK Independence Party. Twenty two years later, in 2015, Sked wrote, 'After I stepped down to return to academic life ... the party came under control of a preposterous mountebank named Nigel Farage, who reoriented it to the far right.'

If anyone was in any doubt of the way the wind was going, the local government elections in the same month that Lamont resigned, the first after John Smith became Labour leader, saw Labour gain 111 councillors and improve their share of the vote by 9 per cent to 39 per cent, while the Conservatives lost 486 councillors and their share of the vote fell by 15 per cent to 31 per cent.

No one had any doubt that when the next election came, Major would be out on his ear, and John Smith would take up residence in 10 Downing Street.

In July, Labour even managed to defeat the government. The issue was the European Union's social chapter, which required those countries signing up to it to ensure their workplaces met with European standards in such matters as the working environment, consulting staff and protection of workers where their employment contract is terminated.

Naturally, the Eurosceptics considered this far too good for British workers, and Major had been forced to negotiate an opt-out. All the other eleven states adopted it. In July in the House of Commons, the government's motion supporting its policy of opting out of the social chapter was defeated by 324 votes to 316.

Of course, the defeat was reversed the next day by the usual stratagem of making it a vote of confidence, so that Conservative

MPs could not vote with Labour without bringing down the government. But it provided the ideal backdrop to Smith's speech at the Labour conference two months later:

> Today, I offer the British people a better way and a clear choice: a choice between Labour's high skill, high tech, high wage economy, and John Major's dead-beat, sweatshop, bargain basement Britain; a choice between Labour's opportunity society which invests, which educates and which cares, and the sad reality of neglect, division and rising crime that is Tory Britain today.

Smith forced a final constitutional change through the conference, bringing in one member, one vote for the selection of parliamentary candidates. His old trade union friend John Edmonds, general secretary of the GMB, supported it with the greatest reluctance, and only after it had been made clear to him that Smith meant what he said: he would resign if he didn't get it.

Smith was also helped by John Prescott, then still much admired among the unions (where he was seen as one of their own) and on the left. Prescott made a heartfelt if confusing plea:

> There's no doubt, this man, our leader, put his head on the block by saying … I fervently believe … of a relationship, and a strong one, with the trade unions and the Labour Party. He's put his head there … give us a bit of trust and let's have this vote supported.

Grizzled old trade unionists know how to translate that sort of thing. 'John's the leader, brothers and sisters, so let's not have any more of this argy bargy.' It came from Prescott's heart, and from the heart of Labour England.

Smith intended the decision to mark an end to Labour's

constitutional debates, so that he could get on with the stuff that mattered. He was not having any further constitutional changes in his leadership. His mind, we're told by politicians who knew him, was on hypothecated taxation – taxes which were specifically for health or education. Hypothecated taxation had always been opposed by the Treasury, but Smith believed it was the way to make sure that the things that really mattered were paid for. It could have meant a new lease of life for Labour England.

This was profoundly depressing for the likes of Tony Blair and Peter Mandelson, who hankered for more constitutional change and a far more radical departure from the things Labour had always stood for, and they watched with dismay as Smith started to build bridges with the likes of Jeremy Corbyn and John McDonnell, with whom they had pretty well sworn eternal enmity.

But no matter what Blair and Mandelson thought, that was Smith's vision. No more constitutional tinkering. Hypothecated taxes and a well-funded education system and National Health Service from day one of a Labour government – a Labour government whose arrival now seemed inevitable with the party led by the solid and trustworthy Scottish lawyer John Smith. The future was clear, and Labour people could feel a sense of optimism about it.

But at 8.05 a.m. on 12 May 1994, John Smith suffered a massive heart attack in the bathroom of his flat in the Barbican, and one hour and ten minutes later he was pronounced dead at St Bartholomew's Hospital.

Smith's aide Hilary Coffman, who had been waiting to take him to an engagement, told Labour communications chief David Hill, who kept it secret for a while so that Smith's father could be told before he heard it on the news. Hill did, however, tell Glenys Thornton, general secretary of the Fabian Society, who told her husband John Carr; and by 10 a.m., Carr was on the phone to Peter Mandelson. 'It's got to be Blair,' said Carr, and Mandelson said, 'No, it's got to be Brown.'

But by the end of the day, Mandelson had changed his mind, and was certain it had to be Blair. Quite how that happened, we don't know. But we do know that Blair, in Aberdeen that morning, knew the moment he heard the news that he would fight for the job, while Brown spent days making up his mind, and then it was too late: the Blair campaign was unstoppable. Brown has never ceased to believe he was deprived of the crown by the treachery of his one-time friend Peter Mandelson.

Blair coasted home, and for the first time in its history the Labour Party had a leader who neither liked nor understood Labour England, and especially that part of it that belonged to the trade unions. His first act was to fire the general secretary whom Neil Kinnock had appointed a decade earlier, Larry Whitty. Whitty had come up in the unions – his previous job had been with the GMB – and he was considered still to be close to them. At the October Labour Party conference, many delegates interpreted Whitty's farewell speech – rightly – as a coded warning not to get so carried away with what Blair called modernisation as to forget what the Labour Party was for.

An idle warning, alas; for behind him as he spoke, against a pistachio background (most people thought it was green but the image makers insisted it was pistachio), were the words NEW LABOUR, NEW BRITAIN. It was against this backdrop that Blair launched the campaign to get rid of Clause 4 of Labour's constitution, which said Labour aimed 'to secure for the workers by hand or by brain the full fruits of their industry ... on the basis of the common ownership of the means of production, distribution and exchange'.

The leader of the GMB union, John Edmonds, reluctantly persuaded his union to support the change because he thought that a defeat for Blair might burst the bubble and enable the

Conservatives to win the next election. But he had no illusions. Labour now had a leader, he told us, who 'feels fear and contempt for the unions'.

'He likes to make us feel we're his buddies – that's his way,' said Edmonds. 'But he can't cope with the idea that when he saw us, he was seeing representatives of the trade unions, not individuals. He's no idea of what unions do or how they work.'

If Edmonds had hoped for some amelioration of the Conservative trade union legislation from a Labour government, he was to be quickly disillusioned. Two months after his election, Blair told a meeting of industrial chieftains, 'There is acceptance that the basic elements of [trade union] legislation, ballots before strikes, for union elections, restrictions on mass picketing, is here to stay.' Well before he had to face the electorate, he had promised CBI chieftains that, although he would have to sign the social chapter, since it was a commitment he could not safely dishonour, he would ensure it was meaningless by blocking pro-worker and pro-union proposals for inclusion in the social chapter. He never told the unions that he had given the bosses that promise, but in government he was as good as his word.

The story of Blair's three years as opposition leader is the story of how the unions, after waiting eighteen years for a government which did not think they were the work of the devil, had the cup dashed from their lips at the last moment.

By-election results were disastrous for the government, encouraging for Labour. The bitter division over Europe was stifling the Conservative Party to death. On 22 June 1995, John Major resigned as leader of the Conservative Party in a bid to reassert his authority in a leadership contest. He was re-elected, of course, but the hoped-for revival of authority was nowhere to be seen. By the end of 1995, defections and by-election losses had brought the government's overall majority in the House of Commons down to three. In the local elections of May 1996, Labour gained 468 council seats and the Conservatives lost 607 seats.

Blair was going to win. Never mind that it was not the victory they had dreamed of. It was victory after eighteen years. Dissenting voices sounded crabbed and ungrateful. But they persisted. Clare Short described Blair's media advisers as 'the people who live in the dark'. Jeremy Corbyn supported her: 'Clare Short is right to draw attention to the appalling power of the spin doctors and the way that modern politics is dominated by totally unresponsive focus groups.' It did not matter. Blair was going to win. That was all that mattered.

Never mind that at the 1996 Labour Party conference in Blackpool, Tony Blair told delegates that Labour 'will be the party of sound finance and good housekeeping' and 'has taken the mantle of the party of law and order'.

He did also throw a few crumbs to Labour's traditional base, telling them that a Labour government would 'scrap the Tory internal market of the National Health Service' and restore 'a unified system of railways with a publicly owned, publicly accountable British Rail at its core'. His government, when it came, did neither of these things.

Major's government staggered on right up to the wire, without an effective Commons majority after December 1996, every day hoping for better times, hoping for a miracle, hoping Labour might implode.

As for Blair, he seems rather to have hoped to get only a slim Commons majority which would provide an excuse for a coalition with the Liberal Democrats, whose policies he found less alarming than those of his own party. No such luck. If John Smith had led Labour into the 1997 election he would, according to Bob Worcester, have had a majority of just under 100. Blair's was an extraordinary 179. He was flying. He could do anything he liked.

CHAPTER ELEVEN

TONY BLAIR AND THE GREAT MISSED OPPORTUNITY

Sometimes the sheer loathing we feel for Tony Blair and his New Labour project puzzles people. What causes it, they ask?

Is it his style? Is it the ostentatiously wealthy way he lives now, and the means by which he has become so rich? Is it what he did to the Labour Party before he became Prime Minister? Is it the way he split the Labour Party? And we say, 'No, not really; we think we could forgive all that.'

And at the last, they say with an understanding nod, 'Of course, it must be Iraq.' But you know what? It isn't really even Iraq, though it's hard to think of another modern occasion when so much harm was done in the world because of the vanity of a Prime Minister and the utter spinelessness of most of his Cabinet.

But no. In the end, it's not even Iraq.

This is what it is.

When Labour took office in 1997, it could do anything it wanted. It could have changed the world, the way Clem Attlee and his colleagues changed the world in three years, between 1945 and 1948. They had every advantage Attlee had and more. They had a big majority – even bigger than Attlee's. And they had a strong economy, whereas Attlee was working with a war-wrecked economy. Attlee had to send John Maynard Keynes to Washington with a begging bowl, and the Washington elite said, 'We can't give them money, they'll only spend it on welfare!'

But Attlee changed the world. He and Bevan introduced the National Health Service, they began a massive house-building programme, they built new schools, redistributed the nation's wealth, they nationalised the coal mines, brought the troops back from Europe and the Far East and struck at the very heart of British imperialism by giving independence to India. The sheer speed of the Britain's retreat from empire was remarkable, and but for the murderous mess of partition, could otherwise be remembered as nothing short of miraculous. People may laugh now at the antics of the League of Empire Loyalists, but Churchill and the British imperialists had to watch then as Ceylon and Burma became independent too.

Someone once called Attlee 'a modest man, with much to be modest about'. (It's normally attributed, probably wrongly, to Churchill). Tony Blair was far from being modest; he was a creature of the TV age, quick-witted, adroit, alternatively charming and, to use one of his dread expressions, 'inclusive'. Two people of diametrically opposed views could leave a meeting with Blair, believing that he was completely on their side. Blair also enjoyed the support of the middle-class chatteratti in London and crucially whole sections of the media, now thoroughly bored of the grey John Major and his endless battles with his foaming Tory Eurosceptics.

The Blair government could have done anything. Literally anything. It could have turned the supertanker of state around, as Attlee did. It could have reversed the trend for the rich to get richer and the poor to get poorer. Instead the government accelerated it.

If all that was too radical, it could have done a few little things to remove some of the burdens Thatcher had placed upon those at the bottom of the heap. It could have provided some homes for the poor, slowed down the sale of council homes, given tenants back a few of the small protections they used to have against the greediest landlords.

It could have taken the railways back into public ownership – the public had been aghast to see the extent of the subsidies being handed over to Richard Branson and others, while fares skyrocketed to make the British railways the most expensive to travel on in Europe. It could have halted the picking apart of the Post Office by the privateers, instead of blaming the European Union. It could have built millions of council houses, instead of just talking about doing it, as Yvette Cooper liked doing, and building nothing.

It could have developed policies for full employment instead of clamping down heavily on the smattering of economically literate Labour MPs who were arguing for the Keynesian policies that would be needed to get there (the Tribune Group of MPs was flooded by supporters of Blair and Brown and two of the most critical, Roger Berry and Peter Hain, were removed as officers from the group, after they had published a pamphlet calling for massive investment, reflation and tax increases to achieve full employment). It could have reversed some of the most iniquitous anti-trade-union laws; and instead of constantly ordering its Members of the European Parliament to vote against their socialist colleagues where there was even the vaguest possibility of upsetting the big corporations and the bankers, it could have cheered their solidarity with working people.

There are so many things that Tony Blair's New Labour government could have done that would not have broken the bank, caused a run on the pound or upset the European Commission, but the point was that in order to have even tried, one would have had to believe in a few of the things the Labour Party was created for – such as some measure of redistribution of wealth. As the late journalist and socialist Paul Foot was wont to say, 'There is no evidence that Tony Blair ever has been a socialist!' But worse, there was not even any evidence of any interest, empathy or understanding from Blair towards the party that he famously told *The Guardian* that he had 'come to love', other than an obligatory nod to Keir Hardie from time to time in speeches mostly soon forgotten for their vacuity but reliably lapped up by an extraordinarily bovine media. It largely continues to lap them up to this day.

Blair wasn't particularly interested in trying to make Britain a more equal place. Indeed, Peter Mandelson famously declared that he was 'intensely relaxed' about people getting 'filthy rich' – as we know now, because he was keen, as was his master, to suck up to and eventually emulate them. Tony Blair had accused his MEPs of 'infantilism' when they opposed his plan to rip up the party's Clause 4 constitutional commitment to common ownership, in favour of some instantly forgettable and fairly inane homily that did the trick for the media of underlining just how he had 'modernised the party'. The nonsense peddled by Mandelson that common ownership committed Labour 'to nationalising the corner shop' could just as easily have come from Margaret Thatcher.

Within a few years, virtually every MEP who had protested Blair's intellectual and verbal vandalism had been dropped as a candidate. This was a pattern to be repeated with a vengeance in the Parliamentary Labour Party over the next decade, with a whole phalanx of shiny, on-message, reliable candidates parachuted into place. Many of these same MPs would go on to form a core of around fifty MPs who were seemingly determined to stop Jeremy Corbyn from becoming leader, throw him out once he had been elected leader and then spend the remaining years doing their level best to prevent a Labour government being elected with him as leader.

Blair's retreat from social democracy alarmed Roy Hattersley, who had been once been regarded as a staunch Labour right-winger, albeit one who truly appreciated the Anthony Crosland school of social democracy. Hattersley, in common with other pragmatic, middle-of-the-road Labour people, could probably have gone along with a lot of what Blair and his supporters were promulgating, if they thought that short-term defensiveness was just a tactic. Former Health Secretary and Chancellor Kenneth Clarke came to a dinner organised by Tribune in the Gay Hussar restaurant in Soho, not long after Labour's 1997 general election landslide. There he volunteered that he was genuinely surprised to have learned that Gordon Brown's promise during the campaign to stick to Tory spending limits wasn't just a ruse to get the party across the finishing line with the media – but that Brown had actually meant it.

Shortly after Tony Blair was elected Labour leader and at around the same time that Mark Seddon took over the reins of the *Tribune* newspaper, the latter received a call from the former inviting him round for tea at his home in Islington. Blair was by then shadow Employment Secretary and a rising star in the Parliamentary Labour Party. His easy manner made him a favourite for TV appearances, often to the jealous glances of his not-so-attractive colleagues. Politics, Paul Begala, a political consultant to the Clinton administration, once said, is 'show business for ugly people' – but Blair knew that he was an exception.

Blair was charming and friendly; his tea slopped from his brimming mug into Seddon's as they sat down in his study. He was anxious to dispel any notion that he and his supporters wanted to wrest *Tribune* away from its bearings: 'We just want to be able to have a chance to put our side of the argument.' As a result, shortly afterwards, through the good offices of *Daily Mirror* associate editor Bill Hagerty, Alastair Campbell became a provocative, fortnightly columnist for the paper. His deceased father-in-law, Bob Miller, would certainly have approved, as Miller had been *Tribune*'s circulation manager for a time in the 1970s.

What many others saw as refreshing – namely Blair's airy dismissal of what he clearly thought as dated shibboleths – correspondingly alarmed the young *Tribune* editor. When it became apparent that Blair could not really see the merits of keeping the Scottish ferry service Caledonian MacBrayne, a vital connector of isolated island communities, in public hands, Seddon came to an early conclusion that all was not well with the new leader.

A subsequent visit to Blair's office in the House of Commons confirmed it, when yellow Post-it notes with the message 'call Peter [Mandelson]' were scattered in multiple locations. In the corridor, his young researchers, including James Purnell, now a senior BBC executive, played cricket with rolled-up copies of Hansard and a tennis ball. Gordon Brown, who quite early on picked up the general level of Labour suspicion, mixed with fear of Mandelson in particular, told a hugely appreciative gathering of Tribune supporters in the South Bank Centre in London, 'Peter asked me for 10p to phone a friend the other day. I said, "Here, take 20p and ring them all."'

Like all the best political jokes, it was recycled – its first known outing was in the 1920s, used by Chancellor Winston Churchill against his Labour shadow, the bitter, astringent Philip Snowden.

Back in the early 1990s, Tony Blair and Gordon Brown were close political allies. The latter had been seared – although not surprised – by the defeat of Neil Kinnock for the second time and had come to believe that the party would have to do more than simply change its appearance, but that the Tories' successful attacks on a largely mythical Labour tax bombshell were the wakeup call.

The arrival of the pair – soon to be caricatured by Seumas Milne in his *Tribune* column as 'Pinky and Perky' – in New York in 1992 as guests of the active Labour Party branch there caused quite a stir. The chair was Ian Williams, who had worked for Neil Kinnock and had played a significant role along with Peter Kilfoyle MP in driving the Militant Tendency out of Liverpool.

Blair and Brown rubbed shoulders with various left-leaning celebrities, including Harold Evans and Tina Brown.

Williams remembers meeting the star-struck pair. 'We tried everything to try and get Tony in particular to see that Bill Clinton's third way triangulation was not only a con trick, but potentially a dangerous one, but all to no avail.' Williams cites the case of Ricky Ray Rector, a self-lobotomised cop killer on death row in Arkansas, whose pre-1992 election death sentence Clinton not only famously refused to revoke – lest he be seen as 'soft on crime' – but which he rushed back for in order to ensure that it took place, Meanwhile, Rector was tucking into a supper of steak, fried chicken, cherry Kool-Aid and pecan pie and presumably wondering why everyone was being nice to him.

Blair came back from New York and wrote a typical, gushy comment piece in the *Evening Standard*, extolling the virtues of 'triangulation'. Not long afterwards as shadow Home Secretary, Blair, whose star was now sharply in the ascendant, began repeating the phrase 'tough on crime, tough on the causes of crime'. This, of course, had the advantage of tickling liberal sensibilities while encouraging others to believe that Blair was the toughie whose time had come. It wasn't his own. He had wanted to use the simple slogan 'tough on crime'. It was Gordon Brown who suggested adding 'tough on the causes of crime'.

Brown for his part, would fall under the spell of Alan Greenspan, chairman of the US Federal Reserve, and with his young assistant, Ed Balls, tell the Treasury Select Committee that there could be an end to 'boom and bust' and that in future, modern economies would be driven by something called 'endogenous growth theory', which to Treasury Select Committee member Brian Sedgemore sounded like a claim to self-perpetuating, organic, economic growth.

If Francis Fukuyama had flummoxed much of the commentariat into believing that with the collapse of communism in the '80s came the 'end of history', back in the early 1990s, apparently serious economists and politicians came to believe that the economic cycle would henceforward proceed in one uphill direction, borne ahead by costless supply-side measures and a well-trained, highly mobile workforce. This was to morph into something called 'globalisation'. If one had reservations about 'globalisation', the accusation of being a dinosaur would never be long in coming. In reality, 'globalisation' required a further bonfire of red tape: bigger tax breaks for the corporations, lighter-touch regulation and monstrous salary and emolument increases for bosses. In Britain, the financial and service sector would be the motor of painless, endless growth. The reality was different: an unstoppable race to the bottom in wages and conditions; more casual employment; and when large waves of migration from mainly south-eastern Europe shook an already weakened, largely non-unionised workforce, the seeds of the current crises of populism and Brexit were sown.

This was New Labour's answer too and it came in the form of light touch regulation. It was to come in tandem with a reworked commitment to the Tories' Private Finance Initiative, henceforward to be known as the 'public–private partnership'. Unsurprisingly, perhaps, the left-wing economist and MP Brian Sedgemore was shortly to find himself purged from the Treasury Select Committee, along with another miscreant, Diane Abbott. Years later, Sedgemore would recall that Brown's special adviser, Ed Balls, had been a member of his Hackney South Labour Party and was a regular at fundraising summer barbecues. 'I used to say, you do the burgers, Ed, and I'll do the economics!'

But it would be a huge mistake to diminish or traduce the seriousness of intent that Gordon Brown – who was to become Britain's longest-serving Chancellor – possessed. The minimum wage, Sure Start, massive increases in health spending – and, of course, he was the man behind ten un-meetable and frankly unfathomable tests that kept Britain from joining the EU's single currency. 'I usually realise that someone is a Tory when they begin by praising me for keeping Britain out of the single currency,' Brown once told Seddon. There were, however, many on the left who had cause to thank Brown for this, too.

Brown had, of course, stepped aside for Blair following the death of John Smith. *Tribune*'s own unscientific poll, carried out by John Cryer (now chair of the PLP) had had Robin Cook as the favourite to succeed Smith, until Cook pulled out, saying that he didn't possess 'the looks'. John Smith had favoured Brown over Blair, while Mandelson professed to support both of them, despite secretly manoeuvring against Brown even in the immediate hours following Smith's massive and fatal heart attack.

Nick Brown, no relation to Gordon, who was to become a future Labour Chief Whip and Agriculture minister, recalls overhearing Mandelson calling journalists on Blair's behalf, even as Margaret Beckett, Labour's interim leader, was weeping tears for John Smith in her office. Brown, it was later revealed, had given way to Blair over a meal at Granita, an Islington Italian eatery, after having realised that his support in the PLP was ebbing. It was here, by all accounts, that Blair blithely promised to give way after seven years for Brown. And Gordon Brown took Blair at his word.

The Granita deal obsessed Britain's commentariat for over a decade, but rarely did they bother to peer underneath and ask themselves what really, in the end, drove these two politicians apart and in such dramatic fashion. For the media it was all about a 'power struggle', but in truth it was a power struggle to decide what to do with power. Gordon Brown had been seared and burned by the Tory tax bombshell attacks on Smith, and believed that Labour's repeated election drubbings showed that traditional Labour policies of redistribution and public ownership no longer chimed with the electorate. But unlike Blair, Brown still believed in equality and redistribution, and he also believed that he would have to use different and sometimes more complicated ways of achieving that traditional social democratic agenda.

The unserious Tony Blair professed to have found something called the 'Third Way', which on closer inspection turned out to be a kind of 'hopey, feely' instruction manual for middle managers. Extensive research by *Tribune* (none of the rest of the media were remotely inquisitive) revealed that it had apparently been the brainchild of an obscure New Zealand Christian socialist, who unsurprisingly failed to answer telephone calls. Blair's own efforts to explain it led to a Fabian pamphlet authored by him that was so thin that it would have blown away on the faintest zephyr. But he managed to find the odd academic, such as Anthony Giddens, to spout on about it, and whole hosts of columnists, many although not all who hovered around *The Guardian* and *The Independent,* lapped it up and began, once again, to accuse disbelievers of being 'dinosaurs'.

One of the most enthusiastic for Blair's ludicrous Third Way was *Independent* columnist Andrew Marr, who briefly came to edit the same paper. As a student, Marr had been a supporter of an obscure Trotskyite sect, Socialist Organiser, and attempted to flog copies of the paper of the same name to students at Cambridge. The cartoonist Martin Rowson recalls members of the reactionary Rugby Club finally throwing Marr and his papers into a pond. But Marr's youthful enthusiasm for revolutionary socialism came to illustrate another weird phenomenon – many of the most fanatical Blairites had been members of similar leftist splinter groups. What bound them altogether was the legendary discipline of 'democratic centralism', or, put more simply, following the line.

CHAPTER TWELVE

A FAUSTIAN PACT AND
A MEETING WITH
HER MAJESTY

As 'groupthink' seized much of what had been Fleet Street, the room for dissent became ever smaller. Soon the Third Way became 'the project', and being a supporter of 'the project' more or less defined how you were likely to be treated, interviewed by the media or whether you would succeed in politics and the media. The former Labour MP and radical (before the word 'radical' was also hijacked by Blairites) Leo Abse was convinced that Blair was in his words a 'complete fraud'. His book, *The Man Behind the Smile: Tony Blair and the Politics of Perversion*, followed in a rich vein of psychological profiles Abse had written, including one devoted to Margaret Thatcher.

A complete news blackout accompanied its publication. It may not even have been published had the publisher realised that the book was going to be effectively ignored. Strangely, Abse's publisher could find no newspaper to carry paid advertisements. Even the *New Statesman* baulked and refused. *Tribune* did, however, run advertisements for Abse's book. Perhaps it was this that encouraged the novelist and right-wing columnist Frederick Forsyth to say in a newspaper interview at the time:

Mr. Blair took a view from the beginning that the project [he makes inverted commas in the air] is about changing this country out of all recognition. Well, I don't buy all this 'I'm a straight kind of a guy' stuff. He's not a straight kind of a guy. He's extremely duplicitous, backed by some seriously ruthless kind of guys with a Project.

In 2012, interviewed once again about the state of dissent during the Blair years, Forsyth offered this:

Ah, but for almost sixty months, the only opposition came from the media – from Mark Seddon at *Tribune*, and, I suppose, Charles Moore [editor of the *Daily Telegraph*] at the other end. And there were forces inside New Labour that actually wanted all this suppressed. And if it is a question of stopping the investigation of Mr Mittal or Mr Hinduja or what Mr Vaz does with his money, then I would find myself side by side with Mark Seddon behind the barricades.

Most in the media had thought that it was immensely sensible and pragmatic for Tony Blair and his new director of communications, Alastair Campbell, to fly half way across the world to attend a conference organised by Rupert Murdoch and News International at Hayling Island, off the coast of Australia. Murdoch's mass-selling *The Sun* had savaged every Labour leader from Harold Wilson onwards. On election day in 1992, it had depicted Neil Kinnock as a light bulb and exhorted, 'If Kinnock wins today, would the last person to leave Britain please switch off the lights.'

So, not unreasonably, Blair was keen that *The Sun* would not rain on his parade. The tactics he employed were the same as those he had deployed with Paul Dacre at the *Daily Mail*, who remained deeply unimpressed, and a mystified Max Hastings at the *Telegraph*, who expressed astonishment that Blair didn't even want to increase taxes 'on people like me', after taking him for what proved for to be a rather ordinary lunch of fish and chips at the Carlton Club. The Blair approach – along with that of Mandelson and Campbell – was effectively to pay homage at the court of the press barons and prove that there would be no threat to media monopolies by the simple expedient of removing any. At Hayling Island, or perhaps on the long flight back, Blair decided to bury Labour's long-standing commitment to limit cross-media ownership – opening the way for Murdoch to move and expand into television should there be a Labour government. This Murdoch duly did when he took over BSkyB.

The late John Smith and his then City spokeswoman, Mo Mowlam, had famously launched what had become known as the 'prawn cocktail offensive' in the early 1990s, in a bid to persuade the City that it could live and work with a Labour government. Efforts were made to reach out to bankers and financiers, to show that Labour was not necessarily hostile to them and some of the party's policies could actually benefit the City.

In many ways, Labour governments had historically been good for the stock market; more government spending expanded the economy, and improved industrial relations were good for business too. Not that this would ever be enough to persuade the pinstriped ex-public school boys of the Square Mile, one of whom was once heard to say in the lavatories, following a speech by Mowlam, 'The trouble with all of this is Labour is like an iceberg – two-thirds of it are underneath the bloody water'. Smith was no Tribunite socialist, although like Wilson he understood the latter's old adage that for the Labour Party to fly it needed a 'right and a left wing', but nor was he the sort of Labour shadow Chancellor and then leader who felt the need to sell the party's soul to win power. His efforts with the City were designed to oil the wheels of the Keynesian approach to the economy he favoured. It was to their benefit, and the benefit of the country as a whole. If they didn't like it, well, tough.

Blair on the other hand surrendered wantonly and deliberately to big business and to Murdoch in particular. He went a whole lot further, because he decided to ingratiate himself with the Dirty Digger. Murdoch, for instance, would find it a whole lot easier than the general secretary of the TUC to meet with Blair and to get to influence the direction of policy. In fact, one former TUC general secretary, the mild-mannered John Monks, once wearily complained that Blair treated the unions 'like embarrassing elderly relatives at a family gathering'.

The unions, which out of loyalty tended to support Blair whenever he found himself in trouble with the party's NEC, or needing some pal parachuted into a safe seat, should have realised what was in store for them when Blair, as shadow Employment Secretary, simply refused point blank to meet the leader of the biggest print union. Tony Dubbins, who led the GPMU, had wanted Blair to recommit to reversing the Tories' anti-union laws and restore the closed shop, but Blair got wind of their agenda and simply didn't show up for the meeting. A few years later, during a strike by railway signalmen, Blair was ambushed by journalists near the BBC's Millbank office wanting to know whether Labour supported members of its oldest affiliate who were out on strike. On Mandelson's advice, he simply turned tail and fled down the street, with the hacks in hot pursuit.

Shortly before the general election, Mark Seddon found himself inside 10 Downing Street, having gone to meet Jon Cruddas, then advising Blair on industrial policy and who was to later become MP for Dagenham. Leaving Cruddas's office, he spotted Blair's assistant Anji Hunter walking down the corridor, arm in arm with the grizzled figure of Murdoch. 'He comes in round the back, so no one can see him,' said Cruddas. 'For Christ's sake, don't breathe a word!' Seddon, who at the time was supplementing his meagre *Tribune* wage with a weekly stint on the *Evening Standard* 'Londoner's Diary', managed to keep Murdoch's visit to Blair secret for one whole day. Another frequent visitor to 10 Downing Street was Rebekah Brooks, née Wade.

Many years later, Murdoch was to fall out quite sensationally with Blair over claims that his wife, Wendi Deng, had had an affair with Blair, who by then was no longer Prime Minister. Blair vigorously denied the claims, but Murdoch and Deng went on to divorce. It was all worlds away from the happier – but still weird – times when Blair was on such intimate terms with the Murdochs that he was named godfather of their daughter, Grace, in 2010. Apparently, he even donned white robes for her baptism in the River Jordan, right where it is thought John the Baptist first dunked Jesus Christ.

As the 1997 general election approached, Blair, Mandelson and others had, effectively, finessed the hard graft of the Neil Kinnock years. A slick, well-oiled party machine, run out of Millbank Tower, presided over a campaign that ran with ruthless efficiency.

Out in the country, there was a yearning to be finally done with eighteen years of the Tories in power. The Major government was tired and bowed and the media was more or less united in its view that Labour would win and win big. The establishment had come to the conclusion that it was probably time to fall in line with the popular view – after all, the Labour Party under Blair had become suitably tamed.

And yet it was sometimes difficult to really feel that a potentially seismic election was actually taking place across huge swathes of the country. This was because party panjandrums in both the main parties had decided that in most of the country, especially in those parts where the votes tended to pile up high for one party or another, there wasn't much point in bothering – people would vote anyway. Instead, all of the frenetic efforts were concentrated in the marginal seats, largely clustered in city suburbs and in the English Midlands.

Blair's reading of the electorate was so poor that he thought almost right up until polling day that Labour might only squeak past the post and then, horror of horrors, the rump of Labour's left in Parliament would be able to hold his hand over the fire. Encouraging him in this belief was Roy Jenkins, who had left the Labour Party in the early 1980s in a failed attempt to supplant it with his short-lived SDP. Another confidant was the self-aggrandising, chuntering windbag who led the Liberal Democrats, Paddy Ashdown. Even if Blair couldn't have abided to have Tony Benn around for tea, what was stopping him from listening to the experience and advice of people who had stayed loyal to Labour, such as Barbara Castle, Denis Healey or Roy Hattersley? Did he not think that some of the union leaders might have some practical, down-to-earth advice? Not a bit of it.

So what were Jenkins, Ashdown and Blair really up to? No good, it turns out. For another aspect of the Third Way that had not been quite so apparent, was a belief that the mould of British politics could finally be broken, if Labour and the Liberal Democrats merged and gave birth to proportional representation.

There are plenty of good arguments for proportional representation, but this troika were less interested in the finer points; what they really wanted was a 'realignment', which would have the hoped-for effect of dumping the trade unions altogether alongside troublesome left-wing Labour MPs and reconstitute something called the 'centre ground'. The centre ground would be largely filled with sensible centrists such as Blair, Ashdown and Jenkins and rule in near perpetuity, because, of course, the new entity would attract more Tories. (And a few ultra-safe Labour seats had already been gifted to former Thatcherite, Tory defectors such as Shaun Woodward and Alan Howarth).

The 1997 general election and those that followed were fought around the centre ground; although in truth the centre of political gravity was now well to the right of where it had once been. It took about twenty years for the penny to drop that the centre ground of politics is usually wherever those who are on the winning side of things at any given time choose to position it. In Britain and much of the rest of Europe, it has moved steadily to the right for four decades.

Abridged versions of some of the meetings in pyjamas between these titans of the centre ground would be fed to lobby hacks by Alastair Campbell, with whole screeds being rolled out in Sunday newspapers such as *The Observer* and *Sunday Times*, even revealing with bated breath what Paddy and Tony might have had together for breakfast.

So when *Tribune* held a pre-election gathering of supporters days before the election at Browns restaurant in London and Robin Cook stood up and predicted a Labour landslide, there was massive consternation in Downing Street. A landslide would leave no possible excuse for a deal with the Lib Dems, and it would enable left-wing MPs to rebel in safety, without risk of bringing down the government. By the following morning, Cook was on the airwaves, eating huge slabs of humble pie, declaring that actually he had meant the complete opposite of what he had said.

Labour duly won by a landslide. Trade unions dug as deep as they could; they supplied workers to help the party, drivers and cars to get its leaders around the country, as well as money they struggled to afford. Members worked tirelessly on the doorsteps and the party's slick and shiny machine did the rest.

Sitting next to Michael Foot and Jill Craigie on Melvyn Bragg's sofa in Hampstead, Mark Seddon watched as the results came in – that is until Blair's Sedgefield result was announced, when Mrs Bragg, who was also watching, asked Seddon to move in order to make way for Melvyn as the 'TV cameras are coming in now'. Another guest, Jenny Stringer, who had worked for both Neil Kinnock and John Smith and who later selflessly looked after Michael Foot in his final years, quietly murmured of Blair, 'lightweight'. Earlier, in the pub, hordes of youngsters were pouring in as the polls closed, many breathlessly telling each other that they had voted Labour. It had been a night to remember.

A measure of the near fanaticism now abroad in Tony Blair's 'new' Labour Party came from a freshly appointed minister, Tessa Jowell, who volunteered that if necessary she would 'jump under a bus' for him. She didn't appear to be joking. Jowell may not have been the first, but she may have been among the first to be described as a Blairite. Blair had announced staccato fashion from Downing Street that 'we were elected as "new" Labour and will govern as "new" Labour'. The brand, it seemed, would henceforward be a programme.

Blair had considered changing the name of the party to 'New Labour', but had realised that this could be a hurdle too far, just as he had also pushed behind the scenes for the Socialist International to be renamed the 'Democratic International'. This way he could bring Bill Clinton and his Democrats on board and swamp the European social democratic parties, who were looking at what had just happened in Britain with a mixture of shock and awe.

Was all of this necessary or desirable? Had the electorate, tired of the Tories and seemingly in the mood for a more egalitarian Britain, really voted for something called 'new' Labour? Blair hadn't been confident of winning big, in fact, as we have seen. Blair, Mandelson and his closest supporters had seen Labour as a useful vehicle – but beyond the election, they hoped to cast off the bits of it that they didn't like. He may have led the Labour Party, but he couldn't stand Labour England.

A helicopter followed Tony Blair's car as it made its way to Buckingham Palace. Queen Elizabeth had welcomed Prime Ministers from Winston Churchill onwards during her long reign. Reportedly, she got on rather well with Harold Wilson. How would she get on with the fresh-faced Tony Blair?

Blair recalled his first audience. 'She was… direct. "You are my tenth Prime Minister. The first was Winston. That was before you were born." I got a sense of my relative seniority, or lack of it.' She declined his invitation to call him Tony. So, later on, did Prince Charles, who was not impressed with the idea that the Prime Minister might call him Charles. 'Sir will do fine,' he said quickly.

The Queen is not thought to have had a high regard for her flashiest Prime Minister. If she could not have Harold Wilson back, she would like Labour to be led by someone she respected and understood. Events following the death of Princess Diana did not improve matters. Neither the Spencer family nor the royal family wanted a big funeral, but Blair believed there was a public demand for it, and insisted the royal family needed to mourn publicly. When the Queen Mother died in 2002, the Palace took steps to prevent Blair taking centre stage at her funeral. Oddly enough the authors think that the Queen would rather warm to Jeremy Corbyn if he became Prime Minister, since opposites attract, and she might enjoy talking to him about his allotment.

Following his audience with the Queen, Blair and his wife, Cherie, were garlanded back into Downing Street by cheering, flag-waving crowds. But here came an early discordant note – the flag wavers were not made up of spontaneous members of the public, allowed into Downing Street to greet the new Prime Minister, they were for the main Labour Party staffers who had been drafted in. The film record was a confection for the media.

CHAPTER THIRTEEN

ENTER THE
CONTROL FREAKS

Tony Blair's new Cabinet contained some reassuring faces for the real Labour faithful. First and foremost was Blair's deputy leader John Prescott. Prescott had manfully borne many a Mandelsonian humiliation in the run-up to the party's election landslide, once peering into a jam jar on television holding an itinerant Chinese mitten crab fished from the River Thames, saying, 'Hello, Peter!'

John Prescott was about as real Labour as it is possible to get. A decent, well-intentioned, if somewhat prickly, Yorkshireman, who Blair knew from the outset would be hugely important to keep the unions and the party membership onside. Prescott sometimes found himself excluded from awayday gatherings of the in-crowd.

Some of those on the hard left, who castigated Prescott for not holding New Labour above the Plimsoll line – something that he could quite easily have done, rather missed the point. John Prescott, like his former flat-mate Dennis Skinner, in fact always believed that the 'worst Labour government had to be better than the best Tory government', and in any case on that brave May morning in 1997, Blair's assertion that 'A new day has dawned, has it not?' reminded even the fiercest doubters that there was now a Labour government – and what is more, it included people like Prescott who the membership trusted. Prescott and other Labour loyalists to this day would find some of the sharper barbs directed at Blair and New Labour unpalatable and unfair. These stalwarts did their best. To Prescott's great credit, he never joined the critics viciously circling the Corbyn leadership. In fact, he went out of his way to offer support and encouragement.

Others from the broad left of the party sat around Blair's first Cabinet, such as the new Health Secretary Frank Dobson, the long-time peace activist Gavin Strang, who held the Transport portfolio, and the redoubtable Clare Short, who became the first Cabinet-level Minister for International Development. Blair had been obliged to give all of these left-wingers ministerial roles, since the Parliamentary Labour Party elected the shadow Cabinet in opposition. Not all were to survive Tony Blair's first Cabinet cull in the following year.

It has become fashionable to compare the rebelliousness of some on the left back then to the antics of sections of the PLP and the Progress group of Blairite supporters today, under Jeremy Corbyn's leadership. But there is both a qualitative and quantitative difference. There was a huge degree of goodwill towards Tony Blair and his new Cabinet from right across what used to be described as the labour movement, even if it was tinged with some fear and concern as to where Tony Blair and his project might head. Blair's critics, including those elected to the National Executive Committee under the auspices of what was known as the Grassroots Alliance, had bitten their tongues during the election campaign and following it, devoted much of their energy to trying to plot an alternative, more recognisably socialist programme while doing battle with the new centralisers at the top of New Labour and in the party's Millbank HQ.

The left of the party simply did not have the reach into the media that the so-called centrists have today. Many of these same contemporary centrists seem to take vicarious delight in self-emoting and offering barely thought-through, often personal criticisms, in the full knowledge and expectation that this will win them media attention. What is now described as the 'mainstream media' was generally as hostile to the left as it is today, although it was arguably less filled with foam-flecked hysteria.

Neither was there a dynamic, ungovernable social media, which for all of its faults allows anyone to offer an opinion or a link to something else. In the 1990s, far fewer would question what was being served up to them on the BBC, for instance, or *The Guardian*. Even fewer had the knowledge of parliamentary and Fleet Street Kremlinology that could trace back stories clearly planted on behalf of, for instance, Peter Mandelson, via, for instance, Patrick Wintour in *The Guardian*.

Readers and viewers are much more educated and alert today to attempts to hoodwink or divert them. And the quality of British political journalism has declined. Compare and contrast the steadfast objectivity of the BBC's former political editor John Cole with his most recent successor, Laura Kuenssberg.

In January 2017, the BBC Trust ruled that a report in November 2015 by Kuenssberg broke the broadcaster's impartiality and accuracy guidelines after a viewer had complained about her item, which featured an interview with Jeremy Corbyn on the *BBC News at Six*. This was edited to give the incorrect impression that Corbyn disagreed with the use of firearms by police in incidents such as a recent terrorist attack in Paris. The BBC Trust said that the inaccuracy was 'compounded' when Kuenssberg went on to state that Corbyn's message 'couldn't be more different' from that of the Prime Minister, Theresa May, who was about to publish anti-terrorism proposals.

The trust said that accuracy was particularly important when dealing 'with a critical question at a time of extreme national concern'. Of course Kuenssberg was relatively young and inexperienced in Labour Party affairs, but this wasn't an isolated incident and neither was she the only senior journalist guilty of both a lack of curiosity and an inability to question the group-think of many of those around her.

Back in 1998, before Tony Blair could really begin to refashion his Cabinet to reflect his own image, Peter Mandelson came unstuck – and not for the first time. He failed to declare a £373,000 loan from wealthy MP Geoffrey Robinson. This, by anyone's standard, was a quite a large sum to forget receiving – but it also had the effect of identifying a plutocratic tendency in the upper echelons of government. At a time when many youngsters couldn't get the banks to lend them money for modest apartments, here was Mandelson attempting to build some bijou extension to a grand home in Notting Hill with someone else's dosh – and interest free.

The John Smith inheritance was slowly and steadily being rolled out by the government, including the plans for a devolved Parliament and a new Assembly in Scotland and Wales. There was no rowing back from devolution, even though the veteran Labour backbencher Tam Dalyell's nagging 'West Lothian question' still remained unanswered. For at least two decades, Dalyell had not unreasonably posed the question, 'How could Scots vote on legislation also affecting England when the English cannot vote on legislation that affects Scotland?'

The biggest advance came through the Irish peace talks and the eventual Good Friday Agreement. Had Tony Blair not taken Britain into a war in Iraq, it is possible that he would be best remembered for his achievements in Ireland. A combination of his general winsomeness and his lack of much historical grasp, as well as his energy, probably made him the best candidate to plough the hundreds of years of accumulated sectarianism.

Blair and his Northern Ireland Secretary, the extraordinarily frank Mo Mowlam, managed between them to wow the hard men of Irish nationalism and the equally implacable Ulster loyalists. Whatever else may be said of him, Tony Blair can take full credit for his performance with the orange and the green traditions of Ireland.

As a legacy, this would be hard to beat. But many observers underestimate the extraordinary role played by the late Mo Mowlam. The grim-faced Ulstermen, led by David Trimble, could not make head or tail of her since her behaviour frequently defied all of their norms. She had taken to wearing a wig during her treatment for cancer and would occasionally delight in removing it at meetings with them – to their consternation.

During the talks, she attended a dinner hosted by *Tribune* in the upstairs room of the Gay Hussar, fiddled with her wig and proceeded to fashion a wrist bangle from the chili pepper table decorations, despite the protestations of the restaurant's manager, Jon Wrobel. Having touched her eyes, she fled in agony to the bathroom in a valiant attempt to flush them out with water, while a group of American diners stood gawping, saying, 'Isn't that the Northern Ireland minister?'

The logic of devolution, whether to Scotland, Wales or even to London, is that once the new institutions have been established, they choose their own leaders. This is where the Blairite vehicle ran into a terrible cul-de-sac of its own making. It soon became apparent that those who were not 100 per cent committed to 'the project' need not apply.

To any rational observer of the Labour scene in early 1999, it was fairly obvious that Ken Livingstone was popular not just among Labour Party members (who had not that long ago elected him to top place in the party's ruling NEC), but among Londoners, too. In fact, an ICM poll commissioned by the *Evening Standard* showed that Ken Livingstone was the overwhelming favourite among Labour supporters to be selected as the party's candidate for mayor, well ahead of the other contenders (Livingstone had 50 per cent of the support; Glenda Jackson, 16 per cent; Frank Dobson, 15 per cent; and Trevor Phillips, 7 per cent).

The poll also revealed that if Livingstone stood as an independent candidate he would defeat Labour's official candidate, which proved to be the case when Livingstone went on to trounce Frank Dobson.

It was also fairly clear that in Wales, the veteran politician Rhodri Morgan, despite his legendary scruffiness, was widely seen as one of the fathers of Welsh devolution. His Welsh non-conformism may have had him out of step with the sharp-suited fixers in London, but he would hardly startle the horses in Wales. Morgan pronounced on London Blairites who were determined that one of their own, Alun Michael MP, should be the candidate. During the campaign to select the candidate for the leadership of the Welsh Assembly, Morgan claimed, 'The Alun Michael campaign has been sponsored from Downing Street. It is quite clear that what he is going for is the coattails of Tony Blair; that is followership, not leadership.'

The party machine had not so long before been arguing strongly for 'one member, one vote', but had now come to the conclusion that going back to an electoral college containing ordinary party members, MPs, MEPs and trade unions could be more malleable. Not all unions would ballot their members who paid the political levy, so it would be possible to at least get some of them to vote for the party leadership's choice.

Proposals for selecting candidates on this basis were put to Labour's ruling NEC, but before many of the members had had a chance to read the documents placed before them, the representative of the engineering and electrical union, John Allen, had called out, 'Move to a vote!' – the vote was duly carried.

The machinery was used to block both Livingstone and Morgan.

At around this time, Mark Seddon received a call at *Tribune* from the Downing Street switchboard. 'The Prime Minister would be grateful if you could come for an informal discussion.' This took place on a white sofa in an office inside No. 10 with Tony Blair, as ever, at his courteous best.

It soon transpired that Blair was really beginning to regret his decision to effectively have Ken Livingstone blocked from running as Labour's candidate – not because he had become a late convert to the latter's left-wing agenda, but because it seemed that Livingstone would have every chance of beating the official candidate, Frank Dobson. Seddon pointed out that Labour's habit of calling upon its own circular firing squad could very well result in a Livingstone victory – so far better, surely, to have Ken in the tent pissing out, than outside pissing in.

In the end, the people got their way, over Blair's dead body. Livingstone became London's first mayor, and was expelled from the Labour Party for standing against its official candidate. Rhodri Morgan became Wales's first-ever First Minister.

Labour's NEC is where the annual beauty contests take place for the much-coveted constituency places and this is where real and raw power struggles take place and took place, even as the Blairites had wrested away any residual policy-making functions from the organisation.

The NEC comprised the leader, who would give a report each month and face questions, usually of a toadying variety. Other members included the deputy leader and elected representatives from the parliamentary party – and later the European Parliamentary Labour Party. It also contained a powerful trade union section, one of whose members would inevitably be elected chair of the NEC.

And then there were the constituency representatives – before Tony Blair and Peter Mandelson changed the rules to keep Ken Livingstone and Diane Abbott out – traditionally MPs, whose election each September conference would give an indication of how far to the left or right the party was heading. Back in the late 1970s, the left dominated the NEC, with those such as Tony Benn, Joan Maynard, Audrey Wise, Frank Allaun, Eric Heffer and Ian Mikardo.

During Neil Kinnock's tenure as Labour leader, the left was in retreat. Increasingly, the unions elected people to the NEC who could usually be counted on to support the leader. By the time Tony Blair was elected leader, what had become known as the hard left was still in retreat.

The first major upset occurred in Blair's first year as leader, when Ken Livingstone beat Peter Mandelson for a place in the NEC's constituency section. As a result, MPs were banned from standing for election. Instead, ordinary party members could stand – the idea being that they weren't so prominent, there would be less media interest in NEC elections and no one would frankly care. This theory was immediately thrown into question when members of the left-wing Grassroots Alliance swept to victory in 1997 – their number included Mark Seddon.

NEC meetings could be interminably boring and long. They could also be hugely entertaining and very revealing. John Prescott, for instance, would come into his own when the leader was away, and he had to deliver the 'leader's report'. Prescott's reports were sometimes flowing streams of consciousness. On at least one occasion a party staffer simply gave up trying to keep up with JP, and quietly put away her pen.

For reasons of the alphabet, Mark Seddon sat next to Dennis

Skinner for most of his eight years' membership of the NEC. Skinner was completely unafraid, and when he spoke, most NEC members would nod in agreement, and then vote against whatever it was he was advocating.

On one occasion, Seddon dared Skinner to ask Tony Blair a question in 'New Labour-speak'. Skinner looked at Blair and growled, 'When are we going to apply blue-sky thinking to the Third Way approach to beacons of excellence at a local municipal level?' The ensuing silence was only broken by the sound of a shocked-looking Blair scribbling ferociously, presumably thinking, 'Fuck, what's come over Dennis?' He stammered into life and said, 'Thank you, Dennis,' before launching into a clipped list of managerial gobbledegook.

The New Labour project required that the NEC be as effectively neutered as the annual conference. This process was euphemistically described as 'Partnership in Power', and was a classic exercise in managerial centralism.

Labour's bottom-up, grassroots democracy was turned on its head, and power was transferred up the line to something called the 'Joint Policy Commission', which supposedly fed into something called the 'National Policy Forum'. Most of the hacks were too lazy to enquire just what all of this meant, i.e. untrammelled power for Tony Blair and his supporters, but it was a system of centralised control more befitting of an old-style Stalinist Communist Party. Its real intention was to marginalise and drive out dissent.

This strategy was designed in a report drawn up as a command and control mechanism for the Labour Party to adopt, apparently by none other than John Birt, friend of Peter Mandelson and then director general of the BBC.

For the bulk of the party and the unions, the Blair/Mandelson project of centralising power at the top of the party could be tolerated just so long as some of the main bread-and-butter policy commitments were being met.

And, on 1 April 1999, the national minimum wage was introduced. It was set at £3.60 for workers over the age of twenty-one and £3 for those under twenty-one. Rodney Bickerstaffe, the leader of the big public sector union UNISON, who devoted his life to battling for the low paid, was key first to the adoption of the minimum wage and then to its implementation. Yet in private moments, Bickerstaffe also understood that while the minimum wage could lift hundreds of thousands from poverty wages, there was always the chance that under certain circumstances it could become an effective maximum wage.

Britain's long romance with neoliberalism had successive Tory and Labour governments presiding over a low-wage, low-skill economy – although as Chancellor, Gordon Brown was keen to see a high-skilled economy grow. Yet British workers tended to work longer hours than those on the Continent and with older, less-productive machinery. Production was lower, union membership had shrunk and was more restricted, and on top of that successive governments had bought into the fiction that the 'invisible economy', the financial sector, was now far more important than the diminishing manufacturing sector.

George Orwell had rebranded Britain as Airstrip One in *1984*, and the Britain of the early twenty-first century was still vastly overspending on defence – in comparison with most of her European competitors. It had also decided to push ahead with another £51 billion overhaul of the Trident nuclear submarine fleet. The nuclear deterrent was actually under the overall control of the United States and, to add insult to injury, at a time when it appeared that the remnants of the once-mighty British steel industry was about to stagger into oblivion, it was announced that some of the steel needed for the new submarines would be sourced from abroad. But no, Airstrip One was most apposite as the low-wage, low-skill UK economy could be best compared, not with Germany, Scandinavia or even France, but the United States.

On 7 June 2001, Labour won a second consecutive general election with a majority of 167. It was dubbed a 'quiet landslide', as voter turnout was significantly down at 59.4 per cent (the first time it had fallen below 60 per cent since 1918) compared to the 71.3 per cent who had turned up at the polling booths at the 1997 general election.

Out of the 641 seats, 620 seats went to candidates from the same party as they had done in 1997. Labour lost five seats overall, with the Conservatives only increasing their total number of seats by one (they gained nine seats but lost eight). One of the five seats that Labour lost was in Wyre Forest, where its candidate, David Lock, lost to Richard Taylor, who stood as an independent Kidderminster Hospital and health concern candidate and campaigned on restoring the Accident & Emergency Department of Kidderminster Hospital.

It was to the NEC that Blair came subsequently in 2004, as the EU expanded into central and Eastern Europe as well as to the Mediterranean and two former British colonies, Cyprus and Malta, introducing ten new member states in all. In retrospect, this was one of the most momentous decisions he would take in government and it would produce very real ramifications for all that would follow, culminating finally in the referendum vote for Brexit.

He made the point that this was essentially a good development – although in his usual forked-tongue way, he acknowledged that there would be ramifications for the UK labour market. Joining the EU would give the new member states the same rights of free movement for their citizens, although by 2007, the alarm bells had rung sufficiently loudly to ensure that Germany, for instance, would continue to institute 'transitional arrangements' to control the flow of workers and therefore to avoid the potential for wage undercutting. Britain's labour market was much less robust than that of Germany, where the unions were stronger, wages were higher and conditions were better.

In 2004, as members of the Labour NEC, Seddon and Dennis Skinner tackled Blair over his refusal to push for similar transitional arrangements, and to at least slow down what would be an inevitable flood of people looking for work from central and Eastern Europe. Blair appeared to believe at the time that Germany would open its borders, along with France and Italy. He blithely claimed that 'only 13,000 or so' workers would be expected to arrive each year in Britain. In fact, the flow turned out to be over twenty times this estimate. In 2004 to 2005, there were 52,600 workers from the accession states and this was only the beginning. Labour canvassers, especially in eastern and central England, began to feel the blowback from voters. Some of it was based in often barely suppressed xenophobia, but for the most part the reaction came from anger felt about increased competition for jobs and under-pressure public services.

The media, which often takes little interest in Britain's underbelly when it makes noises of which it doesn't approve, tended to shove all of this under the carpet. The readers of the *Telegraph* and *Spectator* tended to be happy because nannies were cheaper, as were plumbers and electricians.

This seemingly endless flow of cheap, but often highly skilled labour, brought with it a new middle-class dependency. The political establishment only really began to take note when Nigel Farage and UKIP began to make strides in local and European elections. Successive governments then made a great deal of noise about restricting numbers of migrants, but in the full knowledge that they could do absolutely nothing at all to control free movement of labour from the EU. Both Brexit and the Windrush scandal – since British governments could only take action against non-EU migration, historic or otherwise – can be traced all the way back to Blair's foolhardy refusal to listen. David Cameron's subsequent epic failure to persuade the EU to at least give Britain some belated breathing space over migration was eventually met by a sullen vote to leave the EU.

In many working-class areas during the EU referendum, the betting shops were doing brisk business – because even while the British political and media establishment remained convinced by their own polling that voters would support staying in the EU, good sections of the public had a pretty good idea that it was going to go the other way.

The EU Commission's own miserable refusal to listen to the howls of anger from the southern Europeans who had been poleaxed by the effects of permanent austerity courtesy of the European Central Bank and tied to a disastrous single currency was another extraordinary own goal. Meanwhile, the British political class continued to trill on about the amazing benefits of globalisation, while voters looked often in inchoate ways for something and someone to blame for the deindustrialised semi-wastelands they inhabited. Brexit was their eventual cry of rage, because in their eyes all of the warnings of impending doom from the British establishment simply masked one very inconvenient truth. For millions of people in Britain, it really could not get any worse.

Tony Blair's Labour government had been elected on the premise that 'things can only get better'. In many respects, things were beginning to get better, despite Gordon Brown's decision to stick to Conservative spending plans and Tony Blair's overall timidity. Yet just as the early seeds for Britain's eventual secession from the EU were sown in those early years, so were those for the biggest disaster in post-war British politics, support for George Bush's invasion of Iraq.

CHAPTER FOURTEEN

THE ROAD TO IRAQ

Tony Blair's love affair with war began with the nasty and brutish war that had broken out in the collapsing Yugoslavia, a hotchpotch of multi-ethnic statelets that had held together under the embrace of Marshal Tito's distinctive, non-Soviet, Balkans-style communism since the end of the Second World War.

The break-up of Yugoslavia contained within it deeply disturbing fears of history repeating itself. The First World War had its origins in the fissiparous complications of the Balkans. The failure of the international community to constrain the resurgent Croats and Serbs in particular had ended with the UN standing by as massacres of Muslim civilians shocked the world in Srebrenica and Goražde.

In early 1999, the Serbs were targeting Kosovo, which was still officially part of Serbia, but had an overwhelming Muslim majority. Alarmed at the failure to persuade the UN Security Council to intervene, in late March 1999, NATO launched airstrikes against Serb forces in Kosovo, signalling the beginning of an intensive bombing campaign designed to force Serbian forces out of the region.

At an EU summit in Berlin, Tony Blair said that the aim of the military action was to prevent Serbian forces from perpetuating a 'vile oppression against innocent Kosovar Albanian civilians'. NATO had of course been created to defend its members from attack – it was not modelled as an out of area interventionist force, yet public opinion in Europe was largely appalled at the brutishness of the Serb militias and in Britain, the idea of 'humanitarian interventionism' had a growing band of supporters, especially if it meant frustrating the ambitions of those such as General Ratko Mladić, Radovan Karadžić and the Serbian leader, Slobodan Milošević, who had flipped from being a loyal communist apparatchik, to a menacing populist nationalist.

On 22 April, Tony Blair made what became known as his Chicago speech at the Chicago Economic Club, outlining his 'Doctrine of the International Community', which advocated a greater use of humanitarian intervention, using military force to protect civilian populations. Much of this was now received wisdom from the Clinton administration, but there was an altogether more serious debate proceeding at the United Nations, where the notion of the international community adopting what some called 'Responsibility to Protect' was gaining ground. Its architects wanted to ensure the future Yugoslavias or Rwandas simply wouldn't be allowed to happen, but the key to having each and every member of the UN Security Council on board was consistency. Britain had both played a prominent role in the former Yugoslavia and, at Robin Cook's behest, had scored a fairly quick, cost-free win in Sierra Leone. The events of 11 September 2001 in New York and then Washington, with the attacks on the World Trade Center and the Pentagon, had a profound and lasting effect.

Perhaps it was a combination of all three and a subsequent belief that he could be the persuader with the United States President George Bush that had Blair taking such a lead role in the run-up to the Iraq War. On 29 January 2002, in his State of the Union address to Congress, President Bush first used the term 'axis of evil' to describe those states his administration accused of sponsoring terrorism and seeking weapons of mass destruction (WMDs). These were North Korea, Iran and Iraq.

The big question as to how Tony Blair managed to fall in behind two entirely different notions of 'humanitarian intervention' never really seemed to exercise the minds of much of the commentariat. But there was a world of difference between the humanitarian interventionist model being advanced by the United Nations, which was bound up in international law, aimed at preventing genocide and which found its logical conclusion in what was to become R2P or Responsibility to Protect, and the unilateral military interventionism of the neocons that was supported by Tony Blair. This highly desirable potential advance for humanity as a whole could only ever really hope to gain the acceptance of other countries on the UN Security Council, in particular Russia and China, if it could be divorced from special interests and power politics.

Any real chance of bringing on some of the real sceptics in both of those countries was largely blown away by the Iraq War. For American neocons such as Richard Perle, Paul Wolfowitz and the equally hard-line US UN ambassador John Bolton, such weak-kneed liberalism conflicted directly with the nostrums caught up in their real manifesto, 'The Project for the New American Century', which provides the template for the even greater American exceptionalism and unilateralism of Trump's America today.

But the new century was not going all America's way. It was fast being caught up by the rise of China – whose century it would likely be. But the fact that Blair seemed incapable of understanding these two very different visions of interventionism speaks volumes. The failure of much of the political class and commentariat on both sides of the Atlantic to do so explains why Blair received the support that he did, and possibly explains the simpering media coverage that he continues to receive. This is long after the British public, in particular, came to the conclusion that he was, in fact, a common or garden snake oil salesman. Blair's legendary poor grasp of recent history was sharply on display. The broadcaster Jon Snow recollects mentioning the former Iranian leader Mohammad Mosaddegh, who was toppled by both the British and the Americans in a coup in 1953. Blair had to ask who Mosaddegh was.

On 24 September 2002, the government published a dossier titled 'Iraq's Weapons of Mass Destruction: The Assessment of the British Government', in which it was claimed that 'Iraq's military forces are able to use chemical and biological weapons, with command, control and logistical arrangements in place. The Iraqi military are able to deploy these weapons within forty-five minutes of a decision to do so.'

In the foreword, written by Tony Blair, that claim was repeated:

> Saddam has used chemical weapons, not only against an enemy state, but against his own people. Intelligence reports make clear that he sees the building up of his WMD capability, and the belief overseas that he would use these weapons, as vital to his strategic interests, and in particular his goal of regional domination. And the document discloses that his military planning allows for some of the WMD to be ready within forty-five minutes of an order to use them.

This latter claim came with another splattered across a breathless press, which almost without exception backed the coming war. It was that these same weapons of mass destruction could hit the two run-down British Sovereign Base areas, RAF Akrotiri and Episkopi in Cyprus, within forty-five minutes. This was a lie.

In the House of Commons, following the publication of the dossier, Blair said,

> I cannot say that this month or next, even this year or next, Saddam will use his weapons. But I can say that if the international community, having made the call for disarmament, now, at this moment, at the point of decision, shrugs its shoulders and walks away, he will draw the conclusion that dictators faced with a weakening will always draw: that the international community will talk but not act, will use diplomacy but not force. We know, again from our history, that diplomacy not backed by the threat of force has never worked with dictators and never will.

He repeated the untruthful 45-minute claim made in the dossier. On 3 February 2003, another dossier, 'Iraq – Its Infrastructure of Concealment, Deception and Intimidation', was released by the government. It was to become known as the 'dodgy dossier', and those most closely associated with it, such as Tony Blair, Alastair Campbell and Jack Straw, would for ever after be dogged by it. Robin Cook, now Leader of the House, was to resign from the Cabinet, but after helping to secure a new right of Members of Parliament to vote on the authorisation of the use of military force. This was a rare positive achievement ahead of the juggernaut taking Britain to war. Under a better Prime Minister, Cook's courage and intelligence would have been used and encouraged. Under Blair he was on the down escalator from day one.

A majority of Britons were not persuaded by Tony Blair, his spin doctors, his dossier or his spotty legal advice. There was sympathy and support in spades for Britain's American cousins for the grotesque terrorist attacks that had been inflicted upon them. But few people followed Bush and Blair in connecting attacks launched predominantly by Saudi Wahhabis, some actually living in America, with Iraq and its strongman leader Saddam Hussein.

Opposition was strongest on the left, which managed to rally over a million people to demonstrate against the looming war clouds just as Tony Blair was becoming his most messianic, in London's Hyde Park. The demonstration was joined by, among others, the Reverend Jesse Jackson, Mo Mowlam, Tony Benn and the nonagenarian Michael Foot, replete with his Plymouth Argyle scarf. Another speaker was the MP George Galloway, who was subsequently to be expelled from the Labour Party for 'bringing the party into disrepute'. Tony Benn, Tony Woodley and Mark Seddon were to speak at his defence in the wood-panelled conference room of the Steelworkers' Union in Gray's Inn Road, London. The main charge brought against him at a special sitting of the party's National Constitutional Committee was that he had told Abu Dhabi TV that the war in Iraq was illegal and urged British troops not to obey 'illegal orders'.

The Hyde Park demonstration was one of the biggest demonstrations in British history. Coaches filled with people were still arriving as Hyde Park began to empty. But none of it made a jot of difference.

If it is possible to pinpoint times when a vast number of people began to lose their faith in the British political system and most of the shabby politicians atop the heap, this was surely one of them. Along with the miners' strike and the imposition of the iniquitous poll tax, the day Tony Blair and his Cabinet chose to ignore popular sentiment and lie about the pretexts for war marked the end of the public's trust in Tony Blair.

Mark Seddon didn't believe Tony Blair's claims about Iraqi WMDs from the outset and was one of the first to go public with his doubts on BBC Radio 4, early in 2002. Gut instinct told him that both Bush and Blair in the aftermath of 9/11 and the invasion of Afghanistan were at the very least exaggerating Saddam Hussein's capacities and were seeking a pretext for regime change.

As the months went by and the evidence remained un-forthcoming, and the agenda of US neocons became clearer, it was difficult to divorce the political imperative for regime change coming from Washington and London, as well as the strong-arming of dissent, from the lack of clear facts.

Unconvinced by Tony Blair, Seddon led the opposition to the build-up to war on Labour's official ruling body, the thirty-strong National Executive Committee. Only four members, Seddon, Dennis Skinner, Christine Shawcroft and Ann Black, held the line. Not one of the NEC refuseniks who disbelieved Tony Blair and George Bush over Iraqi WMDs and who were part and parcel of the whole process were asked to appear in front of the subsequent Chilcot Inquiry, which was set up to investigate the events in the run-up to the Iraq War. Seddon offered, but was turned down.

The war-drum-beating David Aaronovitch, who loudly urged Tony Blair on from his arm chair at Rupert Murdoch's *The Times*, was, however, asked to give evidence, although since he played no direct role in anything at all, it still remains difficult to fathom quite why or how. Aaronovitch seemed so convinced that Iraq had WMDs, that he offered to 'eat my hat' live on air on BBC Radio 5 'if they aren't found'. He continues to resist carrying out his promise all of these years on.

Blair was adamant that Saddam Hussein was flouting UN resolutions and had WMDs. He was equally adamant in telling the NEC at the end of September 2002 that 'regime change is not United States policy'.

Seddon took Sir John Chilcot at face value, and sent him what is probably the only record of the meetings at which Blair and various senior government ministers, including Jack Straw, John Prescott, John Reid and Geoff Hoon, faced serious questions about, and direct opposition to, the road to war. We will have to wait another quarter of a century or so for the Cabinet records, and it is doubtful whether a record of meetings from the Cabinet, PLP or European PLP was ever kept.

These minutes, faithfully recorded by Ann Black, provide a powerful snapshot of Blair and his ministers at three key meetings of what is supposed to be the 'sovereign policy-making' body of the Labour Party from September 2002 to 25 March 2003, when Britain, along with America, was five days into 'shock and awe'.

While the Labour Party maintains a somewhat abridged and pruned version of events, Ann Black's record has never been disputed. Seddon attempted to force votes blocking British involvement in the Iraq venture unless it was explicitly backed by the UN and in accordance with international law. Defeated twice, and finally blocked by a 'procedural motion' on the third attempt, he walked out of that meeting.

Unlike the mandarins, ministers, diplomats and military chiefs, none of the NEC members could claim to have seen intelligence reports on supposed Iraqi WMDs. In common with those Labour MPs who wanted to support Blair, but clamoured for facts to make their case to angry constituents, the NEC finally got to read the 'dodgy dossier'. It had to be handed back.

Reporting from inside Iraq in 2002, and then on the eve of war in 2003 for the BBC and *Daily Mirror*, Seddon interviewed Tariq Aziz, Iraq's then Foreign Minister. He was convinced that Iraq would not be attacked, citing the massive global anti-war demonstrations, and he reiterated that his country had no WMDs. 'Tell Mr Blair', said the veteran Foreign Minister, 'that he can come to Iraq and send his own inspectors.' Aziz gave every impression of simply not believing that an attack would actually take place.

Having spent days with other journalists being promised visits to sites identified by America and Britain as having WMDs and being fobbed off with claims that they were 'mushroom farms' or 'baby milk factories', Seddon thought Aziz's protestations sounded lame. But it was when he interviewed the former UN weapons inspector Scott Ritter that his doubts about Blair's claims took root. Ritter, a lifelong US Republican, was clear. Although the UN Special Commission on disarming Iraq (UNSCOM) had been repeatedly frustrated, it had finally done its job. The nuclear programme was eliminated; if chemical weapons still existed there would be proof; Iraq was in compliance with UNSCOM over biological weapons.

In the weeks running up to the invasion, Seddon met with the former Czech Foreign Minister – and a former president of the UN General Assembly – Jan Kavan in New York. Kavan was in regular contact with his old friend Robin Cook and was clear, as was Cook, that military action without a second UN resolution would be in contravention of international law – a fact finally publicly acknowledged by UN Secretary-General Kofi Annan after the Iraq War, by which time it was too late.

That third motion tabled on 25 March 2003 at Labour's NEC, in front of Blair, Prescott and Straw, was a joint effort by Kavan and Seddon, with Cook's likely approval. The promised second UN Security Council resolution had failed, and the NEC motion demanded that 'immediate advice' be sought from both the UN Secretary-General and the president of the UN General Assembly 'on what steps need to be taken by HM Government to ensure that Britain is once again in compliance with the United Nations Charter'.

Blair – a former lawyer – had argued that 'lawyers' opinions tend to reflect their own political perspectives, but the government's own Attorney General [Lord Goldsmith] has ruled that this war is legal'. He went on to say that 'structural questions about the United Nations and the European Union are secondary to those around future relations with the United States. Partnership is infinitely preferable to the French desire for a rival pole of power, which could revive the dynamics of the Cold War.' France had led opposition to the second UN Security Council resolution, and Straw added disingenuously that 'France simply can't cope with the fact that America is also intellectually and scientifically dominant'.

Blair had desperately wanted that second resolution. Throughout all the NEC meetings it was advanced by him as the reason for not binding his hands too early, as it was with the Cabinet and the PLP. On 28 January 2003, after Dennis Skinner had told Blair, 'This will be the biggest mistake you'll ever make,' and others had argued that the Europeans were demanding more time for Hans Blix and his weapons inspectors, Blair said, 'The inspectors can only interview scientists in the presence of "friends" from the Iraqi security service. Backing down over Iraq will make it more difficult to deal with North Korea next.' But he remained optimistic about a second UN resolution, believing that this would win members over.

Back during the September 2002 Labour Party conference, amid scenes of high tension and low farce, Blair had argued against Seddon's first resolution opposing military intervention unless it had the backing of the UN. According to the minutes, he 'argued passionately for keeping the option of unilateral military action by the United States and Britain, in case other countries blocked the move in the UN Security Council'.

Mark Seddon and Christine Shawcroft were determined that the Labour conference would get a chance to vote on the resolution, and if anyone doubted the significance that Blair saw in this, he said, 'The NEC statement will be studied around the world and Saddam will exploit any signs of division.'

An alternative set of words was eventually proposed by the leadership, which stated 'that military action should only be taken in the last resort and within the context of international law and with the authority of the United Nations'.

There was a cigarette paper's worth of wriggle room between wresting power from the UN and allowing for more time to get the UN to come around. Even so, Blair's own words on unilateral action should have set alarm bells ringing. As that debate began, a succession of hand-picked speakers, one of whom accused those opposed to the rush to war of 'being appeasers and guilty of making orphans of the sons and daughters of Cyprus service-men', spoke from notes prepared for them by the Kafkaesque speechwriting unit. The then chair of the Labour Party, Charles Clarke, confronted Christine Shawcroft and Mark Seddon, and demanded that they withdraw the motion altogether. They re-fused but still lost.

Blair, the ex-lawyer, had rested his arguments on legality, while apparently purposely forestalling any attempts to get him to seek the advice of those responsible for upholding the rule of international law, especially once the prospect of a second UN resolution had receded.

What of those Cabinet ministers and opposition leaders who stood by him, some of whom now have reservations about what they did and said at the time, or those who put the 'dodgy dossier' together or, worse still, knew what was going on, but chose to sit on their hands? What of those, such as Jack Straw, who knew that the British intelligence services were effectively col-luding with the Americans when they took information that had been obtained by torture? Mr Straw's Macavity the cat routine may have served him well for decades, but the truth was finally to catch up with him in 2018. Did all the blame for Britain's involvement in Iraq now simply rest on the shoulders of Tony Blair? It didn't, of course, although Blair should have taken the lion's share of the blame and still refuses to do so all these years later. He refuses to apologise and has by all accounts never visited some of those most affected – i.e. wounded British servicemen and women, although perhaps they wouldn't want to see him. Notwithstanding the near universal global condemnation for his role in lighting the blue touch paper in the Middle East to a fire that still rages out of control, the British media still largely treat him as a statesman and continue to hang onto his every banality.

Not so at the United Nations in New York, where former Secretary-General Kofi Annan and his successor, Ban Ki-moon, deliberately kept their distance and kept a close watching brief over Blair's increasingly messianic interventions. The mood cannot have been improved by Clare Short's claim, in February 2004, that British spies were involved in bugging Kofi Annan's office in the run-up to war with Iraq. When asked about the claims at his monthly prime ministerial news conference, Tony Blair replied, 'I really do regard what Clare Short has said this morning as totally irresponsible.' Two days later, the Labour Party chairman, Ian McCartney, told BBC Scotland that Clare Short would not be expelled from the party over her United Nations bugging claims, and said, 'I'm not going to make her a martyr.'

The claims were true, of course. Clare Short had particular cause to feel aggrieved; a serious believer in internationalism – the Department of International Development was largely her creation – Short was bamboozled by Blair into believing his claims about Saddam Hussein's weapons of mass destruction. His promise that Britain would play a major role in the rebuilding of Iraq after the war was soon displaced by the corrupt chaos of its aftermath, the lunatic decision to disband the Iraqi Army and the whole state apparatus, and a vicious spiralling civil war.

She had repeatedly called Tony Blair 'reckless' in a BBC radio interview and had threatened to resign from the Cabinet in the event of the UK government going to war with Iraq without a clear mandate from the UN, but remained in the Cabinet – at Blair's pleading – for two months after her decision eventually to back it. She finally resigned on 12 May.

Her letter of resignation said,

> In both the run-up to the war and now, I think the UK is making grave errors in providing cover for the US mistakes rather than helping an old friend … American power alone cannot make America safe … But undermining international law and the authority of the UN creates the risk of instability, bitterness and growing terrorism that will threaten the future for all of us.

Prophetic words as it turned out.

Labour had been fatally weakened by the Iraq War and its aftermath. That extraordinary coalition of the liberal-left middle class and the working class that, when it comes together, occasionally votes in Labour governments was under severe strain. Many of Labour's traditional left-leaning middle-class votes were heading in the direction of Charles Kennedy's reviving Liberal Democrats.

Kennedy had opposed the war and had spoken at the Hyde Park demonstration. Many of Labour's working-class supporters – whom Peter Mandelson had once airily dismissed by saying, 'They have nowhere else to go' – were, in fact, not to show up on election day at all when it came on 5 May 2005.

CHAPTER FIFTEEN

'A CONTROL FREAK, UNCOLLEGIATE AND DELUSIONAL'

On 5 May 2005, the Labour Party won a historic third successive term of office, but with a significantly reduced majority of sixty-six (down from 167 at the 2001 general election). Labour lost forty-eight seats overall and was returned with the lowest share of the popular vote (35.2 per cent) of any majority government in British electoral history. The Conservative Party gained thirty-three seats, leaving them with 198 overall and a 32.4 per cent share of the vote.

The Liberal Democrats gained eleven seats taking their number to sixty-two, the highest number of seats won by a third party since 1923, when Herbert Asquith's Liberal Party won 158 seats. George Galloway, standing under the banner of the Respect Party, won the Bethnal Green and Bow seat previously held by Labour's Oona King, with a majority of 823.

Blair was presiding over the now clearly rotting fish of a British Labour Party that had largely been shorn its ability to hold him to account – and the wreckage of Labour England. On 16 July 2006, the Prime Minister told BBC One's *The Politics Show*, 'Nobody in the Labour Party to my knowledge has sold honours or sold peerages.' This chutzpah came hard on the heels of three quite memorable sleazy scandals involving cash for peerages.

The first had been on 8 July, when *The Times* reported that Sir Gulam Noon's peerage had been blocked, after the House of Lords Appointments Commission discovered that he had made a loan to the Labour Party but not disclosed this on the forms that were sent to the commission. On 12 July, Blair's old tennis partner Lord Levy was arrested by the Metropolitan Police, who were investigating cash for honours. By 15 July, *The Times* also reported that two government ministers, Science minister Lord Sainsbury and Trade minister Ian McCartney (as Labour chairman, McCartney had signed the nomination forms for the party's new peers), had been questioned by police. This fresh slew of claims came atop earlier 'cash for honours' breaches that involved twelve businessmen from whom the party had received £13.95 million in commercial loans, four of whom (Chai Patel, Barry Townsley, Sir David Garrard and Sir Gulam Noon) were later nominated for Labour peerages. Property developer Sir David Garrard topped the list with a loan of £2.3 million, followed by fashion tycoon Richard Caring and Science minister Lord Sainsbury, who each loaned the party £2 million. Lord Sainsbury, a founder member of the breakaway SDP, was later to continue his disruptive intervention by funding Progress.

In December of that year, Downing Street announced that Tony Blair had been interviewed by police as part of their inquiries into the cash for honours affair. He was not interviewed under caution, indicating that he had been treated as a witness rather than as a suspect.

By the beginning of September 2006, the bells were tolling for Blair – because once he began to warn colleagues to 'stop obsessing' over the timetable for his resignation, it only acted as a green light to encourage more of them to do so. Labour's plotters, led by Tom Watson, did not exactly cover themselves in glory, some preferring the anonymity of social media chat rooms to do the damage and loosen Blair's grip.

In the same month, the former Home Secretary Charles Clarke lumbered into view and accused Gordon Brown of 'lacking courage and vision, of being a control freak, uncollegiate and delusional'. He also argued that Brown's failure to become leader in 1994 had haunted him ever since: 'Gordon would have been humiliated in the [leadership] election in 1994. But that has coloured their [Blair and Brown] relationship for years. It is a complete delusion in Gordon's mind that if he had only run, he could have won.'

Clarke's spiteful outburst helped mark his descent into 'embittered, also ran, could have been' territory. He would have loved to run himself, but knew he didn't stand a chance. It was far from clear that had Brown run for the Labour leadership, he 'would have been humiliated'. The Newcastle East MP Nick Brown, who would have been Gordon's campaign manager had he chosen to run, believes that Gordon would have stood a chance only if he had put himself forward as a candidate on the day of John Smith's death, as Blair did. Nick Brown, with long experience of being Chief Whip, knows that of which he speaks. That Gordon Brown was a more substantial political character tended to be reflected in the rather stoic way that he tended not to hit back at detractors like Clarke.

The Blair–Brown struggles were meat and potato to the media, which for the most part tended to avoid actually examining the issues that had pulled the pair apart. For Blair and his acolytes, Labour was always essentially a vehicle for power. For Brown, deeply schooled in the unions and the party, it was about trying to deliver a social democratic policy agenda in times that were still largely hostile. Brown was loyal to Labour. It is difficult to say that about Blair.

Blair's leadership staggered on into the following year. But Brown's moment, when it came, would not be as he imagined. He became Prime Minister without any internal contest and that wasn't a healthy state of affairs – his rival, John McDonnell, had been unable to secure the requisite nominations. But even here, when it was clear to all that Brown would be a shoo-in, the recriminations over allegations of McDonnell supporters being 'leant on' dogged him.

Brown's more stolid and serious demeanour could, under different circumstances, have fitted quite well with the more austere times, but the Brown premiership just didn't seem to gel – south of the border, at least. Brown himself was later, in self-demeaning mode, to say that his failure to connect was down to a more old-fashioned desire not to parade his emotions. Oddly, most Britons had probably had enough emoting from Tony and Cherie, so this seems a somewhat self-deprecating answer. In truth, a majority had probably tired of the endless scandals involving tawdry New Labour donors and some of the recipients of their largesse. Blair had left office in the knowledge that the public's affections for him and his party were in a state of free fall.

Some of these reasons were spelled out by Lord (Meghnad) Desai, an LSE Keynesian economics professor and long-time critic of Brown. He argued that Gordon Brown needed to make himself more presentable to the electorate. Of Tony Blair, he said, 'Blair was like champagne and caviar, Brown is more like porridge or haggis. He is very solid, very nourishing but not exciting.'

In an interview with the *Evening Standard*, Lord Desai went on to say that 'Gordon Brown was put on earth to remind people how good Tony Blair was', describing the Prime Minister as 'indecisive', 'weak' and 'a worrier'.

To later pick on Brown for his failure to call an election in the midst of a major foot and mouth crisis in the country was power to the cause for the Blairites, because they would have done, perhaps finding some crass way of turning a disaster into an opportunity. Or perhaps not, because by then the tide was turning.

Not long following Labour's inevitable election defeat – one that was not as bad as many of the commentators had predicted, but was still pretty bad overall – Tony Blair penned his memoir *A Journey*. It was a fairly tawdry spectacle; a former Prime Minister peddling his memoirs, the vulgarity and venality of which demeaned the office he once held.

Unsurprisingly, Blair gave vent over Brown. However 'impossible' he may have been to work with, whatever his 'emotional flaws' and serially frustrated ambitions, the heap of ordure dumped by Blair onto the colleague he once claimed to be almost married to signalled a new low.

Did Brown deserve this? He didn't. And why is so much credence given to what Blair himself would once have described as tittle-tattle, as he usually did to the NEC whenever some great scandal had broken?

The worst you can say about Brown is that in crucial moments of his political life, he was frozen by indecision. In 1994, it cost him the premiership. For when else, in the whole of British political history, has there been a politician who was within touching distance of the premiership but hesitated because it might cause a row in the party? By the time Brown made up his mind, the decision was no longer his to make.

In a different age, retiring statesmen wrote candidly and lucidly about great matters of government and international diplomacy. But now Blair produced the political equivalent of chick-lit. Brown maintained a dignified silence. That is his way – in public, at least. We doubt he could have churned out anything as racy as Blair's *A Journey*, even if he had wanted to.

Instead, he busied himself completing the final chapters to a book on the world economy – a serious subject that couldn't be more different from Blair's 700 pages, which included breathless references to Princess Diana, the cast of *EastEnders*, the singer Charlotte Church, Bono and Des O'Connor.

In stark contrast, Brown and his wife, Sarah, announced that they would embark on several charitable projects connected with the developing world. This, they said, would be unpaid work. True to his word, Brown and his wife threw themselves into campaigns around global education. UN Secretary-General Ban Ki-moon made Brown his Special Envoy for Global Education and used to say that Brown was 'the most effective envoy' he had ever appointed.

Brown never had the chutzpah to establish anything like the Tony Blair Faith Foundation, a curious hybrid organisation that combines charitable work with lobbying and expensive, glitzy PR.

One of the most remarkable claims in Blair's memoirs is that it was he, rather than his Chancellor, who came up with the revolutionary idea to make the Bank of England independent and strip it of its regulatory powers – a decision hailed as Brown's finest. We may disagree with Brown's assessment of his plan as a radical and progressive departure, but it was certainly his plan. Blair's rewriting of history, together with a cruel personal jibe, is treated with dignified silence from Brown.

Then there was Blair revealing his fury that Brown openly dared to initiate an internal Labour Party inquiry into the notorious cash for peerages scandal. In his memoirs, he accuses a 'venomous' Brown of political blackmail, saying his Chancellor would desist from pressing for an inquiry only if he, Blair, shelved controversial pension reforms. On this unpleasant episode, too, Brown has continued to maintain a dignified silence. Brown's eventual autobiography was, of course, much more circumspect, although he reclaimed his decision over the Bank of England.

Blair's hobnobbing with the rich and powerful was nauseating enough, but it was his cavalier attitude to political fundraising – and the sleazy philosophy of 'who gave what and for what in return' – that was truly shocking.

No wonder Blair was incandescent with Brown for threatening an inquiry over political backhanders; he knew just how combustible and politically life-threatening the findings of such a probe could be to his reputation. Handing over peerages in return for cash donations to a political party is a criminal offence, and has been since Lloyd George tried to pack the House of Lords with his cronies.

Blair should be grateful to Brown for his loyalty when it came to his silence over his ruinous foreign policy decisions that bled the Treasury dry, and committed Britain to a disastrous war in Iraq and another seemingly without end in Afghanistan.

We wish that Brown had spoken out over Iraq. (Mark Seddon went to see him to make the case for not going to war in Iraq, but had to make do with a lecture about the benefits of the Private Finance Initiative.)

The fact that Brown never went public with his concerns – or exposed the obvious truth that Blair hadn't a traditional Labour bone in his body – will, of course, mystify those who think he could have exploited this weakness by pushing to replace him as Prime Minister much sooner. We are among that number. Perhaps this was another moment when he was frozen by indecision. There's no way of being sure.

Of course, there have been many psychological studies of the Blair–Brown relationship. Blair's autobiography says they were initially 'like lovers desperate to get to lovemaking', then a married couple who argued, and finally hated rivals. But it can only be Blair's narcissism that makes him describe his Chancellor as having 'zero emotional intelligence'.

Having observed Blair and Brown from close quarters for many years, we conclude that the latter naively believed so many of the promises Blair made about their partnership. He believed Blair when he said Brown was the true successor to John Smith. He believed him again when he pledged to stand down in his favour in 2003.

It was only when the penny finally dropped that Blair was simply humouring him and that Peter Mandelson had switched sides and was backing Blair to succeed John Smith in 1994, that Brown decided to surround himself with courtiers equally capable of the dark arts of political plotting as those who were helping Blair. Courtiers such as Charlie Whelan, Ian Austin and Damian McBride.

Ultimately, history is proving kinder to Brown, as both of us predicted in various newspapers columns and interviews at the time.

CHAPTER SIXTEEN

ED STONE RULES

So how did Professor Ralph Miliband's younger son become Labour leader, rather than his older son? The short answer is that Professor Miliband's older son, David, voted for war in Iraq.

In 2010, Tony Blair's supporters still thought it was business as usual, and that the worst enemy they had to face was Gordon Brown. The high priests and priestesses of Blairism – now almost forgotten (though far from impoverished) grandees like Patricia Hewitt, Jack Straw, Geoff Hoon, Stephen Byers and Charles Clarke – had no idea how toxic the Blair brand had become.

Since 2010 was certain to be an election year, naturally they began the year by mounting a well-publicised coup against Brown. When that failed, former Labour Party general secretary Peter Watt told the media that Brown lacked the 'emotional intelligence' to be a 'modern leader'. He presumably got the line from Tony Blair. Or he may have taken it from Alastair Campbell or the long-time Blairite *Observer* columnist Andrew Rawnsley, who had so cruelly attacked Brown for being 'fatally flawed'.

These people believed that the Blair legacy was not safe in Brown's hands. They seem honestly to have believed Brown to be dangerously left wing. They had no idea what was coming. The next few years must have seemed to them like a long and dreadful nightmare.

Brown led a visibly fractured party into the election, and lost. But it could have been worse. The May 2010 general election produced a hung parliament for the first time since February 1974. The Conservatives had 306 MPs, Labour had 258, the Liberal Democrats fifty-seven and the Democratic Unionists eight.

Probably the biggest beast to lose his seat in East Anglia was Charles Clarke, which is yet another thing Clarke will never forgive Gordon Brown for. These two men have known and loathed each other ever since the mid-'70s, when Clarke was president of the National Union of Students, and Brown an Edinburgh University student who defied the establishment by getting himself elected rector. Being the student-elected rector gave Brown a status in student politics rivalling that of the NUS president, and Brown did not hesitate to speak out when he didn't agree with Clarke.

A son of the manse, Brown knew his duty, which was to stay in Downing Street until opposition leader David Cameron was in a position to command a parliamentary majority. So he stayed, in spite of jeering editorials saying he was trying to cling to power after being rejected by the people, shamefully written by journalists who knew the truth.

His other duty was to resign as Labour leader, which he did at once. The Liberal Democrats could in theory have joined with Labour to form a government with an overall majority of one, and Liberal leader Nick Clegg had made it clear that if there was any chance of this, Brown had to go. Vince Cable on the other hand bleated about not wanting to form a coalition with the Tories and kept up lines of communication with Brown.

But on 11 May, five long days after the election, it was clear that the Liberal Democrats and the Conservatives had a deal. The Lib Dems were to be full coalition partners, with Clegg as deputy Prime Minister. This, in the event, was to destroy the progress the Liberal Party and its successor the Liberal Democrats had made since its lowest point of six seats in the 1951 election. In the late 1970s, the Liberals had gone into a pact with Labour, which had given them far more wriggle room.

It seems hugely doubtful that the one Liberal Democrat who had really managed to cut through with the people, Charles Kennedy, would have gone into a Tory-led coalition. But Kennedy had been unceremoniously dumped by his party's panjandrums as his drinking problems spiralled. Kennedy was no enthusiast for the Cameron–Clegg deal, but sat it out in Scotland, fearing the worst for his party.

So at last, Gordon Brown and his wife and young children walked out of Downing Street for the last time. The Queen, after watching the exit, discreetly sent a message to her outgoing Prime Minister, extending an unprecedented invitation for him to bring his children with him when he went to hand her his resignation.

Three years earlier, the Blairites had searched desperately for a candidate for the leadership who was not called Gordon Brown. The growing army of Blair haters in the Labour Party now searched for a candidate who wasn't David Miliband. This time, they were successful.

The man who found him was none other than Neil Kinnock, to whom the Blairites had once looked for inspiration. Kinnock persuaded the very young, almost untested, Ed Miliband to run for the leadership against his own brother. Kinnock told him, 'If you don't mind David standing against you, why should David mind you standing against him?' 'It's not that simple,' said Ed, and Kinnock replied, 'Nothing is ever that simple.'

Kinnock and Ed Miliband understood how deep the disillusion went. Labour, said Ed, had 'lost trust catastrophically' as a result of the Iraq War and the MPs' expenses scandal – and because, as he put it, 'we lost touch with the values that made us a progressive force in politics and lost touch with the people we were meant to represent'. New Labour was 'the party of bankers' bonuses'. Others rallied around Ed, including Roy Hattersley and crucially some of the trade union leaders, determined that a line be finally drawn under the New Labour years.

Just forty-one, and an MP for only five years, Ed had, crucially, not been in Parliament to vote on the Iraq War. He had been taking a Fulbright scholarship in the United States. Had he been there, he would have been forced, either to vote against the war, which would have brought ruthless career-destroying permanent exile from Blair's front bench, as it did to John Denham, or to vote for it, which, as his brother found, would never be forgiven among Labour members.

Before the month of May was out, four more candidates had appeared. There were frontbenchers Ed Balls and Andy Burnham, and there was the usual no-hoper from the far left. In fact, this time there were two.

There was John McDonnell, who told the Public and Commercial Services Union's annual conference in Brighton that he was standing to prevent the contest becoming 'the sons of Blair v. the son of Gordon Brown ... All of the other candidates so far are all from the New Labour stable. They are all implicated in the policies that basically lost us the last election.'

And there was Diane Abbott, who said, 'The other candidates are all nice and would make good leaders of the Labour Party but they all look the same.' She had a point.

McDonnell failed to get the required number of nominations. Abbott did get them, because other candidates 'lent' her their supporters – she was nominated by MPs who had no intention of voting for her.

But only two candidates were in with a chance. The choice was loyalty to Blairism with David, or a moderate break with it in Ed. Peter Mandelson, by now Lord Mandelson, said Ed would lead the party into an 'electoral cul-de-sac, by winding the clock back to an era before Tony Blair'.

On 25 September, Ed Miliband became the twentieth leader of the Labour Party, narrowly defeating David. Despite the elder Miliband winning a majority of the support among MPs and party members, Ed Miliband's standing with the trade unions proved decisive. Ed Balls was third, Andy Burnham fourth and Diane Abbott fifth.

The battle between the brothers had been bruising. As the results were announced, a picture of the two in an oddly staged hug and embrace commanded the front pages. David regarded himself as more experienced and qualified. He must have been shocked by the upstart nature of the challenge from his younger brother. The rest of the country tended to think that the whole contest was distinctly odd and in many respects they were probably right. And despite the apparent support on the left of the party and in the unions for Ed, it was hardly ever enthusiastic.

Someone muttered to Neil Kinnock, 'Now we have our party back.' Kinnock insists he replied, 'It's always been our party.' Perhaps he did. The leader of the GMB, Paul Kenny, said, 'New Labour is gone. It is a product of history. It can join Madame Tussauds.' Tony Woodley, the joint general secretary of Unite, called the result 'a clear sign that the party wants change, to move on from New Labour and to reconnect with working people'.

In his first speech as leader, Miliband said the decision to go to war in Iraq was wrong. Blairites on the platform were white with fury. Nothing worse could happen to them, they felt, than that the new leader should attack them in this way. They didn't know what was yet to come.

Two former ministers, Alan Milburn and Margaret Hodge, noting that Ed's strongest support was in the unions, said that the party's links with the trade unions should be broken. Clem Attlee would have pointed out caustically that they did not say that when the union vote was going their way. Milburn and Hodge largely got their way in the end, and perhaps in future they will be more careful what they wish for.

For a short time, Ed Miliband looked like the man who was going to bring Labour England back to life. The fact that he owed his leadership to the unions seemed actually an advantage, for the unions were part of the heartbeat of Labour England, and were loathed by the grandees of New Labour.

He seemed like an Attlee figure: small in stature, not a great platform orator, shy even, but thoughtful and decisive. He wasn't a natural media performer and for a party that had prided itself for so long on the medium, he didn't appear to have benefited from much in the way of media training. His photo opportunities were often poorly conceived, but no matter, as he appeared confident and genuine – even if he may also have looked and sounded young and green.

While Labour seemed to be recovering its sense of direction, the Liberal Democrats were floundering. Nick Clegg's gamble of going into full coalition with the Conservatives was unravelling at what must have seemed to the Liberal leader like terrifying speed.

Just six months into parliament, in December 2010, half the Liberal Democrat MPs, including Nick Clegg, voted for an increase in student tuition fees. They had not only signed the National Union of Students' pledge never to vote for such an increase; Clegg had made a special parade of doing so with a specially designed visual to show that they really, really meant it. They spent the whole of the rest of the parliament apologising for this breach of faith. They were never forgiven. They have still not been forgiven.

The one big gain they had hoped for, the prize for which they had sacrificed a great deal in their negotiations with the Conservatives, their best hope for being a player in British politics again, was a referendum on the alternative vote system, and that was lost just five months after the student fees debacle, when they had not quite been in government for a year, on 6 May 2011.

In by-elections and local council elections they were performing catastrophically.

It was already clear that the Liberal Democrats had blundered irrevocably. Earlier, out campaigning in a by-election in Clegg's leafy Sheffield Hallam constituency – well, leafy before the city council started felling many of the trees – Mark Seddon was genuinely surprised at the local frustration directed towards Cleggy. One of the reasons soon became apparent. Shortly after the general election, David Cameron's government had effectively blocked assistance for local steelmakers Sheffield Forgemasters to bid successfully for a major order for the parts for the nuclear industry. Clegg had come under pressure to fight Sheffield Forgemasters' corner in the Cabinet, but according to locals, had failed miserably to do so. A petition criticising Cleggy had punters lining up to sign. This was before his great betrayal of all of the students in university towns up and down the land who had voted so enthusiastically for him and his party.

Miliband, meanwhile, seemed to have things rather his own way. He achieved what many of his predecessors would have liked, the end of the system by which Labour MPs elected the shadow Cabinet. Henceforth he could choose whomever he wanted. Opposition seemed confined to the far left, with Jeremy Corbyn saying, 'I do not see the need for this change, it increases the power of patronage, it reduces the accountability of the leader to Labour MPs.' At Labour's conference in September 2011, Miliband was cheered for saying, 'I'm not Tony Blair.'

Perhaps the day things started to go wrong for Ed Miliband was 22 February 2012. Late that night in the Strangers' Bar of the House of Commons, the Labour MP for Falkirk, a former career soldier called Eric Joyce, who had spent yet another convivial evening in the bar, took a dislike to a group of Conservatives sitting nearby. He headbutted and punched Stuart Andrew MP, after punching Phil Wilson, a Labour assistant whip who had tried to impede his progress towards Mr Andrew.

Two Conservative councillors stepped in to try to protect Mr Andrew, so Mr Joyce punched one of them and headbutted the other, then fought off two more Conservative MPs who wanted to calm him down, before smashing a door window.

Joyce had been an enthusiastic Blairite, vigorously lambasting those who opposed Blair's foreign adventures. He had been parachuted into the heavily industrial and working-class Falkirk after it had been vacated by the respected pro-devolution left-winger Dennis Canavan. Canavan had been blocked by New Labour from running for the new Holyrood seat covering the same area, despite securing the backing of 97 per cent of local members.

Suspended from the Labour Party after his arrest, Mr Joyce apologised and announced that he would serve out his time in this parliament, but would not stand again. So Falkirk Labour Party set about choosing his successor. And that is where the fun began.

The battle for what was thought to be a safe Scottish seat swiftly turned into a trial of strength between the Blairite Progress and trade union Unite. Unite's candidate was former nurse Karie Murphy, office manager for Tom Watson MP, Labour's election co-ordinator. She was also, as the *Daily Mail* put it every time they mentioned her, a 'close personal friend' of Unite leader Len McCluskey.

Unite officials began recruiting members to the Falkirk Labour

Party and paying their subscriptions, allegedly with the idea that those members would support Ms Murphy. Progress quickly cried foul, despite the fact that they were suspected of doing the same. The local party, as with many working-class Scottish constituencies, had been in decline for years and was virtually moribund. This was despite the fact that Grangemouth refinery was a major local employer and still a redoubt of Unite. Many of the union members were active, but not in the local Labour Party of Major Eric Joyce. Karie Murphy was young, energetic, left-wing and was promising to fight the union's corner in Parliament. Ironically, signing up members en masse had been tried some years previously in Trimdon Labour Branch in Tony Blair's Sedgefield constituency. The agent, who later became an MP, Phil Wilson, wrote an article about making Labour a 'mass membership party again', by the simple expedient of selling membership cards for £2.

The row rumbled on for more than a year, at the end of which the Labour Party nationally decided that no members who joined the party after 12 March 2012 (when Eric Joyce resigned from the party) would be allowed to vote in the election of a new candidate.

McCluskey wrote to his members accusing the Labour Party of running a smear campaign against the union and threatening legal action. McCluskey said, 'It is certainly our belief that Labour needs more trade unionists in Parliament, as opposed to seats being handed out on a grace-and-favour basis to Oxbridge-educated special advisers.'

It was everything Miliband could do without. It further divided Labour, for the two sides – the trade unionists and the Blairites – dug down in their trenches and glowered at each other, and they have done so, more or less, ever since. It placed Miliband in direct confrontation with his most powerful backer,

Len McCluskey. And it focused public attention on the political influence of trade unions, which was precisely where Labour did not want it focused, for the combined efforts of the Thatcherites and the Blairites had ensured that voters saw trade union influence as something very sinister indeed.

And it led him straight into that graveyard of modern Labour leaders, the party's internal structures. For in the wake of Falkirk, having accepted that bad things happened, he had to say how he was going to make sure they didn't happen again.

So in July 2013, he set out proposals to reform Labour's links with the unions, describing the Falkirk selection process as 'part of the death-throes of the old politics'. He wanted, he said, to change the way individual trade unionists are affiliated to the Labour Party.

> I do not want any individual to be paying money to the Labour Party in affiliation fees unless they have deliberately chosen to do so. Individual Trade Union members should choose to join Labour through the affiliation fee, not be automatically affiliated … Men and women in Trade Unions should be able to make a more active, individual choice on whether they become part of our Party.

This, he hoped, would increase, not decrease the membership. It would be a revival of Labour England, for it would 'genuinely root us in the life of more of the people of our country'.

The initial reaction among many in the trade unions was horror. They feared that union influence, in the party they had created and funded, was under threat. This was also the view among many who worked for Unite. And yet, interestingly, Len McCluskey did not seem to share the general disquiet. He had in fact worked out that, quite by error, Ed Miliband had presented a great opportunity to unions such as his if they were to go out and vigorously recruit new members and registered supporters.

This was to lead to an entirely new way of choosing Labour's leader. The electoral college, in which 40 per cent of the votes were cast by the trade unions, was to be abandoned in favour of one member, one vote (OMOV). And this was to be compounded by a system under which non-members could take part if they registered as a supporter, by paying a nominal fee.

Ironically, a key figure in picking this new system was Labour's general secretary, Ray Collins. Collins was a trade union man through and through, having served a succession of general secretaries at the TGWU and its successor, Unite. The plan would certainly remove some of the influence of the unions' leaders determining who would lead the party – although most unions balloted their political levy payers before casting their votes in leadership elections. But it would also effectively take some power away from the union executives in determining how much money should be handed to Labour as part of the political levy. So under OMOV, union general secretaries would have a much greater say in how much was given to the party.

Finally, Miliband had done something Tony Blair approved of. 'It's bold and it's strong,' said the former Prime Minister. 'It's real leadership, this … He's carrying through a process of reform in the Labour Party that is long overdue and, frankly, probably I should have done it when I was leader … This is big stuff and it takes a real act of leadership to do it.'

Miliband must have listened to this with a sinking heart. Didn't he have troubles enough already, without Blair supporting him?

As it turned out, the battle over who got the Falkirk nomination was worthless: come the 2015 election, the once safe seat was lost to the SNP, and has yet to be won back by Labour.

But the crowning irony, in a situation replete with irony, is that these changes, forced on Miliband by Mandelson and Blair, were what later made a Jeremy Corbyn leadership possible. And yet, the only opposition came from a small, still voice piping up that it was unfair to full party members. The voice belonged to Jeremy Corbyn. The debate rumbled on until 1 March 2014 when Miliband's changes were adopted by a special conference.

These sorts of debates are a graveyard for Labour leaders. Miliband knew it. What he really wanted to do was talk about policy. A clever and erudite man, Miliband had the happy notion of One Nation Labour. This, it was hoped, would have some resonance in a country that has become so unequal, except that, like a lot of what Miliband said, it didn't really seem to strike a chord with those for whom it was intended.

The man who hoped to become Britain's first Jewish Prime Minister stole the idea directly from Jewish-born Conservative Prime Minister Benjamin Disraeli, also the first One Nation Tory.

Miliband also resisted growing pressure to match the Tory promise for a straight in–out referendum on EU membership. Then, charging straight into the enemy's camp, he wrote in the *Daily Telegraph* about the 'squeezed middle': 'The greatest challenge for our generation is how to tackle a crisis in living standards that has now become a crisis of confidence for middle-class families. I know our country cannot succeed and become collectively better off without a strong and vibrant middle class.'

And he made one big personal contribution to history. When, in the Syrian civil war, President Assad used chemical weapons, Prime Minister David Cameron and US President Barack Obama discussed bombing Syria. Ed Miliband could have supported the idea. But he didn't. He told the House of Commons, 'This is fundamental to the principles of Britain: a belief in the rule of law and a belief that any military action we take must be justified in terms of the cause and also the potential consequences ... I am very clear about the fact that we have got to learn the lessons of Iraq.'

The government's motion was defeated by 285 votes to 272. Cameron could not participate in war, and Obama decided against attacking without British participation.

The man who had averted war was Ed Miliband, and there seemed a real possibility that he might become Prime Minister. This seemed to confirm to Fleet Street that he was the most dangerous left-winger possible, and his rise to the premiership had to be halted at all costs.

And so the campaign against him became personal. Very personal, very nasty – and nakedly anti-Semitic.

He was attacked for his stature (he is not very tall), his voice (it's a bit nasal), his appearance (which seems perfectly normal to us, but newspapers managed to make him look and sound like a gargoyle), even his erudition, which was described as geekiness. And on 28 September 2013 the *Daily Mail* ran one of the nastiest attacks ever published – an attack, not on Miliband, but on his late father, Professor Ralph Miliband. It was headlined 'THE MAN WHO HATED BRITAIN'. We will return to this article in the chapter on anti-Semitism.

On 1 October, the *Daily Mail* published a response by Ed Miliband: 'Fierce debate about politics does not justify character assassination of my father, questioning the patriotism of a man who risked his life for our country or publishing a picture of his gravestone with a tasteless pun about him being a "grave socialist".' It also printed an abridged version of the original article and an editorial under the headline 'AN EVIL LEGACY AND WHY WE WON'T APOLOGISE'. In the end, however badly they behave, newspapers always have the last word.

The following May, while out campaigning in the run-up to

the local and European elections, Miliband was photographed rather inelegantly eating a bacon sandwich. It played to the image of an awkward, odd man that was being carefully fostered by national newspapers – as well as to something much darker.

Two months later, in a speech at the Royal Institute of British Architects, he said,

> David Cameron is a very sophisticated and successful exponent of a politics based purely on image. I am not going to be able to compete with that and I don't intend to. I want to offer something different … I am not from central casting. You can find people who are more square-jawed, more chiselled. Look less like Wallace. You could probably even find people who look better eating a bacon sandwich.

Miliband's embarrassment didn't end there. A much-publicised walkabout in Glasgow during the midst of the Scottish referendum campaign was a riotous shambles, with Miliband being pushed and shoved. In shades of Neil Kinnock's treatment by the media, photos taken from the worst angles were the ones that made it into the press. Miliband's media handlers didn't do their boss many favours either. Around that time, the BBC interviewed David Cameron, perched on the edge of the Cabinet table in Downing Street, an impressive background all within camera shot. Ed Miliband, who was interviewed for the same news package shortly afterwards, was put in an overlit room and stood in front of three bulging and sagging bookshelves containing tattered copies of Hansard. Miliband didn't need to try and become a character from central casting, but his people could have helped a bit more than they did.

In September 2014, just after Scotland voted to reject independence, Miliband chose to perform a terrifying high-wire act: to deliver his speech to his party's conference without notes, without autocue – without anything. He was literally going naked into the conference chamber.

He said his government would boost pay, apprenticeships and housing; impose a mansion tax and a levy on tobacco companies for a £2.5 billion-a-year fund for the NHS; raise the minimum wage to £8 or more by 2020; and lower the voting age to sixteen.

But it's what he forgot to say that mattered. He forgot to deliver key passages on the deficit and immigration control. His enemies in the media managed to report only what he did not say.

Immigration mattered. There was an ugly mood about. The idea that this urban sophisticate who led Labour did not care about immigration enraged some of his party's natural supporters.

Less than a month after the conference, two by-election results underlined this. Douglas Carswell, who had defected from the Conservatives to UKIP, held Clacton, and Labour's Liz McInnes only narrowly held off UKIP to keep Heywood and Middleton in Greater Manchester. UKIP's vote in Heywood and Middleton increased by 36.1 per cent – one of the largest increases in vote share ever recorded.

All the same, the smart money was on a Miliband government emerging from the general election on 7 May, probably governing with the support of the Scottish Nationalists, who were set to sweep the board in Scotland. And, as is happening more and more often these days, the smart money was completely wrong. David Cameron came out of the election with an overall majority of twelve seats, and was able at last to govern without the Liberal Democrats. Nick Clegg was unceremoniously jettisoned – and joined in quick succession by the slippery Vince Cable, who lost his seat.

No one had seen that coming. Not the press, not the pollsters, not Cameron and certainly not Miliband.

What went wrong?

Miliband's obvious decency was swamped by some pretty serious attempts to look cool and be trendy – not least in the firstly furtive and then explicit courting of, among others, the non-voting celebrity Russell Brand. There was something curiously disconcerting and slightly queasy about these contrived meetings. Did the country's prospective new Prime Minister really have to pander to lightweights like Brand?

To the Blair loyalists, Labour's defeat was proof of what happens when a dangerous red revolutionary like Ed Miliband gets his hands on the leadership. The party, they thought, had chosen the wrong Miliband. His brother, David, was constantly serenaded as the lost leader across the water in New York.

To the left – to Jeremy Corbyn, for example – it was Miliband's failure to adopt radical policies. Banging on about One Nation was all very well, but it lacked any real sense of meaning or resolve. Ed Miliband had moved the party away from New Labour, but its programme for government seemed pretty thin. Even when it had the chance to say 'we promise to renationalise the railways', the party baulked.

To the Scottish Nationalist Party, it was Miliband's repeated refusal to pledge to talk to them about an anti-Tory front.

To English nationalists – a growing if disorganised group – Miliband's defeat was because everyone knew that, whatever he said, he would talk to the SNP because he would need their support to form a government.

To any good election tactician, the strange decision by Miliband's team to place their man in front of an 8-foot granite structure with his pledges written on it, instantly dubbed the 'Ed Stone' by the press, had something to do with it.

The Ed Stone included the Labour leader's contentious claim to be tough on immigration that few in the Labour Party believed he meant, but then neither did most of the public. By then it had become apparent to most that all political promises to cut migration ran straight up against the EU policy of free movement, and just as long as Britain remained an attractive proposition to workers from East and central Europe, there was nothing the politicians could do. The Ed Stone, or rather a version of it, had been cooked up as an idea for Labour's referendum campaign in Scotland and was on that occasion sensibly dropped.

To this day, the whereabouts of the Ed Stone remains a mystery. Our guess is that it was smashed up and dumped into landfill before the risk of it becoming a place of weird pilgrimage manifested itself.

CHAPTER SEVENTEEN

LABOUR'S MOST RELUCTANT LEADER (EVER)

Miliband didn't hang about. He resigned the very next day, and the leadership election was on.

His successor, for the first time in the history of the Labour Party, was to be elected by a simple vote of all party members. To get onto the ballot paper, a candidate needed the backing of 15 per cent of the Parliamentary Labour Party, which meant thirty-five MPs. It was quite unlikely that any candidate from the left would fulfil this requirement. If there was to be a candidate, it was quite unlikely that it would be Corbyn. Before Corbyn took the plunge, John McDonnell, Diane Abbott, Jon Trickett and others ruled themselves out.

The self-regarding Streatham MP, Chuka Umunna, eliminated himself from the contest via a short video shot in Swindon. Umunna's main contribution to the debate was that Labour 'hadn't taken wealth creators seriously enough during the election campaign'. 'Wealth creators' is New Labour code for very rich people. By early July, he had withdrawn from the race, citing 'intrusive media'.

Meanwhile, Andy Burnham appeared to be picking up early momentum as the party's non-establishment candidate. Len McCluskey was said to favour him, and up and down the country party members were looking for a candidate who could continue in the political trajectory forged by Ed Miliband. There appeared to be no desire to return to anything approaching New Labour. Yvette Cooper and the Leicester MP Liz Kendall struggled from the outset. Both were seen by many members as epitomising a continuation of New Labour.

Even then, Corbyn himself hardly sounded like a man who thought he was on the brink of victory. 'We had a discussion among a group of us on the left about how we might influence future developments of the party,' he told *The Guardian* the day he announced his candidature. 'We decided somebody should put their hat in the ring in order to promote that debate. And unfortunately, it's my hat in the ring. Diane and John have done it before, so it was my turn.'

You could have got odds of 100–1 at any bookie against him becoming leader.

When nominations closed on 15 June, Andy Burnham had the highest number of MPs supporting him – sixty-eight – and was the hot favourite to win. Yvette Cooper had fifty-nine and the loyal Blairite Liz Kendall, forty-one.

Jeremy Corbyn only scrambled over the thirty-five nominations hurdle two minutes before the noon deadline, and only then with the help of MPs who did not intend to vote for him but thought, in the interests of democracy, that he should be allowed to put his name forward and be soundly beaten.

Slowly, as if in a bad dream, these MPs woke up to the horrifying possibility that Corbyn might actually win. And if he did – well, he himself was spelling out the horrors that might lie ahead. At a seminar with economists and trade unionists in London, Corbyn said that under his leadership, Labour would raise taxes on the rich, clamp down on corporate tax avoidance and use up to £93 billion of corporate tax reliefs to create a national investment bank. This is exactly what most Labour Party members and voters out in the country wanted to hear. He said, 'Rather than remove spending power from the economy and damage growth and future prosperity, Britain needs a publicly led expansion and reconstruction of the economy. You don't close the deficit fairly or sustainably through cuts. You close it through growing a balanced and sustainable economy that works for all.'

It would not have fazed Clem Attlee – he would probably have felt it was a decent start, but a little timid. But it scared the pants off Tony Blair, who rushed to give a lead and steady the ship: 'We lost in 2010 because we stepped somewhat from that modernising platform,' he told Progress. 'We lost in 2015 with an election out of the playback from the 1980s, from the period of *Star Trek*, when we stepped even further away from it and lost even worse. I don't understand the logic of stepping entirely away from it.'

Frontrunner Burnham seemed unable to decide whether he was chasing the left-wing or the right-wing vote. Early on, while still considered a man of the left, he horrified Labour folk, not just the left, by calling Miliband's mansion tax 'the politics of envy'. It's a standard Tory sneer at any proposal to reduce the gap between rich and poor, and anyone who uses it brands himself an enemy. If Burnham understood Labour England, he'd have known that.

'Burnham's strategy had been to pitch to the left,' a Miliband aide told Corbyn's biographer Rosa Prince. 'The election freaked him, so he tacked right. Big mistake. Everyone in the Westminster bubble was saying that Labour lost [the general election] because it was too far to the left. Andy, despite saying he wanted to go outside the bubble, couldn't see beyond what they were saying.'

There was something going on that no one knew about – not Burnham and not Jeremy Corbyn either. One of the very few people who had recognised it before was the late Michael Meacher, who died in October 2015, and who in 2010 had brought back the old '70s Bennite organiser Jon Lansman as his parliamentary aide.

'What Michael really brought me in to do was to work on bringing the left together,' Lansman told us. And Lansman was the key figure in the project. Born in 1957 to an Orthodox Jewish family in north London, educated at Highgate School and Cambridge, Lansman came to socialism through a visit to Israel. He had his moment in the spotlight as the very young, very clever, very quick and utterly ruthless chief fixer for Tony Benn in the late '70s and early '80s.

His wife Beth Wagstaff's tragic early death from breast cancer, in 1999, left him with three young children to bring up by himself, which took him out of the political spotlight for almost two decades.

He started with Meacher by seeing it as the sort of job he had done for Tony Benn in the '70s – manoeuvring and using the rules to leverage advantage for the left. But he and Meacher started to see that something very different was needed, and that something was what got Corbyn elected. They later christened it Momentum.

'Momentum is very different in character from previous organisations on the left of the Labour Party,' he says.

> It's different because we brought in people from different cultures, people who had not previously been involved with politics, ex-Green Party people and others. There were a lot of returners – people who had left Labour in despair. So it's much more pluralist, we do not have a single ideological position. We want to

pass on the good things that we agree on. We provide a space in which people organise.

Peter Mandelson once boasted of putting the left into a sealed tomb. He would have succeeded if Progress was still running the show.

So Lansman, who in the '70s was seen as the ultimate sectarian, operating in dark corners, is now championing a sort of political activity which is far removed from that – though perhaps not quite totally removed: each year there is a Momentum slate for Labour's NEC.

Across the country, local constituencies and union branches were having nomination meetings. With the emergence of Corbyn on the ballot paper, many members felt that this time around there was a very real choice. Burnham began losing his advantage. Even in New York, the branch of Labour International switched its likely backing from Burnham to Jeremy Corbyn. The local chair, Ian Williams, a former speechwriter to Neil Kinnock and veteran of the battles against the Militant Tendency on Merseyside, was clear why this happened. 'We saw and heard Jeremy's appeal, and members liked it. They thought it was authentic.' Corbyn, never a great speaker and accustomed to going around the country with speeches written on the back of a proverbial fag packet, suddenly found his meetings were packed out. Many members were prepared to support, others were joining because of him. Others felt that he needed to be given the strongest vote in order to hold whoever might emerge victorious to left-wing policies. Some saw him as an interim Labour leader, who would want to step aside within a couple of years once the party had been returned to its members, and to be replaced with a younger version of Corbyn.

In the meantime, however, Len McCluskey and Unite had shifted their earlier support from Andy Burnham to Jeremy Corbyn. This for the hard-headed realists in the unions was not about the vagaries of a debate for future travel, it was about gaining power and in Jeremy Corbyn they saw the leader with the best chance of doing it.

By the time the left's opponents among Labour MPs saw what was going on, it was too late. In August, a panicky Huddersfield MP, Barry Sheerman, called for the leadership contest to be halted over fears that those registering to take part included members of the Socialist Workers Party, the Green Party, the Conservatives and UKIP. He saw with horror that 553,954 people could vote in the leadership contest, and fewer than half of them – 292,973 – were members. There were 148,182 affiliates (trade union members who had opted in to paying the political fund) and 112,799 had registered to vote.

Around 56,000 voters were forbidden from taking part. Among those who had their vote rejected, after it was discovered that they were members of other parties, were Mark Serwotka, general secretary of the Public and Commercial Services Union, film director Ken Loach and Toby Young, who urged Conservative voters to register to vote for Corbyn in order to consign Labour 'to electoral oblivion'. Lord (Michael) Young of Dartington, an architect of Labour's winning 1945 manifesto, would have been horrified to see that his son, Toby, was frequently trying to harness his great reforming reputation to further his own mean and reactionary political endeavours.

The nature of the party was changing dramatically. 'In 2014, the biggest cohort of Labour party members was in their sixties. By now [2018], it is people in their twenties. The next biggest cohort is people in their fifties. It is much flatter,' says Lansman.

In truth, there is a generation missing. Labour's doughnut lacks people in their forties and early fifties – the Thatcher and Blair generations.

Momentum itself is now very big, and looks, from our 2018 vantage point, to be pretty well entrenched. It is not going to disappear any time soon, and is likely to outlive Corbyn's leadership. It has 40,000 members and is still growing at the rate of more than 1,000 every month, and there are 250,000 people on its database. In 2019, its income is expected to top £1 million for the first time, and most of this comes from individual subscriptions: less than 5 per cent comes from the trade unions. Momentum's critics both inside and outside the Labour Party appeared to fail to understand that the organisation is organic; a grassroots response with its own policy prescription and policies reinforcing a Labour Party that has moved in its direction. Its critics like to bang on about Trotskyists and entryists, as though this were all some rerun of the 1980s with Labour and the Militant Tendency. Most Momentum members would likely be hard put to explain what Trotskyism is; their values are overwhelmingly rooted in something altogether more familiar – the much abused deep roots of a Labour England that had never entirely shrivelled and gone away.

So was it the saturnine skills of Jon Lansman that got Corbyn elected? Certainly he and Simon Fletcher were the main campaign organisers. But the fact is that what Lansman and Meacher saw was real: a vast army of people – largely but not exclusively young – who were tired of excuses for leaving the same old unfair society in place. Corbyn was different, and better, and the extraordinary rock-star progress through the country of this late middle-aged, mild-mannered bearded leftie was not something anyone could create. It was real and organic. Labour England, which people thought dead, had simply changed shape.

Corbyn won big. Burnham came a poor second, Cooper third and Kendall a distant fourth. He was suddenly, not just a party leader, but at the head of a movement. Where could he take it?

CHAPTER EIGHTEEN

THE STRANGE REBIRTH OF LABOUR ENGLAND

2015–2018

Jeremy Corbyn's astonishing victory in the 2015 Labour leadership election showed that the commentariat and the pollsters could be profoundly wrong. For many, even for some of those who were not his natural supporters, it was a pleasure to see the control freaks and technocrats, the spin doctors and professional politicians of the New Labour years roundly defeated.

The upsurge in members meant that when it came to selecting Labour Party candidates, the members would henceforth choose them and not the party machine. As a direct consequence, the quality of many of Labour's parliamentary candidates would begin to improve dramatically.

More profound than any of this was the signal that Labour's revival sent not just to Britain, but to the rest of the world. The near political and economic consensus, and the market fundamentalism and essentially neoliberal model that had held sway since the late 1970s, was finally going to be challenged. There was some life left in Labour England.

For the hundreds of thousands who had joined, here was a

party, a new movement with deep roots in the old, with which they could identify.

It was for redistribution, for restoring the fractured public and welfare services. It would no longer accept the grotesque inequality that was blighting so many lives. In the words of Len McCluskey, at a private meeting of Labour MPs, 'Labour made the journey from being a party that had largely gone from meekly whimpering about austerity to a party completely opposed to austerity within nine months.'

When Tony Blair became Prime Minister, much of Europe had left-leaning governments. But by 2015, the European left had lost its way and was largely out of power and impotent. In the most recent French presidential elections, there wasn't even a socialist candidate. In Germany, the once mighty SPD were forced into a tail-between-the-legs post-election deal with the Christian Democrats. In Portugal and Spain there were left-wing governments, but the further east in Europe one travelled, the more xenophobic, right-wing and nationalistic governments tended to become. The traditional socialist and social democratic parties were in disarray and fading fast.

In the United States, Donald Trump had managed to cap-ture the disillusioned, blue-collar vote, by often stealing Bernie Sanders's clothes on opposing the free trade agreements signed in the Clinton and Obama years that many workers blamed for the draining of their jobs south of the border, and to China. Hillary Clinton had believed that it was her dynastic turn to become President; her wing of the Democratic Party seemed to completely fail to see what was coming and was wedded to the same old policies of triangulation. Liberals on both sides of the pond began to obsess about populism, failing to appre-ciate that it was the political and economic agendas of both the 'new' Democrats and New Labour that had helped fuel it. The populist leaders were the bastard offspring of a complacent liberal elite who had arrogantly assumed that working-class voters had nowhere else to go.

But in Britain, there was a youthful enthusiasm, a feeling that once again anything could be possible. Some of this optimism would come to be laid at the door of the much maligned Momentum. Momentum managed to harness youthful support by tapping into the passions and creativity of a generation that had been short-changed.

Instead of rolling out the red carpet to this wave of youthful enthusiasm, grumpy older Labour MPs banged on about the Militant Tendency, comparing Momentum to the rather dull, small Trotskyite group that mutated into something else years ago.

'Jeremy Corbyn is a phenomenon,' Gordon Brown acknowledged. Yet the Corbyn phenomenon and the rising up of Labour from the ashes were of little import to the mainstream politicians and media who railed against the emptying out of the political process. They would refuse to accept that a mass party was rising right in front of them.

Local constituency parties that had been moribund for years reported surges in membership and supporters, with the majority of these in London and the south. Even in traditional Tory suburban and rural areas, local party officials reported a huge increase in membership.

Labour's right-wing worries about having lots of members just in case they start demanding things. When it became apparent that many of these new members and supporters had joined Labour precisely because they wanted to vote for Corbyn, the party's right wing tried to find ways of stopping them from voting.

Corbyn had this to say:

People want to have a debate about Labour's direction. I didn't want a leadership contest. I wanted a policy debate in the party. The National Executive decided that we'd have a leadership contest and so this is a very important way in which we can discuss the direction of the party.

Jeremy Corbyn, the reluctant candidate who just wanted a 'debate', began to look just a little like Clement Attlee, that 'modest little man with plenty to be modest about'.

Jeremy Corbyn was probably not the ideal candidate to be Leader of the Opposition. But he was the best standing – and more importantly he captured the zeitgeist. It is refreshing to come across a political leader who is capable of being both self-deprecating and honest about his own shortcomings. Was he the strongest candidate on the hustings and in the campaign? The vast majority of members thought so and so did we.

He isn't a great speaker, certainly not when one considers some of the great Labour orators such as Neil Kinnock or Michael Foot. Nevertheless, huge crowds began to gather as he prepared to speak in draughty halls and civic centres. Lines of people would snake around buildings to the obvious surprise of the odd journalists who might have turned up. It was not the medium that drew the crowds; it was the message.

But much of the media wasn't curious. There was a lofty snootiness about the great unwashed who might be at risk of making 'the wrong decision'. Which may explain why most of the commentators completely missed what was happening in unfashionable, down-at-heel towns all around the country.

What is loosely described as the 'commentariat' is not a complicated beast. It is largely drawn from a narrow base of individuals who spend a great deal of time reaffirming their collective view of the world. The American journalist Glenn Greenwald has observed, 'There are exceptions, but this is the crux of British punditry: banal, predictable, bitter, rhetorically flamboyant attacks on the easiest and most marginalised-by-Oxbridge targets, followed by self-affirmation because other like-minded groupthink British pundits praise it.'

Corbyn's policies not only appealed to Labour's electorate; they also began to register with the wider public, unfamiliar with hearing such commitments. There was nothing particularly revolutionary about them; they weren't extreme, unworkable or anything else that the *Daily Mail* or the Blairites might throw at the public. Corbyn was espousing a fairly traditional democratic socialist, Labour argument, albeit one that had been pushed to the periphery during the Thatcher–Blair ascendancy.

Years of purges and parachuted candidates, often of fairly pedestrian quality, had left the Labour benches almost denuded of MPs who believed anything in particular. In Jeremy Corbyn, the new party members felt that they had someone sincere and authentic.

Here was someone who had been against the Iraq War, and who would do his best to avoid dragging Britain into future Middle East quagmires. Here was someone who believed in public ownership, believed in the redistribution of power and wealth, was against the almost permanent austerity of both the Tories and the European Central Bank, and enunciated lots of practical policies to save the public realm from complete destruction.

And after Harriet Harman, who had been standing in as interim leader during the election process, marched MPs into the lobbies with the Tories to support their Welfare Bill, the worm turned finally and decisively in favour of this serial rebel from the backbenches.

It was probably at this precise moment that the then front-runner for the Labour leadership, Andy Burnham, lost the election; for after an agony of indecision, he trooped into the lobby behind Harriet Harman. Jeremy Corbyn rebelled and voted against the Bill. There was no doubt which side the majority of members and supporters took.

If Burnham had voted with his instincts that day, he would probably be Labour leader by now – and the next Prime Minister.

Jeremy Corbyn had never harboured great personal ambitions, nor did he actively seek power for himself. This makes him unusual and in the words of Gordon Brown 'difficult to deal with'. He couldn't be offered preferment; he couldn't be offered a place in the House of Lords. He had no interest in these things. Nor was he interested in handing out peerages and baubles, which probably earned him some even more bitter enemies. He had to be dragged into appointing a handful of Labour peers, such as Shami Chakrabarti, to make up the numbers. He told a close colleague that if he did have to name any new peers, they would mostly be ethnic minority women.

He had spent twenty or so years in effective political exile. He was the type of Labour MP Tony Blair in particular disliked the most; an unbiddable socialist, an inveterate peacemonger, a scruffy reminder of everything that Blair had wanted to bury for good. A vegetarian, allotment-holding, bicycle-riding, bearded lefty.

In fact, Jeremy Corbyn is what many believe to be the archetypal *Guardian* reader. So why were *Guardian* columnists so hostile towards him? *The Guardian*'s long sulk over Corbyn has cost it dear with many of its most committed readers. Its estrangement from a Labour Party now much more in tune with its own long-held editorial view is one of the mysteries of our time.

Corbyn's majorities grew and his local party was healthy and resistant to the various moves to make his life difficult or have him replaced with a New Labour clone.

No issue, big or small, escaped Jeremy Corbyn's attentions while he was in political exile. If he had not been an MP you can imagine him as one of those earnest types you see on demonstrations, festooned with badges affirming their commitment to women, LGBT rights, Palestinians, vegetarianism, the Birmingham Six and much more besides.

He may now regret his own propensity to speak at almost any gathering of like-minded internationalists. It means that he is now best known – courtesy of endless media columns – for sharing platforms with Hamas, which back then called for the destruction of Israel, and with Sinn Féin at a time when its policy was still 'the Armalite in one hand and the ballot box in the other'.

Corbyn has paid a heavy price for such dalliances, some of which were clearly wrong, though benignly intentioned. Few of his detractors, least of all the permanently primed, circular firing squad in the Parliamentary Labour Party, gave him any credit for his stand against apartheid over the years or his support for repressed people across the world. Corbyn, unlike most ministers in most British governments, took the United Nations and international law very seriously. He helped lead the revolt against the Iraq War and the permanent war in Afghanistan. Without him, who would be championing with gusto the plight of the Chagossians of the British Indian Ocean Territory and many other places his detractors have probably never heard of – still less care about?

On BBC Radio 4's *Today* programme, Andrew Mackinlay,

the former Labour MP for Thurrock, said that he believed that the party was rigging the system against Corbyn: 'I think that we would not be having this discussion this morning if all the indications were that Kendall or Cooper or Burnham were in the lead.'

The party's membership, which not that long ago had barely been around 120,000 and was in steep decline, had blossomed. In most organisations this would be cause for celebration. In Labour headquarters there was deep gloom. Huge efforts, expensive but largely unsuccessful, were directed into winnowing out the smattering of entryists, who would have had next to no influence on the eventual outcome.

The wonder was why hundreds of thousands of people would actually want to join a party that immediately sends their applications to a compliance unit, successfully blocks their imagined right to vote and appears to believe they are being groomed by a malign bunch of septuagenarian Trotskyists based in Crouch End.

It was reminiscent of the old Ogmore Labour Club in south Wales when the legendary Sir Ray Powell MP presided over all. Then the refrain was: 'So you want to join the Labour Party, lad? Sorry, we're full up!' As Labour's leadership contest came to an end, it became apparent that the party's panjandrums had done everything in their power to stop the eventuality of a Corbyn victory. They were the modern day equivalents of Cnut the Great, who tried in vain to halt the tide coming in.

On the day of the announcement of the results, cameras caught serried ranks of suited delegates, faces dejected and downcast, inside the QE2 Centre in Westminster. Jeremy Corbyn's supporters were outside, loudly waving banners. The perennial outsider had to come outside to greet them.

And, this being the unforgiving Labour Party headquarters

at work, there was no car to take the new leader back home. He simply walked down the road and took part in a separate demonstration in Whitehall.

The contrast between how the left treated Labour's new leader, Tony Blair, on his election as leader in 1994 with how the Blairite right treated Corbyn is stark. Blair's election was treated with respect by almost everyone in the party. Left-wingers such as Clare Short, Frank Dobson, Michael Meacher and Gavin Strang said that they were happy to serve under Blair. Corbyn and his friends did not resort to sour, personal briefings to the press. They just got on with organising conferences, writing pamphlets and talking to one another in Quaker meeting houses and badly heated Labour halls.

That's not to say, of course, that the Bennites, including Corbyn, have been guiltless in Labour's civil wars. They were on occasion enthusiastic volunteers for Labour's circular firing squad. But, in 1994, they gave Blair a fair chance and a following wind.

But, in 2015, an immediate and menacing silence greeted Corbyn's victory. It wasn't long before that silence gave way to a great deal of noise and anger.

In the immediate aftermath of his victory, a shadow Health minister, Jamie Reed, resigned, citing his opposition to the new leader's policy over Trident. (Corbyn has been against nuclear weapons all of his life.)

A number of other members of the shadow Cabinet – Yvette Cooper, Rachel Reeves, Chuka Umunna, Chris Leslie, Emma Reynolds, Tristram Hunt, Mary Creagh and Liz Kendall – also confirmed they would not serve under Corbyn. Tristram Hunt, who had been parachuted into the safe seat of Stoke-on-Trent Central at the behest of his friend Peter Mandelson, was to leave Parliament to become director of the Victoria and Albert Museum in London. Chuka Umunna, who had thrown his hat into the leadership ring, only to withdraw it days later citing the 'pressures of media scrutiny', mused publicly about setting up a new party, which presumably he would be gratefully asked to lead. He was reported to be thinking of calling it 'Back Together', blissfully unaware that this was also the title of a track by a 1970s disco combo band, fronted by Roberta Flack and Donny Hathaway.

By late summer 2018, the Labour whips were fairly certain Umunna and MP Chris Leslie were in informal discussion with Liberal Democrats and possibly some Remain Tories about setting up yet another centre party. This was confirmed by press reports that suggested Liberal Democrat leader Vince Cable had missed a vital vote on Brexit because he was attending a meeting to discuss establishing a new party. To add to the confusion, some pro-Remain Tories were hoping to reach a deal with Labour to form a National Government, hold a second referendum on the EU and bring in proportional representation. Their price appeared to be Corbyn's head.

Chris Leslie seemed to see his role as Corbyn and McDonnell's critic in chief. Eventually, even former Blair loyalists such as ex-Cabinet minister Caroline Flint began to weary and told him so in no uncertain terms. Other prominent members of Labour's current and overactive circular firing squad included: Ian Austin, Jess Philips, Wes Streeting, Neil Coyne, Mike Gapes and John Mann. Many of whom might form the nucleus of a new centre party that will try to prevent Labour from forming a government.

A number of them are likely to be deselected, as new parliamentary boundaries have to be adopted. But since, unlike Roy Jenkins, David Owen and Shirley Williams, they are relatively unknown to the public, this group of MPs will be forced to rely on better and more reviled figures such as Blair, Clegg and the serially dull John Major. Their faith remains in David Miliband, who they seem to believe can return from the United States to vanquish all. Some of the plotters have even identified a constituency for Miliband, Vauxhall, appropriately close to Parliament and represented by Kate Hoey, one of Labour's very few hard-line Brexiteers. And yet the far bigger longer-term threat to both Labour and the Tories remains on the far right, from a revived UKIP that will perhaps work hand in glove with the English Defence League.

There has, in short, been a planned and co-ordinated attempt right from the very beginning by those that the media suddenly took to describing as Labour moderates or centrists to strangle Jeremy Corbyn's leadership at birth.

It all rather helped Prime Minister David Cameron to sound like a statesman instead of a slimeball, when he described Jeremy Corbyn's election as Labour leader as a threat 'to our national security, to our economic security and to the security of your family'.

Within weeks of Corbyn's dramatic victory, Simon Danczuk, the hitherto barely known MP for Rochdale, announced that he was prepared to run against Corbyn as a 'stalking horse candidate'. 'My only intention is to secure a better leader for the Labour Party and to give us some chance of winning the next general election,' he said. 'At the moment, I and many of my fellow MPs simply cannot see that happening under the current leadership ... I do not have any expectation of winning myself, but would hope to open up the field for serious contenders such as Chuka, Dan [Jarvis] or Emma [Reynolds].'

Up until that moment, Danczuk had largely been known for his work in exposing the paedophile and former Rochdale MP Cyril Smith. By cruel irony in December 2015, Danczuk was suspended from the Labour Party following allegations of sending sexually explicit text messages to a seventeen-year-old girl. He resigned from the party in May 2017, after being blocked from standing as a Labour candidate. After losing his seat at the 2017 general election, running as an independent, he ruled out a return to politics.

Once elected, Corbyn faced all sorts of problems that he had, quite reasonably, always supposed would never be his to worry about, and he arrived ill-equipped to deal with them. The biggest was to assemble round him a personal office, without which a modern opposition leader cannot function. It is perhaps not entirely surprising that at first he made a mess of it, and eventually opted for the safest, most conservative option.

Jon Lansman and the other key figures in Momentum felt with some justice that they more than anyone else had delivered Corbyn's victory and had earned a place at the top table – and that having given him good advice so far, their advice might still be considered worth listening to.

Momentum was, as we saw in the last chapter, what the late Michael Meacher had first employed Jon Lansman to create. This was not the rigid sectarian Lansman whom Labour had known and failed to love in the rough and tumble of the Bennite years, and Momentum was not the intolerant and unforgiving organisation Lansman had run for Tony Benn in the '80s. Having fought Denis Healey unrelentingly in the 1980s, Lansman had come to admire him. 'I learned the lessons of marginalisation,' he says. Many of its supporters were new to politics; many more were new to Labour. It is, perhaps, some indication of what the new Labour England might look like.

But Momentum, too, found itself excluded from the inner

circle. The story of Corbyn's leadership is also the story of how Momentum fought the old guard for Corbyn's ear, and lost.

In addition to Momentum, Corbyn started with two or three very bright young women, very loyal to him, whom he had known for years, and who quickly took up some key posts in the new leader's entourage. They gradually realised they were not being listened to. They drifted away to other political jobs, desperately disillusioned – but very private and discreet about their disillusion.

So by a strange and wrenching irony, Corbyn, who had come to the job because something new was stirring in the land, took what must have looked at the time like the safe option, and surrounded himself with the oldest of the old guard.

Two senior appointments came from Unite and its general secretary, Len McCluskey, sowing the seeds of discord with some in Momentum. Unite and Momentum have more recently sometimes found themselves backing opposing candidates in parliamentary selections, the most recent being in Lewisham.

McCluskey sent Karie Murphy, veteran of the bitter battle over the Falkirk parliamentary nomination, to be Corbyn's office manager. And prior to the 2017 general election, he sent his chief of staff, Andrew Murray, to be Corbyn's chief strategist. He joined Seumas Milne, a former *Guardian* comment editor and columnist who was running Corbyn's communications. This was a formidable trio who were not likely to tolerate any nonsense from youthful, probably flaky, Momentum folk or bright young women with a modern sort of idealism.

Murray was a lifelong member of the Communist Party of Great Britain (CPGB) – he left it to join the Labour Party six months before he went to work for Corbyn. He and Milne had cut their political teeth in the '80s in an outfit called Straight Left, a faction within the CPGB which wanted to hang onto the party's old hard-line views, and resisted the idea that communists should be permitted to criticise the Soviet Union.

Straight Left were the most old-fashioned and hard-line of Britain's communists, with that fierce adherence to the party line which early communists believed was the key political virtue. Murray has been compared to Rajani Palme Dutt, the grim old communist 'theoretician' who ensured that the CPGB did not deviate from the Soviet line, from the 1920s to the 1960s. Francis Beckett interviewed Murray for a book on British communism and asked him about a story Beckett had heard from a former communist. Murray said the story could not be true, because it had been told by someone who had deserted the party.

Milne had worked for *The Guardian* for many years, and his many opinion pieces, especially on the Middle East and Russia, were to provide a happy hunting ground for Corbyn's enemies when Milne went to work for the Labour leader.

In 2018, the Labour Party finally appointed a new general secretary, and Jon Lansman threw his hat in the ring. In a tense telephone conversation, Corbyn told Lansman his application was unwelcome and should be withdrawn. Lansman reluctantly withdrew, and another Unite official, Jennie Formby, got the job. She was the preferred candidate of Len McCluskey.

It all feels like the triumph of the old politics over the new. And indeed, Corbyn's people are running him in very much the way that Neil Kinnock's office ran him. We have seen that Kinnock's close advisers never quite trusted their man not to make a mess of it; they wrapped him in cotton wool, kept everyone else away from him, and managed to hide his many attractive qualities from the electorate.

The old political hands around Corbyn are doing exactly the same. 'They are policing him far too heavily,' one senior political journalist told us. His speeches are now carefully scripted and rationed. Journalists, even friendly ones, are not allowed near him. Interview requests are routinely turned down. A sympathetic profile of Corbyn on Radio 4 appeared without an interview with Corbyn.

It is all very foolish. Corbyn got where he is partly because he comes across as a calm, principled and sincere man, which he is. Not letting journalists and the public see this is monumentally self-defeating.

One of the reasons for Jeremy Corbyn's popularity was his hostility to the series of near-permanent wars that successive British governments had allowed themselves to be drawn into. Since the humiliation of Suez, those governments – with the exception of the Harold Wilson Labour government that refused to get involved in America's fruitless war against the Viet Cong – have tended to act as the tail that wags the dog.

Partly this is because British governments really do like to believe that there is a special relationship between Britain and America. It has meant that Britain, ever since the war in Korea in 1950, has spent more on defence than her European allies, despite not really being able to afford to do so.

The 'something must be done' brigade had been making a great deal of noise about the deadly civil war gripping Syria. 'Something must be done' was, according to veteran MP Frank Dobson, the besetting sin of Blairism, based on an invalid syllogism. 'Something must be done. This is something. Therefore this must be done.'

There was a solution to that bloodbath, but it required close co-operation between Russia, Syria's traditional ally, the United States and other regional actors including Iran, Turkey and

Saudi Arabia and through the United Nations. It would have had to begin by appreciating that Bashar al Assad's Alawite minority, which rule the country with an iron fist, feared mass annihilation from the Jihadists and others.

But the Syria situation was horribly complicated and not capable of being solved by some airstrikes with the British joining in with a couple of ageing Tornadoes based in Cyprus, pretending to be a global power.

Innocent civilians and the Kurds needed to be protected, against Assad's brutality. And the Alawites needed protection from the brutish callousness of the various Jihadi groups lined up against him, some of whom were receiving US weaponry – and then using it against other American-backed forces. But that would only come if the US and Russia willed it to happen.

Public opinion was firmly against getting involved in air attacks over Syria that would do little to end the civil war. On 16 November 2015, following the terrorist attacks in Paris on 13 November, Jeremy Corbyn said that the retaliatory attack by French warplanes on ISIS targets in Syria will not change anything and that the solution has to be 'a political settlement in Syria'.

On ITV's *Lorraine* programme, he added, 'We have to be careful. One war doesn't necessarily bring about peace; it often can bring yet more conflicts, more mayhem, and more loss.' He criticised the media for failing adequately to cover other terrorist attacks in Beirut and Turkey.

Later that month he told the BBC's *Andrew Marr Show* that the decision on whether to support air strikes in Syria will be made as a 'party', referring to more than 70,000 responses he had received from Labour Party members to a survey designed to canvas their opinions which had been launched on 27 November:

'Labour MPs need to listen to that [membership] voice, they need to try and understand where people are.'

Sensing his problems within a Parliamentary Labour Party that was in denial of his victory, Corbyn allowed a free vote of Labour MPs over the use of military action. He would speak in Parliament and oppose it, but the shadow Foreign Secretary, Hilary Benn, would close the debate by supporting it. This was something of a confession of weakness on Corbyn's part. He knew that a vociferous section of the PLP were dead against his position.

Benn's speech was hailed by the media but it was a dagger aimed at Corbyn. Following a ten-hour debate in the House of Commons, MPs voted 397 to 223 to authorise air strikes against Islamic State in Syria. Sixty-six Labour MPs voted with the government. At the time of writing, and despite a second round of British-supported bombing this time without a parliamentary vote and which followed a chemical weapons attack thought to have been instigated by Assad's forces, the Syrian civil war was still grinding on.

Labour's pro-intervention MPs were right to say that the party historically was not a pacifist one. But Labour politicians had historically been profoundly influenced by the United Nations and the primacy of international law. Labour England had joined the fight against the Kaiser's armies and Hitler's Nazis. But Labour England had also proudly associated itself with the struggles of the colonial peoples and championed the replacement of an imperialist British Empire with a Commonwealth of equal nations.

Labour England had largely been against joining in foreign ventures, especially when it was unclear what Britain's interests in them might be, or if there wasn't a believable plan for ending them.

Harold Wilson had famously and wisely refused President Lyndon Johnson's request for military assistance in the Vietnam War, for instance.

But Corbyn's opposition to getting involved in the Syrian civil war without the imprimatur of the United Nations, and his intention to apologise for Britain's participation in the invasion of Iraq, had him and Labour back in step with members and voters. The Iraq War had driven thousands away as members and millions away as voters. Now many felt that they could at last return home.

For much of the London-based media, the story wasn't so much about the revival of a Labour Party; it was about reacting to the incessant noise emanating from sections of the party's backbenches in Parliament. Sending journalists to hang around Parliament's Portcullis House in Westminster is a cheap way of garnering copy. Add to that the ease in which gossip and opinion often masquerading as fact swirl around on social media and you have a combustible mix.

Once upon a time, the press and broadcasters by and large believed that it was important to source a story properly before running it, but the modern day curse of reports accompanied by the giveaway 'sources close to X claim', says it all.

This sloppy approach encouraged the rumour mill while giving cover, in the case of the Labour Party, to a running commentary on Corbyn.

His critics for the most part were happy to give vent, frequently fastening onto any passing issue, whether they had much knowledge of it or not. The early months of 2016 were a feverish period of catcalling, plotting, timed resignations and some sackings. In early January, the shadow Minister for Transport, Stephen Doughty, even managed to announce his resignation live on air on the BBC's *Daily Politics* show. It later emerged that this event had been engineered by Doughty and the BBC's political editor, Laura Kuenssberg, and it would seem with the knowledge of broadcaster Andrew Neil.

The cosy Westminster club encouraged all of this; most of the political journalists only really knew the MPs from the Blair–Brown era. They took their lines from them.

There was a far bigger problem for the Labour Party. The slump in newspaper sales had forced a shake-out of print journalists, many from the traditional right-wing stable. Some ended up working for the big broadcasters. Those same broadcasters had often tended to take their stories from the newspapers, but now this process had become even more pronounced. Unsurprising-ly, many Labour supporters increasingly looked elsewhere for alternatives and there was plenty of choice now being provided on social media.

There was always going to be a problem for sections of the Parliamentary Labour Party who had been vehemently opposed to Corbyn and the new emerging movement around him. Many would cite the fact that Corbyn himself had probably rebelled more times against the whip than any of them. But serial rebel Corbyn was just a near lone gun on the backbenches and not a shadow minister.

Either way, discipline in the Parliamentary Labour Party was virtually non-existent and its weekly meetings were often prone to quite extraordinary displays of bitterness and vituper-ation. Some Labour MPs would complain that Corbyn simply wouldn't answer their questions. Corbyn must have been weary-ing of the incessant snarkiness.

Presiding over this weekly tumult and torture was PLP chair-man John Cryer. He must have often wondered what on earth was going to happen next. On one occasion, former Labour min-ister Liam Byrne was reported to have simply lost himself to a screeching, inchoate, white-faced, rage directed at Corbyn. Another PLP meeting was consumed by the fireworks from two old volcanoes that had never stopped exploding against one another; former Labour leader Neil Kinnock and veteran left-winger Dennis Skinner, who was a strong supporter of Corbyn.

If the PLP was a minefield, so largely was party headquarters in Victoria Street, Westminster. Known as 'Southside', some of the party officials made little attempt to hide their hostility to the new regime. Labour's legendary circular firing squad now included some of their number as the leaks multiplied and as attempts were made by rich donors to foist a leadership challenge.

Vast amounts of time and effort were wasted and spent on legal advice over potential leadership challenges.

With this cacophony of criticism, it is a wonder that the party continued to perform reasonably well in local government elections and in by-elections in Sheffield and Greater Manchester. The new Labour leadership was often unable to muster a majority on the party's ruling National Executive Committee.

CHAPTER NINETEEN

CORBYN AND THE
CIRCULAR FIRING SQUAD

David Cameron's louche decision to call a referendum over Britain's membership of the European Union, essentially to keep his own Eurosceptics on board, did not go according to plan. Cameron was ultimately destined to be consumed by his own hubris. The Prime Minister had yelled across the dispatch box at Jeremy Corbyn: 'It might be in my party's interest for him to sit there. It's not in the national interest. I would say – for heaven's sake, man, go.' But after British voters opted for a Brexit, Cameron was the one to go, replaced as Prime Minister by Theresa May. Labour's circular firing squad then turned its guns on Corbyn, accusing him of not trying hard enough for the Remain side in the EU referendum, but he survived the coup attempt.

Labour's attitude towards the common market, then the EEC, then the EC and finally the European Union had shifted with the sands. The party's 1983 manifesto said that Britain should leave, though this went largely unnoticed at the time. By the late 1980s and early 1990s, buffeted by the chill winds of Thatcherism and buoyed by the arrival to the European Commission of Jacques Delors, an interventionist and Keynesian French socialist with a plan, Labour had become the pro-EU party. Thatcher was busy travelling in the opposite direction.

Most Britons didn't tell opinion pollsters that membership of the EU was one of the great issues that preoccupied them. British voters tended to be cooler towards the institution than those on the Continent, but that may have been partly because of the ferocious hostility of Britain's tabloid press to the EU. Tony Blair made little effort to counter the welter of anti-EU bile, and neither did Gordon Brown.

The EU Commission did not exactly cover itself in glory either, proving inflexible to the strains being caused after the banking crash, particularly in the European labour market. The European single currency – effectively vetoed in the UK by Gordon Brown – was undoing the soft underbelly of weak, fairly corrupt southern European economies, while the European Central Bank was insisting on economic policies of near-permanent austerity.

When the EU referendum was eventually called, Labour's so-called heartlands, the emptied-out old mining and industrial areas, took the opportunity to stick up a collective two fingers at both Cameron and the EU. Warnings that quitting the EU could damage these same industrial areas even further failed to dissuade people from voting Leave. As far as many of them were concerned, things couldn't get any worse than they already were. Some two-thirds of Labour MPs represented constituencies that voted to leave the EU, often by very heavy margins.

Even had Jeremy Corbyn and John McDonnell gone on the sort of barnstorming tour that their PLP critics now say that they had wanted them to do, it would probably have made no difference to the result.

Labour's new leadership did, however, make the sensible decision not to share pro-EU platforms with pro-EU Tories. That had worked out disastrously when Labour MPs joined forces with Unionist Tories during the Scottish independence referendum – it handed Labour's Scottish heartlands to the SNP.

Brexit was created by David Cameron, and if Cameron is right and it is a disaster, then it is his disaster. Cameron and his smug Chancellor, George Osborne, had thought they had the vote in the bag from the moment that they called it. Cameron had even gone to bed on the night of the referendum, before the results were even announced, so convinced was he by the pollsters and commentators that he had won.

Labour folk who now try to blame it on Corbyn are simply whitewashing a complacent and arrogant Conservative Prime Minister. But that did not stop Barking MP Dame Margaret Hodge and her colleague Ann Coffey MP from submitting a motion of no confidence in Corbyn. Coffey told BBC News, 'The result of the referendum was a disastrous result for us and the leadership must bear a share of the responsibility for that. It was a lacklustre campaign, it didn't contain a strong enough message and the leader himself appeared half-hearted about it. If you have got a leader who appears half-hearted, you can hardly be surprised if the public feels the same way.'

Angela Eagle, who had praised Corbyn for the energy and commitment that he had shown during the referendum campaign, went back on her words after Britain had voted to leave and accused him of not doing enough. She would later emerge as a challenger to Corbyn alongside the ambitious Welsh MP Owen Smith.

Writing in *The Guardian*, the shadow Chancellor, John McDonnell, responded by saying, 'At a time of such economic uncertainty, with the Tory party split clean down the middle, Labour members and voters will not forgive us if we descend into infighting and introspection only a year after Jeremy Corbyn won his landslide victory as our leader.'

Corbyn himself went on *Channel 4 News* and declared, 'I'm carrying on. I'm making the case for unity. I'm making the case of what Labour can offer to Britain.'

When questioned about the proposed vote of no confidence, he replied:

Margaret [Hodge] is obviously entitled to do what she wishes to do. I would ask her to think for a moment. A Tory Prime Minister resigned, Britain has voted to leave the European Union, there are massive political issues to be addressed. Is it really a good idea to start a big debate in the Labour Party when I was elected less than a year ago with a very large mandate, not from MPs – I fully concede and understand that – but from the party members as a whole? Of course, I want to lead this party. Of course, I want to lead this party in order to put forward an alternative and lead this party to win the election as soon as it comes.

On 25 June, veteran backbencher Frank Field told the BBC Radio 4 *Today* programme that Corbyn 'clearly isn't the right person to lead Labour into an election, because nobody thinks he will win. We clearly need somebody who the public think of as an alternative Prime Minister.'

There was a time, many decades ago, when trade union leaders had been powerful enough to step in when Labour was tearing itself to pieces; the union bosses would calm everyone's nerves and right the ship. That time has long gone. Leaders of the big trade unions issued a joint statement calling on the party to 'unite as a source of national stability' and saying that 'the last thing Labour needs is a manufactured leadership row of its own'. It had no effect.

The failed coup attempt, barely a year after Corbyn had been elected leader, was an extraordinary and very public act of self-immolation. Former leaders, former ministers and backbench MPs tripped over themselves to heap yet more opprobrium on

Corbyn. No doubt Corbyn was buoyed by long-time friendships with people like John McDonnell and Diane Abbott, but there was also a new mass membership out in the country now, a mass membership that was frustrated and angered by the absurd spectacle gripping Westminster.

That absurdity was repeated as farce as attempts were made to force Corbyn to seek the support of 20 per cent of his MPs in order to stand as a candidate for his own job. The party's constitution clearly put the onus on challengers to do that, not the incumbent. It took Michael Mansfield QC all of five minutes to demolish the expensive case dreamed up by Corbyn's opponents.

When the coup finally came, shadow Cabinet minister Hilary Benn was sacked. Nineteen shadow Cabinet ministers resigned, as did twenty-eight junior shadow ministers and eleven parliamentary private secretaries.

Those who then stepped up to the plate and joined the shadow Cabinet in these quite extraordinary circumstances are still largely in place today. They did their new jobs without the battery of office and other support that had been available to those who had walked out, because most of the junior ministers had walked too.

Some new shadow Cabinet members ended up effectively spanning a number of portfolios. Others put their health and wellbeing on the line, such as Easington MP Grahame Morris, shadow Secretary of State for Communities and Local Government.

But who was to challenge Corbyn for the leadership? In the end, the short straw was drawn by Owen Smith. Or rather the ambitious Smith drew his own short straw. Angela Eagle, who had launched a characteristically devious bid for the chance to fight Corbyn, was forced to stand down in favour of Smith.

At the time, Owen Smith probably did not think that he had

drawn the short straw – it must have felt like the opportunity of a political lifetime – but short straw it most certainly was. Smith never for a moment looked like winning, and always sounded like the voice of reaction. This was often unfair, but if you are trying to depose a popular left-winger, it's what happens.

In the early autumn, at the party conference in Liverpool, Jeremy Corbyn was announced as the winner of the Labour leadership contest. Corbyn secured 61.8 per cent of the vote of the vote while Smith won 38.2 per cent.

If 2016 was a year lost to the Labour Party due to a failed coup, 2017 was to be a shock election year, as Prime Minister May sought to entrench her position and win an impregnable parliamentary majority that would enable her to push through Brexit.

Now was the time, May thought, to push a dishevelled Labour Party over the edge and into electoral oblivion. There were plenty of Labour panjandrums who were as keen as mustard to try and help her. Here, for instance, was the 'Prince of Darkness', Baron Mandelson of Foy in the county of Herefordshire and of Hartlepool, as reported in *The Guardian*.

'I work towards undermining Jeremy Corbyn every single day. I resent the idea that I should just walk away and pass the title deeds of this great party over to someone like Jeremy Corbyn.'

We must have missed the moment when we handed over the title deeds of our party to Lord Mandelson.

After months of internecine warfare, resignations, denunciations and the downright treachery of people like Mandelson, it is hardly any wonder that there was not much optimism in the shadow Cabinet, let alone among the poor bloody infantry – and we include ourselves in that.

Jeremy Corbyn was not as scruffy as Michael Foot and managed to spruce himself up for his appearance at the Cenotaph on Remembrance Sunday. But Corbyn's mumbling of the National

Anthem at a Westminster Abbey memorial service for Britain's Second World War dead (he was far from the only mumbler), his support for the peace movement, and his long-time left-wing credentials as a serial rebel seemed to mark him out as another 'loser' in the Foot vein.

Labour's 2017 manifesto was for some commentators (and not a few Labour MPs) yet another 'suicide note' and the party was making the same mistake by appealing to a loyal but rapidly diminishing base.

This white noise was heavily contributed to by a whole phalanx of Labour MPs who seemed to think that their continuous whining would somehow vindicate them.

Tom Baldwin, a former communications adviser to Ed Miliband, later revealed in a book that party officials made use of the startling flexibility of social media advertising to hoodwink their own leader. Campaigns the leader demanded, for example on voter registration, were considered by Labour HQ to be a waste of money, so they planted the advertisements only in places where they would be seen by Seumas Milne and the small coterie of journalists he favoured.

They seem to have been sure that Labour's defeat was to be so seismic that Jeremy Corbyn would be gone by the morning following the general election result.

John McDonnell said that during the election campaign, the more that people got to see and hear Corbyn, the more support he was likely to pick up. Theresa May had obviously hoped that by calling a snap election not many people would see or hear the Labour leader. But May's decision to call the election was both transparent and hugely irritating to voters who, by and large, don't like to be bothered unless they have to be.

Of course, as soon as the election was called, Corbyn and May got equal air time. And it took very little time for voters to decide who was the candidate with empathy. A turning moment came when Theresa May sent Amber Rudd to deputise for her in the BBC TV debate.

Out there, in England, a different election was clearly playing out and one that owed something to the raw energy of youth and the imagination of a whole new breed of activist who, like Bernie Sanders's supporters in America, knew how important social media could be.

In late 2015, Mark Seddon had connected staffers in Corbyn's offices with key Sanders supporters in New York and elsewhere whom he had got to know over the years while living and working in America. Relations were developed over the coming months, ideas, activists and much else shared. Corbyn was later to credit Bernie Sanders for helping to achieve Labour's astonishing result in early May.

Peter Stefanovic, a lawyer born and bred on a council estate in Buckingham, is perhaps fairly typical of a new breed of hugely effective social media activists. He told Mark Seddon that he had become a convert after hearing Jeremy Corbyn speak. 'He talked about the issues that matter and with an authenticity that the Tories simply did not understand.' Stefanovic is convinced that had the election campaign run for another two or three months, Labour would have won a majority.

'You have to understand,' he said. 'Corbyn re-energised a whole new generation of people. Take a look at that manifesto for instance – a promise to build 1 million new council homes or get rid of tuition fees. These were very popular.'

Stefanovic campaigns actively on a host of issues: the NHS, the trade unions and compensation for ex-mineworkers who are still struggling to get industrial compensation. Over one period of twenty-eight days, Stefanovic sent 449 tweets and had 14.4 million impressions; there were between 2 and 3 million visits to his Facebook page and 20 million views of one of his short and pithy campaign videos.

He explained to us that when celebrities such as Hugh Grant or Lily Allen retweet his material it goes stratospheric.

Stefanovic is tall, hugely engaging and utterly genuine. Media corporations would kill to get the sort of following that he and some others have. 'Don't forget also,' he said, 'that today we can trawl a massive TV and film archive, which just wasn't accessible a few years ago.' In other words, it is possible to keep tabs on politicians who make false claims or who are guilty of straight-forward hypocrisy.

The mainstream media has a selective memory. Stefanovic pointed out that it was social media activists like him who caught out Health Secretary Jeremy Hunt in a film clip. Hunt, Stefanovic said, had claimed that '30,000 new mental health workers had been recruited since 2010, when the real figure was 7,000'.

Stefanovic believes changed lifestyles mean that people now consume news in different ways. 'Look at the Canary or Squawk-box,' he says, 'they probably have as many people visiting them on a daily basis as the BBC.'

Diane Abbott got it about right. 'The addition of 3.5 million votes in 2017 was such a huge advance for Labour, for Jeremy and for Corbynism,' she wrote in *Labour List*. 'To put this in context, no Labour leader added so many votes at a general election since Clement Attlee in 1945. Tony Blair certainly didn't. His gain of 2 million new votes in 1997 was the basis for Labour's landslide. But he lost 4 million votes over the next two elections. Public spending restraint followed by illegal wars is not electorally popular.'

Just as the campaign sank Neil Kinnock in 1992 and earned John Major another five years in Downing Street, so in 2017 the campaign threatened to sink Theresa May and place Jeremy

Corbyn in Downing Street – then a far more unthinkable prospect than it is now.

The 2017 campaign was – no one denies it, not even Tony Blair – a triumph and it was Jeremy Corbyn's triumph. If he never achieves anything else in politics, this will always be his triumph, and no one will ever be able to take it away from him.

CHAPTER TWENTY

CORBYN'S JEWISH PROBLEM

At first, after Theresa May's humiliating performance at the 2017 general election, it seemed that nothing could keep her divided, incompetent government in power until 2022, let alone beyond that.

Labour's problems at least seemed manageable. There were relentless attacks on a Labour leader with precious few friends in his parliamentary party. Corbyn was accused of being a Kremlin stooge and being soft on Vladimir Putin. BBC's *Newsnight* photoshopped his trademark Lenin-style cap, turning it into a Russian *ushanka*, with the old Soviet hammer and sickle used as a backdrop.

He was accused of working hand in glove with a former Czech secret agent and of being in league with the hard-line Stalinists who once ruled from Prague. He was called a 'traitor' by sections of the right-wing press, a claim then shouted from the rooftops by some Tories, until one of them foolishly spelled out the charge – that Corbyn had betrayed his country for money. A letter from Corbyn's lawyer finally produced a grovelling apology and an end to these lies.

But just eleven months on from the election, it was dreadfully clear that one issue in particular could help preserve May's government through the messy, fractious Brexit process, even past the next general election. And that was anti-Semitism.

In the council elections in May 2018, Labour made a number of gains, but lost badly in Barnet, north London, an area where it had been expecting to win. The Conservative victory was stupendous: Barnet went from being a hung council to one with a Conservative majority of thirteen seats.

The Conservative council is not popular in the borough, and its policy of handing local services over to the outsourcing company Capita, known by its many critics as Crapita, has few friends outside the right-wing ideologues who lead the council. So how did the Tories win, and win big?

Unlike most political questions, this one has a single and generally accepted answer. Barnet has the biggest proportion of Jewish voters of any council in the country, and the Conservatives owed their victory to the perception that the Labour Party is riddled with anti-Semitism, and that Jeremy Corbyn cheerfully tolerates anti-Semitism and is perhaps even touched with it himself.

The Conservatives knew their best hope lay with this perception, which is why during the campaign Theresa May spat out the words 'Labour's vile anti-Semitism' as often as she could squeeze them into a sentence.

A few days later, on 14 May, John Humphrys on the BBC's *Today* programme interviewed the new president of the Board of Deputies of British Jews, Marie van der Zyl. Humphrys, normally considered a fierce interviewer, did not even question van der Zyl's central thesis: that Labour is an anti-Semitic party, indeed the only anti-Semitic party. This, it seemed, was established fact: Humphrys only had to ascertain from her what she was going to do about it.

Should she, Humphrys wanted to know, tell all Jews not to

vote Labour? She didn't feel she needed to. In Barnet, she told him with satisfaction, 'the people have spoken'.

Barnet's Labour leader Barry Rawlings wrote, 'In Golders Green, which has a large Jewish population, turnout was above 70 per cent compared with below 40 per cent in other polling districts. Non-Jewish residents voted against us in solidarity with their Jewish friends, neighbours and loved ones ... Some members didn't want to put up posters for fear that neighbours might think they didn't care about anti-Semitism ... Doors were slammed in our faces and leaflets were taken out of our hands and torn up in front of us.'

Other cities with substantial Jewish populations have also been affected; in Greater Manchester a Jewish Labour Party member has resigned after thirty-six years, and told us, 'I never experienced anti-Semitism before in the Labour Party. Not until Corbyn's tenure suddenly gave voice to it, gave permission for anti-Semitism to seep out of the woodwork.'

Polling in early 2018 put Labour's share of the Jewish vote nationally at about 13 per cent.

Now all this is very serious, especially for folk like the authors of this book; we are talking about our political party here, one to which we have dedicated a substantial portion of our lives.

If it is now the perceived reality that Labour is anti-Semitic, Labour cannot hope ever to win power, because it is not only Jews who are disgusted by anti-Semitism. And if the perception is true, or even partially true, then Labour not only cannot, but should not, win power, and the political lives of the two authors of this book, as well as those of many other people, become meaningless.

We are in the Labour Party because we believe in equality and fairness. You can't believe that and be anti-Semitic, not unless you have the sort of brain that can believe two opposing things at the same time and still function. Almost all Labour Party members would proudly describe themselves as being against anti-Semitism, Islamophobia, racism and homophobia. This has not always been the case within the Conservative Party. We think the spiritual home of anti-Semitism is not on the left, but on the right.

We would love to believe that the left has always been entirely free from it, but of course we know perfectly well that it hasn't. Karl Marx's own writing – as David Rich points out in his book *The Left's Jewish Problem* – is peppered with anti-Semitism.

More recently, anti-Semitism surfaced on the left (as well as on the right) in the period between the two world wars, the 1920s and 1930s, and in a rather instructive way. After the First World War, horribly mutilated ex-soldiers could be seen begging on the streets of London, while men who had not fought but who had instead sold arms for the war machine were rich and growing richer.

The gulf between the rich and the poor had never seemed so immense. On the left, there was holy rage against what the Conservative leader Stanley Baldwin called 'hard-faced men who look as though they had done very well out of the war'. By 1920 most people were expecting revolutionary change in the way Britain was governed.

So far, so good, but as the hoped-for change failed to materialise, and as two Labour governments under Ramsay MacDonald came and went without reducing the extremes of wealth and poverty, the efforts of a few hard-line anti-Semites began to bear fruit, and those 'hard-faced men' began, in the minds of some on the left, to assume Jewish characteristics.

And so, when Oswald Mosley (a former Labour minister) came to found his British Union of Fascists in 1932, he was joined, not just by a whole regiment of Colonel Blimps from the right, but also by some people from the left. And a few of them stayed with him when his organisation became openly and avowedly anti-Semitic.

Those who stuck with fascism slowly dropped all the other beliefs that had once taken them to socialism, and by the time the Second World War broke out, they had become generally right wing in their political outlook. It's a journey that is still undertaken by anti-Semites. Dave Rich noted that in the 1980s, someone called Harry Mullin started by writing anti-Semitic pieces for the far-left *Labour Herald* newspaper, until he moved to the British National Party.

The recently published diaries of Collin Brooks, Lord Rothermere's chief lieutenant and editor of one of his newspapers, reveal that Brooks was a member of English Mistery, one of the nuttiest of the pro-Nazi groups, and that he and Rothermere remained pro-fascist and anti-Semites even after war had broken out. In 1938, the *Daily Mail* fulminated against 'stateless Jews from Germany' who were 'pouring into this country'. Late in 1939 Brooks was describing the Secretary of State for War, Leslie Hore-Belisha, as 'this pushing Jew-boy'.

Campaigners for a deal with Hitler started by saying Britain should not fight a 'war of Jewish finance' or a 'Jews' war'. But they got cleverer. Professor Richard Griffiths, an expert on the far right, writes that they used the terms 'usury', 'money power', 'alien' and 'cosmopolitan' as coded references to Jews.

After the horrors of the Holocaust had been revealed, no politician could thrive, at least for a while, by promoting anti-Semitism. But during the 1990s, the *Daily Mail*, the same newspaper that had supported Mosley in the 1930s with its infamous 'Hurrah for the Blackshirts' headline, was edging its way back towards a genteel sort of anti-Semitism.

It wasn't overt. Here's an example of how it worked. In 1996 the *Daily Mail* monstered a harmless further education lecturer called Val Goulden for the crime of having won an industrial tribunal against her employer. *Mail* hacks unearthed the damning facts that Goulden was divorced and a single mother, and they doorstepped her elderly and frail former mother-in-law.

When the hacks came to write the piece, they produced their ace. Goulden, they revealed, was not the real family name. Val Goulden's father was actually lorry driver Wilfred Gouldmann, who had 'mysteriously' changed the family surname.

Of course there was no mystery. Like many Jews of his generation, Val Goulden's father had changed the surname to something more English-sounding, hoping to protect his family from persecution. You think the clever people who run the *Mail* couldn't work that out? Of course they could. You think their readers didn't see the subtext? Of course they did.

Anti-Semitism was also making a comeback on the far left, mainly in student politics. Dave Rich's book chronicles in detail the move against Jewish societies in student unions during the 1980s, which was presented as anti-Zionism but sometimes morphed into anti-Semitism. What you can say about Israel without being anti-Semitic, and what you cannot say, is a deceptively simple question. Trying to answer it is like walking through a minefield.

Right-wing anti-Semitism moved to a new ugly level when Ed Miliband became Labour leader in 2010, and looked likely to become Britain's first Jewish Prime Minister in the country's history.

Miliband was quickly identified by right-wing newspapers as a paid-up member of what they called the 'north London metropolitan elite'. This phrase was quickly identified by one of Britain's foremost experts on anti-Semitism, Professor Colin Holmes, the author of *Anti-Semitism in British Society* (and, more recently, a biography of Lord Haw Haw); Holmes saw it as a code for 'Jew'. Since Jeremy Corbyn's election as leader of the Labour Party, there has oddly been no repeat of this phrase, even though Corbyn has represented a north London seat, Islington North, since 1983.

Miliband was in good company. Danny Cohen, until 2015 the BBC's director of television, was furiously attacked by newspapers for firing Jeremy Clarkson, and *The Times* marshalled its tanks behind those of the *Mail*, calling Cohen a 'fixture of the north London metropolitan elite'. The comedian David Baddiel tweeted, 'Surprised Times sub-clause doesn't add: "and y'know: a rootless cosmopolitan of East European stock."' Dave Cohen, author of some of the *Horrible Histories* series of books, tweeted, 'Times calls Danny Cohen "part of North London Metropolitan elite". We hear what you're saying guys.'

The tradition is that of Dornford Yates and Bulldog Drummond, memorably satirised by Alan Bennett in his play *Forty Years On*: 'That bunch of rootless intellectuals, alien Jews and international pederasts who call themselves the Labour Party.' Clarkson is a perfect enemy for a member of the north London metropolitan elite – a public-school-educated British Bulldog Drummond figure for our times.

The campaign's lowest point was the *Daily Mail*'s attack on Miliband's distinguished academic father, Ralph.

The *Mail*'s article begins by telling us, correctly, that Ralph Miliband was an immigrant Jew fleeing Nazi persecution. A couple of paragraphs further on, just in case we've forgotten that he wasn't really English, we read about 'the immigrant boy whose first act in Britain was to discard his name Adolphe because of its associations with Hitler, and become Ralph'.

It follows Miliband to the London School of Economics (then being run from Cambridge to avoid wartime bombing), where he was certainly taught by several tutors, but only one of whom is mentioned: Harold Laski. This was a man 'whom some Tories considered to be a dangerous Marxist revolutionary'. Well, perhaps that's how 'some Tories' saw the distinguished Jewish political scientist Professor Harold Laski. For the record, he was Labour Party chairman in 1945, and a Zionist who fell out with his party leaders because of his passionate support for the emergent state of Israel. He was also the son of a Jewish community leader and the younger brother of Judge Neville Laski, who was president of the London Committee of Deputies of British Jews, presiding elder of the Spanish and Portuguese Jews Congregation and vice-president of the Anglo-Jewish Association.

'…One is entitled to wonder,' said the *Mail*, 'whether Ralph Miliband's Marxism was actually fuelled by a giant-sized social chip on his shoulder as he lived in his adoptive country.' What exactly is the purpose of the last seven words of that sentence?

'The word Jew doesn't have to be mentioned,' says Professor Holmes.

> All you have to do is make it clear that Ralph Miliband was a refugee from Nazism, and then to suggest he has no loyalty to the hand that succoured him. His allegiance was to Moscow. He was one of those rootless cosmopolitans. That theme of Jews owing no allegiance can be found throughout the history of British anti-Semitism. The depiction of Miliband drew strength from the prehistory of such sentiments linked to Jews, treason and Bolshevism.

The Board of Deputies of British Jews considered protesting to the paper, but decided against this. Apparently they felt that the evidence of anti-Semitism in the article was not strong enough. To us, the article seems far more clearly anti-Semitic than many statements for which some Labour figures have recently been branded anti-Semites.

Even though there was no official statement from the Board of Deputies of British Jews, one of its two vice-presidents, Alex Brummer, did comment on the article. Brummer also happened to be the *Daily Mail*'s City editor, and he spoke up for the paper and defended the article. Brummer later wrote that anyone who claimed that it was anti-Semitic owed the *Mail* an apology.

But hang on. This was a political article. Why was the City editor defending it, rather than the political editor? Presumably Brummer spoke for the paper because the political editor, James Chapman, was not Jewish. For that same reason, the deputy editor, Jon Steafel, also defended the article publicly, rather than the *Mail*'s editor, Paul Dacre. The article carried the byline of Geoffrey Levy, though it was certainly the work of many hands.

It looks as though a policy decision was taken that only Jewish names should be associated with the article. So the *Mail*'s top brass must have realised that it would be considered anti-Semitic.

It wasn't just the *Daily Mail*. Calling Ed Miliband 'weird' was another coded message, and the argument that we should have had David Miliband as leader, not Ed, because David looked and sounded better, was a coded way of saying that David looked and sounded less Jewish.

On 21 May 2014, while campaigning in the local and European elections, Ed Miliband was photographed rather inelegantly eating a bacon sandwich at New Covent Garden Market. The picture appeared in London's *Evening Standard*, unleashing a cascade of mockery and becoming the source of a thousand internet memes.

No one ever spelled out the subtext, which was that of course he can't eat a good old English bacon sandwich properly, he's a Jew. But those who read it understood. If it had been the left mocking a right-wing Jewish politician in this way, it would surely have been the subject of an accusation of anti-Semitism, and sparked furious (and justified) protests from the Board of Deputies of British Jews.

And yet, come the 2015 election in Finchley – a constituency which includes Barnet, and has the biggest proportion of Jewish votes of any constituency in the country – Labour canvassers found, not anger at anti-Semitic attacks on its leader, but a belief that anti-Semitism was a Labour virus. In vain the canvassers pointed out that Labour was offering, not just the first Jewish Prime Minister, but a Jewish MP in Sarah Sackman (who proved a first class parliamentary candidate – calm, thoughtful, attractive and fiercely clever).

The constituency was awash with rumours of Labour canvassers saying anti-Semitic things on the doorstep in Finchley. None of these rumours were ever substantiated.

We got an insight into how such rumours might start from a polling day rumour – it made the front page of *The Sun* – that Labour canvassers in Finchley had telephoned observant Jews in the borough, telling them they must not vote for Conservative candidate Mike Freer because he was gay. Many people believed that Labour had done this. It helped propel Freer to victory.

The rumour was started by Freer's campaign team. Freer has not responded to our requests for his evidence, but he did respond to Sarah Sackman. She wanted, she said, to speak to Freer's informant and investigate what had happened, adding that she would be happy to do so in Freer's presence.

Mike Freer wrote back, 'The constituent on the telephone did not wish to be identified and my councillors do not wish to discuss the matter further ... I doubt we will ever get to the bottom of what did or did not happen.' We doubt it too.

Partly because of these rumours, Finchley did not elect its first

Jewish MP in 2015, and Britain did not elect its first Jewish Prime Minister. Soon after the general election, Jeremy Corbyn inherited Miliband's mantle as well as his problems, and brought his own history into the mix. Corbyn's attitudes to the Middle East, and in particular to Israel, have for decades made him suspect among some of Britain's Jewish community.

He inherited a party which was not free of anti-Semitism. As Kieron Monks wrote in *Prospect* magazine, 'Activists, councillors and MPs have been exposed for offences that include praising Hitler, posting cartoons of hook-nosed Jews, and attacking Holocaust victims. Many cases have resulted in suspension or expulsion, and dozens more are going through the party's disciplinary process.' David Hirsh's book *Contemporary Left Anti-Semitism* is scathing about Corbyn's past. Corbyn, writes Hirsh, has met men who repeated blood libels against the Jews; he has appeared on Iran's government-owned television station, Press TV; he has said that 'once again the Israeli tail wags the US dog' and much, much more. Hirsh wonders 'how it is possible for a man with such a relationship to anti-Semitism to be elected twice to lead the Labour Party, and what it tells us about recent political and cultural developments in dominant currents of the contemporary left'.

He quotes Corbyn as saying, 'Our Jewish friends are no more responsible for the actions of Israel and the Netanyahu government than our Muslim friends are for those of various self-styled Islamic states or organisations.' Hirsh finds deeply offensive the apparent comparison of Israel with ISIS.

You can see his point, though it's obvious that's not what Corbyn meant. But then Hirsh writes, 'We cannot know if Corbyn and his team failed to predict that this form of words would be heard in this way – or if they decided to make this inflammatory analogy, conceivably as a nod to those who feel threatened by his general condemnation of anti-Semitism.'

Well, yes, actually, we can know. Unless we believe that Corbyn cynically exploits anti-Semitism for political ends, which is what Hirsh is implying, we can know. Hirsh knows it in his heart, too, because he never makes the charge explicit. That this appalling implication can appear in a book by a respected academic is an indication of how toxic the debate has become.

Some of Hirsh's reasons for feeling so strongly about Corbyn personally appear to have nothing to do with anti-Semitism. There are several pages about Corbyn's general political approach, and the place he occupies on the political spectrum. 'There is a rich and exciting fantasy,' Hirsh writes, 'that Corbyn can sweep to power with his new radicalism.' But 'if Labour cannot win with an Ed Miliband, and it has lost interest in winning with a Tony Blair, then perhaps it is ready to lose courageously and honestly with a Jeremy Corbyn'.

Now, this is a perfectly respectable political analysis. We don't happen to share it, but we know sincere people who do. In fact, it's identical to Tony Blair's own analysis of the situation. But it has nothing whatever to do with anti-Semitism.

For Hirsh, Labour must be prevented from ever forming another government until Corbyn ceases to be its leader. There is no way back for the party while it is led by Corbyn, 'with his Stalinist political biography, his commitment to the politics of Israel-demonisation, his decades-long association with anti-Semitic politics and terrorist movements, and his softness to any movement which positioned itself as anti-imperialist'.

This is not, however, the view of the Board of Deputies of British Jews. Its then president (still the outgoing president as we write) Jonathan Arkush thinks that precisely because of his past, Corbyn could be a potent force against left-wing anti-Semitism.

'It's no part of our wish to see Jeremy Corbyn removed as Labour Party leader, but rather our fervent hope is for him to be part of the solution,' Arkush told us. 'Our appeal to Jeremy Corbyn is to make this his issue.'

Hirsh believes Corbyn has crossed the line that separates legitimate criticism of Israel from anti-Semitism, and is beyond redemption. Arkush insists that he and his board do not accuse the Labour leader of anti-Semitism.

Or at least, he did. Arkush was very clear on this point when we interviewed him. But a few days later, we saw him quoted as saying that Corbyn believed anti-Semitic things. Had he been misquoted?

Arkush answered our question quickly and courteously – a trick that Corbyn's office could usefully learn. He wrote:

It is possible to have a view that is anti-Semitic (for example that Jews are too influential) without being an anti-Semite – someone who dislikes Jews because they are Jewish.

While this may sound rather hair-splitting it is a carefully thought out position within communal leadership circles first, because we consider it to be correct and second, because we would not accuse someone of being anti-Semitic lightly.

Corbyn is a classic example – I do not consider him to be an anti-Semite. However, if he holds the view that the Jewish people (uniquely) are not entitled to the fundamental human right in the UN Charter of self-determination, that is an anti-Semitic view. As I think I said to you, I think Corbyn has a blind spot to anti-Semitism and he may have no insight that denying Israel's legitimacy – if he does, as implied by his having held leading positions in the Palestine Solidarity Campaign (PSC) and Stop the War – that is an anti-Semitic view.

Jonathan Arkush is a lawyer by trade. It seems to us that there isn't really any difference between an anti-Semite and one who has anti-Semitic views. We don't think Arkush can have it both ways.

We sent Arkush's statement to Corbyn's office to get a comment on it. The comment, when it came, was from 'a Labour Party spokesman', and seemed to underline the fact that Corbyn and the Board of Deputies of British Jews have lost patience with each other:

> These are unfounded and outrageous personal attacks without any evidence to support them.
>
> Jeremy has been absolutely clear that he is a militant opponent of anti-Semitism and is committed to driving it out of our movement. Our party has deep roots in the Jewish community and is campaigning to increase support and confidence in Labour among Jewish people in the UK.
>
> Jonathan Arkush's attempt to conflate strong criticism of Israeli state policies with anti-Semitism is wrong and undermines the fight both against anti-Semitism and for justice for the Palestinians. It should be rejected outright.

Online discussion has been rancid and ugly, with wild and terrible accusations and counter-accusations. Some Labour people have been branded anti-Semites who most certainly are not. Those who criticise Corbyn – often thoughtfully – are sworn at and called 'vile'. As for those who attack him, here is a statement widely available on the internet: 'Jews are being hounded out of the Labour Party.'

A Jewish teacher and blogger with a large number of followers writes of Corbyn's 'fascist leanings'. In common with fascist ideology, the teacher claims, 'Mr. Corbyn is viscerally hostile to the western liberal-democratic political tradition, supporting instead those bent on its civil and violent subversion.'

This sort of rubbish, repeated in different forms all over the internet, comes straight out of the Donald Trump school of propaganda. If you repeat something often enough, it does not matter if it is the opposite of the truth: enough people will believe it to make a difference.

But the fears of the Jewish community are genuine and well grounded. Anti-Semitic persecution has returned to Europe. Look, for example, at Ukraine and Hungary. Western Europe has experienced a resurgence of anti-Semitic incidents – look at France. The need for Israel to be there as a haven for Jews is clear, and you can see why Jonathan Arkush insists that claiming Israel has no right to exist is an anti-Semitic statement.

That anti-Semitism is growing again in Britain is beyond question. The first half of 2016 saw an 11 per cent rise in anti-Semitic incidents reported to the Community Security Trust (CST), compared with the same period the previous year. Anti-Semitic incidents in London rose by 62 per cent in the first six months of 2016.

According to a Home Office select committee report, most anti-Semitic abuse and crime 'has historically been, and continues to be, committed by individuals associated with (or motivated by) far-right-wing parties and political activity'.

But the committee was disturbed that it had also penetrated the Labour Party. It reported, 'In April 2016 and the months that followed, Naz Shah MP, Ken Livingstone and a number of other members (reported numbers vary from eighteen to fifty) were suspended from the Labour Party amid accusations of anti-Semitism.' One of these people was Salim Mulla, a Labour councillor in Blackburn, who shared footage of a Palestinian boy being arrested, with this comment: 'Apartheid at its best. Zionist Jews are a disgrace to humanity.' More than half of Britain's Jews consider themselves Zionists, and the committee condemned the use of the word as a term of abuse.

Naz Shah issued a public apology after the publication of Facebook posts dating from before her election in 2015, in which she endorsed the notion of relocating Israel to the United States and drew comparisons between Israel and the Nazis. Ken Livingstone then gave a number of media interviews to provide a defence for Shah that she neither sought nor wanted. All we need say here is that, as Labour NEC member and Momentum founder Jon Lansman put it to us, 'Ken has a disturbing tendency to use Nazi analogies.'

In May 2018, Livingstone resigned from the Labour Party. Some believed that he went before he was pushed. This gave him the last word, during which he once again claimed that pre-war Zionists had worked with the Nazis, an analysis as cursory as it is deeply insulting.

Jeremy Corbyn set up an inquiry into anti-Semitism and other forms of racism perpetrated by members of the Labour Party. The inquiry was chaired by former Liberty director Shami Chakrabarti, while Professor David Feldman, director of the Pears Institute for the Study of Antisemitism at Birkbeck College, London, served as vice-chair. Feldman was roundly attacked by David Hirsh, among others, for agreeing to be a part of what Hirsh already believed was going to be a whitewash.

The report made recommendations for changes to the Labour Party's disciplinary processes, and concluded that the party was 'not overrun' by anti-Semitism, Islamophobia or other forms of racism, but that, 'as with wider society', there was evidence of 'minority hateful or ignorant attitudes and behaviours festering within a sometimes bitter incivility of discourse'.

The report was attacked as a whitewash, and Chakrabarti was pilloried for accepting a peerage from Corbyn soon afterwards. This seems to us to exemplify the toxic atmosphere that now surrounds this debate.

Shami Chakrabarti is one of the most high profile and re-spected Asians in Britain, rightly seen as a woman of courage and integrity. She was already a paid-up member of the great and the good. She did not need to tell grubby lies for Jeremy Corbyn in order to earn the right to call herself Lady Chakrabarti. The suggestion that she did so is both absurd and offensive.

'It's nonsense to see her report as a whitewash,' says Jon Lansman. 'We have come to think of racism as about power and wealth, but it can be against people who are not poor or powerless. Shami Chakrabarti got that – she is the daughter of a wealthy Hindu.'

At the launch of the Chakrabarti Report, something happened which we want to look at closely. A journalist from the *Daily Telegraph*, Kate McCann, questioned Corbyn about a 'Momentum member' handing out a leaflet calling for anti-Corbyn MPs to be deselected. This was a campaigner called Marc Wadsworth, who was present at the launch of the report and who broke in to say, 'I saw that the *Telegraph* handed a copy of a press release to Ruth Smeeth MP, so you can see who is working hand in hand.'

Ruth Smeeth expressed outrage and walked out, and ac-cording to some accounts she was in tears. She later said, 'It is beyond belief that someone could come to the launch of a report on anti-Semitism in the Labour Party and espouse such vile conspiracy theories about Jewish people, which were ironically highlighted as such in Ms Chakrabarti's report.'

Wadsworth's trade union, the National Union of Jour-nalists, said that the media had 'slanderously accused him of anti-Semitism'.

Labour's National Constitutional Committee (NCC) met to decide whether Wadsworth should be expelled, and about forty Labour MPs and peers accompanied Smeeth to the hearing, apparently to ensure she was able to be present to give evidence, though we are not aware of any physical threats made to her. She did have to get through a noisy picket, at which we are told some of the demonstrators were shouting 'Free Palestine', but going through noisy and hostile groups of demonstrators is the small change of life as a Labour MP, or even a Labour activist: both the authors of this book have done it many times.

The committee expelled Wadsworth for bringing the party into disrepute – not for anti-Semitism.

Subsequently at Labour Party meetings, the authors have heard more than once passionate denunciations of 'anti-Semites like Marc Wadsworth'. Even the normally judicious Jonathan Arkush used the phrase when we interviewed him. It has become generally accepted, as fact, that Marc Wadsworth is an anti-Semite.

Wadsworth may have behaved appallingly – in fact, we are rather inclined to think he did. Some of his online supporters may well be anti-Semitic, as Ruth Smeeth claims. Perhaps, as she also asserts, he knew she was Jewish, though he insists he did not, and we haven't seen the evidence for Smeeth's insistence that he was lying.

But did the words Wadsworth used justify labelling him an anti-Semite? Smeeth has so labelled him, and her claim has been repeated as fact over and over again. Wadsworth will now never be free of it.

We studied carefully the words quoted above, and could not see in what way they were anti-Semitic. The meaning of those words is clear: Wadsworth is accusing Smeeth of colluding with a right-wing newspaper to damage Labour's left-wing leadership. That is all he is accusing her of.

We asked Smeeth to comment. Her constituency communications manager, Glen Watson, got in touch with us and provided several examples of Mr Wadsworth's bad behaviour, which we do not dispute. But all Watson said to substantiate the charge of anti-Semitism was this: 'During this event Mr Wadsworth singled out Ruth, a Jewish MP, with a baseless accusation of working hand in hand with the right-wing media. The accusation of Jewish collusion with the media is a common anti-Semitic trope.'

This doctrine means that if anyone accuses an MP who happens to be Jewish of collaborating with the media, it's automatically anti-Semitism. This has to be dangerous, illiberal rubbish.

Clearly, Wadsworth behaved badly and Smeeth was upset by his behaviour; she also has experience of anti-Semitic online abuse. So in the heat of the moment, she described what he said as being anti-Semitic. In the cold light of the following day, she could have withdrawn the charge, her evidence for it being non-existent. But she failed to do this, and still refuses to do so. And the charge is now widely accepted as fact. This seems to us both an appalling injustice to Wadsworth, and a cheapening of the charge of anti-Semitism.

Jeremy Corbyn should have said something to correct this injustice, but he is in so weakened a position on this issue that he is not able to state the obvious. If Corbyn had done what Arkush had been hoping for, and made the issue his own, then whenever a charge of anti-Semitism was made unfairly, Corbyn could have called it out. He could now be making the running on anti-Semitism, robustly confronting it where it exists and refusing to be rushed or bullied when a charge is made unjustly. The relationship between Corbyn and Arkush would be a much more equal one – Corbyn could afford himself, from time to time, the luxury of telling Arkush he was wrong. Instead, Corbyn has been reduced to keeping his head down and hoping it will all blow over. It won't.

There are – much to the annoyance of the Board of Deputies

of British Jews – several groups of left-wing Jews which take a very different view from that of the board. These groups are quite small, but they represent a strand of Jewish thinking. One of them, Jewdas, differs from the others in that its members are religious and members of synagogues, and in the fact that it joined the board of deputies in calling for Ken Livingstone's expulsion from the Labour Party.

And it was this group – because it has members in his constituency – that invited the Labour leader to its Passover dinner in 2018. Corbyn accepted, much to the fury of the board of deputies.

'They satirise the Haggadah [the text read at Passover],' says Jonathan Arkush. 'Their loyal toast is "Fuck the Queen". They poke fun at Passover and satirise it. What is Jeremy Corbyn saying to the Jewish community in spending the evening with them?'

Jewdas accuses the board and the mainstream Jewish press of 'cynical manipulation by people whose express loyalty is to the Conservative Party and the right wing of the Labour Party'. It says, 'Critics of Israel were shunned by their friends and families. A narrow Conservative clique took over our major communal bodies, newspapers and schools.' Jewdas calls the anti-Semitism row 'a malicious ploy to remove the leader of the Opposition and put a stop to the possibility of a socialist government'.

It says of the Board of Deputies of British Jews:

> People could flirt with Nazis and threaten our communal life all they wanted, as long as they stood up for Israel ... As far as they were concerned, Corbyn was already beyond the pale before he started ... The evidence was already there in the fact that he championed the cause of the Palestinians.
>
> But they did find evidence. He has met with people who are anti-Semites. He used ill-advised language ... They reached

through every last bit of his history and uncovered what they could. Some of it was compelling. Some of it less so. All of it was treated as if it was a new edition of the Protocols of the Elders of Zion.

The Labour leadership will recover from this mess, but this fiasco may well leave scars that cannot be healed within the Jewish community.

The board of deputies' chief executive has written that Corbyn must 'shun' Jewdas and the other left-wing organisations such as Jewish Voice for Labour.

In this atmosphere, the first meeting between Corbyn and the board of deputies and Jewish Leadership Council in June 2018 was bound to be wary, mistrustful and suspicious.

CHAPTER TWENTY-ONE

LABOUR ANTI-SEMITISM
– VIRUS OR TORY RAMP?

The meeting between Corbyn and the Board of Deputies of British Jews was preceded and followed by media statements, as both sides tried to seize control of the media agenda. The board won this battle. The Labour leader's media operation is not what it was under Alastair Campbell.

Corbyn was flanked by Seumas Milne, Labour's new general secretary Jennie Formby, and Andrew Gwynn MP, shadow Minister without Portfolio. Jennie Formby said that Labour's processes had not previously been fit for purpose, but they would be soon. Labour was recruiting lawyers to make them so.

There's a strange subtext to this. Formby's election as general secretary of the Labour Party had greatly ruffled the feathers of some staffers in the party's headquarters. Many staffers had been deeply hostile to Corbyn, and now, with a general secretary in clear sympathy with the direction of the party under his leadership, some of them decided to abandon ship. As the departures gathered pace, other senior party staffers claimed that complaints about anti-Semitism that had been made to the party were left unattended and allowed to gather dust. More importantly, they were allowed to fester.

Corbyn said little at the meeting and seemed tired. Seumas

Milne did most of the talking, and became animated on the subject of Israel. He accused Israel of what he called 'ethnic cleansing' for removing Palestinians from their historic homeland. Jonathan Arkush countered with 750,000 Jews expelled from other Middle East countries in 1948. It was that sort of meeting.

His hosts wanted Corbyn to remove himself from three Facebook groups, and block some of his Twitter followers. Some things the board wanted, it got, but it didn't get a Labour Party ombudsman who would be responsible jointly to the party and the board. If Labour agreed to that, it would also have to agree to the same for a lot of other communities. And it would be the only political party to state publicly its inability to operate its own procedures – an impossible statement to make for a party bidding to run the country.

So is Labour stuffed with anti-Semitism? Or is it all a Tory ramp? Neither of these things is true.

It is true that Jewish representative organisations, including the board of deputies and the *Jewish Chronicle* newspaper, have proved unwilling to hold the right and the Conservatives to the same standards as those to which they quite properly seek to hold Labour and the left. They did not, for example, at any time during the five years of his leadership, make any attempt to defend Ed Miliband against anti-Semitic attacks. The *Daily Mail* article on Miliband's father merited not even a mild protest to the editor. The Board of Deputies of British Jews discussed it, apparently, and decided not to make one.

In May 2018, when a Conservative councillor tweeted that he was 'sweating like a Jew in an attic' he was suspended and the board of deputies immediately issued a statement congratulating the Conservative leadership on its decisive action. Labour's swift action – and it has taken swift action against anti-Semitism in some cases – does not get the same treatment.

Conservative Party links with anti-Semitic parties in eastern Europe have gone virtually unnoticed, and the board of deputies shows no appetite for holding the Tories to account for them.

In the European Parliament, the Conservatives deserted the Christian Democrat grouping with which they were once associated, to join the European Conservatives and Reformists Group, which includes hard-line anti-Semitic parties from eastern Europe. Boris Johnson congratulated Viktor Orbán and his party, Fidesz, on their election victory in Hungary, referring to them as his 'friends'. These 'friends' ran an election campaign widely criticised for its relentless anti-Semitic undertones.

As no less an authority than Deborah Lipstadt, the preeminent historian on Holocaust denial, told Jane Eisner, editor of the American Jewish paper *The Forward*, in 2016, 'It's been so convenient for people to beat up on the left, but you can't ignore what's coming from the right.'

On the other hand, it is not true that Jewish community organisations are stuffed with closet Tories wishing to do down Corbyn's Labour Party by fair means or foul. Jonathan Arkush was perfectly sincere when he told us: 'Our overriding concern as communal leaders must be to protect and defend our community and work for the good of the society in which we all live.'

Part of the reason why the main Jewish community organisations and its press tend to notice left-wing anti-Semitism more easily than they do right-wing anti-Semitism is probably because left-wing anti-Semitism is much more likely to be connected with Israel. Perhaps, too, it is because such organisations tend, by and large, to be run by people of a conservative frame of mind, more at home with Theresa May or Tony Blair than with Ed Miliband or Jeremy Corbyn.

The editor of the *Jewish Chronicle*, Stephen Pollard, holds strongly conservative views which he expresses trenchantly and stylishly in right-wing newspapers. Here he is in the *Daily Mail*, celebrating Labour's 2015 election defeat:

'Even the union barons' darling, doe-eyed Andy Burnham – who has spent the past five years trotting out left-wing platitudes about greedy capitalists and asserting his knee-jerk hostility to the private sector at every given opportunity – is now saying how big a fan he is of business.'

Perhaps this provides a little context for Pollard's description of Labour as 'a party of bigots and thugs'.

Dr David Hirsh, as we noted earlier, seems puzzled and distressed by Labour's progress leftwards since what he sees as its glory days under Tony Blair.

There's no plot. But there may be an instinct to believe the best of the right, and the worst of the left.

Perhaps – we have no means of knowing – Corbyn thinks that there is a plot. Perhaps he thinks that, no matter what he does or says, he is never going to get a fair deal. That might help to explain why he has handled the issue so very clumsily.

Corbyn could, as Arkush points out, have placed himself at the head of a great campaign against anti-Semitism. He could have taken the lead, and thereby avoided the impression that he was being pushed every step of the way. And it would have done no harm, psychologically, if every so often Corbyn had condemned anti-Semitism without adding the phrase 'and all other forms of racism'.

Without advisers such as Seumas Milne and Andrew Murray, perhaps he could have done this. But these two ideologues would likely have crushed any such idea, had Corbyn suggested it.

Much might have been different if Corbyn had kept his old friend Jon Lansman by his side. 'Jon Lansman gets it,' says Jonathan Arkush. Lansman, brought up as an orthodox Jew, is currently sporting a full beard because of the recent death of his father, obeying the Jewish tradition that the bereaved son does not shave for a year.

The bitter swirl of anti-Semitism claims was not simply whipped up by the Tories. Corbyn and the Labour leadership are guilty of very real failings. There have been some appalling and intolerant things posted on social media, some of them by members of the Labour Party, others not. Some in the media rushed to cloak Jeremy Corbyn in a racism that he has always found deeply repellent.

Perhaps the foghorn sounded louder partly because expectations were higher for Labour. Jewish socialists have played, and continue to play, a major role in the party's affairs. Labour's circular firing squad were perhaps so busy taking pops at each other that they allowed these desperately serious claims to fester.

Inactivity, a failure to get to grips, and the fact that the party suddenly had over half a million members, with many new to politics altogether, meant that it wasn't always clear who was out there and what they were all doing. People were also able to conceal their identities when they used increasingly unforgiving and vituperative social media sites. Clare Short told us, 'Some critics of Israel slip into anti-Semitic language – which is, of course, intolerable but some supporters of Israel are weaponising the accusation of anti-Semitism against critics of Israel and supporters of the Palestinians.'

Jonathan Arkush's term of office has now come to an end, and his successor, Marie Van der Zyl, seems set to take a harder and more irreconcilable line. She never misses a public opportunity to identify Corbyn's Labour Party as a danger to Jewish people, which we (and many Jewish people) consider to be deeply unfair.

Both sides are hooked on the question of Israel. Arkush says, 'The far left is full of bigotry about Israel. And the problem is that we find bigotry about Israel always morphs into anti-Semitism.'

But surely it's not anti-Semitic to criticise Israel? No, it isn't, concedes Arkush. But it becomes anti-Semitism, he argues, when Israel is demonised (for example claiming Israel is uniquely evil or responsible for all the ills in the world); or when it delegitimises Israel (arguing that Israel has no right to exist); or when it is a case of double standards and Israel is judged more harshly than any other country. The United Nations Human Rights Committee is especially guilty of this, Arkush claims.

This sounds reasonable, but it is often used to push back the boundaries of what can legitimately be said about Israel. The Board of Deputies of British Jews, having accepted that criticism of Israeli government actions is not anti-Semitic, seems then to want to claw back that ground. The arguments made by Arkush seem to be designed to allow the board to severely limit what you can say about Israel without being called an anti-Semite. Can you, for example, support a call to remove investment from Israel to mark disapproval of some of its actions?

If Corbyn ever laboured under the delusion that the problem would go away, by the summer of 2018 he must surely have been disillusioned. The definition of anti-Semitism, agreed in 2017 at a conference of the Berlin-based International Holocaust Remembrance Alliance (IHRA), is one that he was happy to accept – but Labour's new code of conduct on anti-Semitism does not replicate in full a list of examples of anti-Semitism published by the IHRA.

Corbyn is wary of being forced to expel people who make legitimate criticisms of Israel. The Board of Deputies of British Jews and some of Corbyn's backbenchers are concerned that criticisms of Israel can morph into anti-Semitism.

That's what it's about. It could be solved if there was any mutual respect or trust. But there isn't, and as we put this book to bed, former Labour minister Margaret Hodge chose to confront

Corbyn on this issue behind the Speaker's Chair in the House of Commons, calling him a racist and an anti-Semite.

Hodge and Corbyn have form, both having been involved in Labour politics in Islington – Hodge is a former leader of Islington council. They have been fighting each other for decades. In the early Blair years, the two publicly debated Blair's proposal to abandon Clause 4 of the party's constitution in Islington, and Hodge angrily accused the hostile audience of romanticising the idea of being in opposition, of having their heads in the sand and of being stupid. Of the hundred or so people present, only two voted with her.

Her charge of racism and anti-Semitism against Corbyn is untrue. If there was a single phrase over the course of his enduring political career that could justify such a charge, it would have been disinterred by now.

Hodge has deliberately manoeuvred Corbyn into a position where he is forced to take action against her. Her lawyers at Mishcon de Reya are already in bad-tempered correspondence with Labour HQ. John McDonnell, who can see a dark pit when you place it in front of him, wants the party to drop its action.

If it chooses not to, we will watch Hodge and Corbyn debating the finer points of what constitutes a legitimate criticism of Israel and what is deemed anti-Semitic. Hodge has constructed a megaphone through which they will do it, and she can keep it at top volume for as long as the proceedings take to rumble their way through Labour's disciplinary process. If she is determined that Labour under Corbyn can never succeed, she has chosen a very effective course of action.

Meanwhile, Dr David Hirsh has presented us with something he calls the 'Livingstone formulation'. He takes it from Ken Livingstone's words in 2006: 'For far too long the accusation of anti-Semitism has been used against anyone who is critical of the policies of the Israeli government, as I have been.' This, he says, is used to close down debate.

The point Hirsh is making here is that when you accuse someone of anti-Semitism, they can say, 'You're only saying that because I'm critical of Israel.' This then closes down the debate.

Hirsh has a point. There are occasions when the argument is used in exactly the way he describes, and he proves it by citing some examples. But here's the problem. Hirsh's development of the statement into a formula is itself used to close down debate. Sometimes, people do exactly what Livingstone describes: they hear a criticism of Israel, and they then close down debate by calling it anti-Semitic. Now Hirsh has provided a way in which that debate, too, can be closed down. If I criticise Israel too severely but insist that I am not anti-Semitic, you can simply say, 'Ah, the good old Livingstone formula again.'

As John Kampfner, chief executive of Index on Censorship, wrote in 2009,

> The school of thought that says Israel has nothing to reproach itself for, that Hamas is solely to blame and that anyone who thinks otherwise must be hostile to Israel is strong on the blogosphere. People are entitled to that view, but it should not lead to self-censorship by editors.

And editors are self-censoring. The debate makes everyone frightened of the issue. The weekly magazine *The Economist* noted at the end of May 2018 that the *New York Times* had tweeted, 'Dozens of Palestinians have died in protests as the US prepares to open its Jerusalem embassy.' Someone tweeted back with dark humour: 'From old age?' The Palestinians had, of course, been killed by Israeli soldiers. You can justify Israel's action if you like, but as *The Economist* says, the tweet from the *New York Times* was self-censored for fear of causing offence. '#havedied' quickly became a hashtag campaign. Even the liberal *Guardian* newspaper drew the line at a cartoon by Steve Bell that depicted Prime Minister Theresa May entertaining Israeli Prime Minister Benjamin Netanyahu, while an image of a young Palestinian medic, shot dead by an Israeli sniper, burned in the Downing Street fireplace.

The debate has become toxic. It's all abuse and bullying and point-scoring. It long ago ceased to concentrate on protection of British Jews on one side, and the creation of a better and more equal society in Britain on the other.

Whether Jewdas is right to say that all this will leave lasting scars in the Jewish community, we have no means of knowing. But it does look as though it could do lasting damage to our politics. Theresa May leads one of the least competent and most reactionary governments of our lifetime. She is obliged to do anything the Democratic Unionist Party requires of her. The damage this is doing is appalling.

It would be the most wrenching, horrible irony if the rebirth of Labour England were to falter because Labour was seen as racist.

CHAPTER TWENTY-TWO

FORWARD MARCH

In the final days of the 2017 general election campaign, Labour's headquarters in Southside, Victoria Street, appeared to be in near meltdown. Convinced that the party was set for an appalling drubbing, resources were rushed to seemingly safe seats that were under threat; target seats were forgotten about and highly marginal constituencies abandoned.

Even those around Corbyn began to grow despondent, some talking of a rout in the Midlands that might even sweep away Labour's deputy leader Tom Watson (which may have been wishful thinking on their part).

One typically downcast activist was the perennially upbeat and influential *Guardian* writer Owen Jones, who tried to buoy up others and who also pointed out that the party might still perform well in London. But if Labour was only going to do OK in London, what chance did it stand elsewhere?

One of Corbyn's final stops on the last night of the campaign was at a big, desolate roundabout in Harrow, north London. Perhaps 1,000 people were gathered, waiting to hear him speak as the battle bus edged towards the pavement and a slight figure – grey hair, grey beard, grey suit – gingerly stepped onto the pavement and took the microphone, with no apparent enthusiasm.

He said all the things he'd been saying for weeks, but he

couldn't disguise the exhaustion and hopelessness in his voice. Most of the people in the crowd wanted to hear that message. But very few of them went away thinking they would ever hear it again from the man who had delivered it.

When Corbyn had finished, he climbed slowly back on board the bus and the bus moved on. He had at least two more meetings to address before the polls closed. And even then, party leaders don't get a lot of sleep on election night. Winners don't mind. Adrenalin keeps them going. But if you're losing, only will power keeps you going. The iron will that had kept the 69-year-old Michael Foot going on election night in 1983 was going to have to be reborn in 68-year-old Jeremy Corbyn in 2018. It would be a few sleepless, torturing hours yet before he could get some blessed rest, following which he would write his resignation statement.

But Corbyn, we are told – and it's easy to believe this – suddenly woke up at exactly 10.00 p.m., when the BBC released its exit poll, which correctly predicted a hung parliament. No one has seen him look as tired since.

Just before 10.00 p.m., key staffers from the leader's office and that of John McDonnell claim that their electronic entry cards mysteriously stopped working at Labour's London HQ. Who had given this order? We still do not know. But fairly soon after the election, Corbyn began moves to get a new general secretary appointed.

Stephen Kinnock MP used his election count in Aberavon to declare that Jeremy Corbyn would likely have to consider his position. But this was before Kinnock's count had been completed and he discovered that his majority had increased. His wife, former Danish Prime Minister Helle Thorning Schmidt, had been caught on camera berating him before he went on air: 'What exactly are you going to say? Have you thought about what you are going to say?' She sensed that her husband was about to stride straight into a minefield. Schmidt, the consummate professional, knew something about hostages to fortune.

Labour didn't win the general election, but neither did it collapse as virtually every commentator had confidently predicted that it would.

In the cold light of day, and now with normal service restored to electronic entry cards, it soon became apparent that there had been an extraordinary surge of support, particularly among young voters. That Labour had captured constituencies such as Kensington & Chelsea was nothing short of extraordinary, as was the storming of Canterbury and the near toppling of the Home Secretary, Amber Rudd, in her Hastings & Rye constituency. In Scotland, Labour staged a partial recovery and the much-feared meltdown in the Midlands never happened.

However, the party did not do well in some of the former Midlands mining areas that had supported Brexit – and also the breakaway Union of Democratic Mineworkers during the 1984–85 strike. Labour's vote once again declined in Dennis Skinner's Bolsover constituency and the party lost North East Derbyshire altogether. Older voters in traditional blue-collar towns had proved more impervious to the strange rebirth of Labour. And four London constituencies with big Jewish populations – the so-called bagel belt – resisted Labour's sweep of the capital.

The UKIP vote had collapsed, and with it the fear that much of that vote would go to the Tories. Many UKIP voters had returned to Labour – but clearly not enough of them. Reaching out to what are often described as traditional, older working-class voters would have to be one of the key tasks ahead. For years New Labour's panjandrums had discounted those who didn't vote. Corbyn's Labour Party knew that if non-voters became voters either again or for the first time, astonishing things could happen.

The election result had proved that a new-look Labour Party, one which was serious about making Britain a more equal place, could actually encourage many people who had given up on voting to come out and do so. These were the people who Peter Mandelson had once said 'have nowhere else to go', but who had gone somewhere else – away altogether. Now many of them had come to the conclusion that the Labour Party was seriously back on their side.

Lord Mandelson managed to take a day off from plotting Corbyn's downfall to admit that he had underestimated him. But he resumed his normal malevolent service shortly after-wards. And while much of the media focus continued to be on Corbyn's temporarily silenced backbench critics, a new phalanx of seriously minded Labour MPs, often the victors in seats the party thought it hadn't had a hope of winning, such as Crewe or Brighton Kemptown, took their seats.

So Labour England had not only begun to put down new roots, in the shape of a mass membership, it had thrown out some pretty substantial growth on top as well.

The party's radical manifesto certainly played its part. In fact it played its part twice. The deliberate leaking of the manifesto, which was done to cause damage to the Labour campaign, ac-tually had the opposite effect. When the manifesto was officially launched, the media was obliged to cover it all over again.

Election manifestos have become increasingly incidental and marginalised in recent years, but Labour's seemingly retro man-ifesto caught the zeitgeist. Corbyn and his closest political allies may have come from the party's hard left, but the manifesto comprised the sort of policies that would have been familiar in intent if not detail to Harold Wilson or Tony Crosland.

Once again, social media was to play a powerful role with voters, with Labour's promises to abolish university tuition fees and build new council homes proving very popular. Peter Stefanovic points to some of the hugely popular and often funny memes that did the rounds, gathering hundreds of thousands of views. These were put together on an ad hoc basis by volunteers and supporters.

The influence of Britain's newspapers was waning. Young people were getting their news from a variety of sources. So some newspapers became even more hysterical in their multiple denunciations, which only made people even more determined to go to the polls and do the opposite of what the newspapers were instructing them to do. Following the election Corbyn pointedly thanked the editor of the *Daily Mail*, Paul Dacre, for a pre-election issue that had devoted a dozen or so pages to attacking him – and suggested that Dacre should double the number of pages next time. Oh for a picture of Paul Dacre chewing wasps!

And yet Labour's strange rebirth, while happening in an organic, often disorganised way around the Labour Party, was not happening in quite the same way around that other essential component, the trade unions. Weakened immeasurably by the multiple assaults of Thatcherism and barely given time to breathe freely again under Blairism, some of the big general unions were still failing to recruit enough new members to stem the losses of older members, although a few such as the GMB were achieving some success in organising and representing new members in the gig economy.

Some of the small, single-industry unions, such as the rail union RMT, were doing a whole lot better, but this was in an industry that had remained unionised.

The big unions were also still trying to work out how or whether to embrace the host of small, independent unions that had risen up in the gig economy. Multiple Tory attacks on collective bargaining rights, abilities to organise and even measure that prevented unions from balloting its members by email, all had had a deep and profound effect. It remains the case to this day that it is comparatively easier for unions to organise and function in some American states than it is in Britain. It speaks volumes that one of President Donald Trump's earliest meetings on assuming office was with union leaders, albeit specially selected leaders. Unite leader Len McCluskey has never formally met with Prime Minister David Cameron and he is still yet to meet Theresa May.

Something clearly wasn't always working.

It had something to do with the great wave of trade union mergers that had taken place in the 1980s. This had left far fewer small craft unions, and a very few big general unions that were not always nimble enough to respond to what was happening in the workplace. Those few small craft unions that survived – the Fire Brigades Union (FBU), the train drivers' union, ASLEF, the National Union of Journalists and a few others – are today adjusting better to new conditions than their bigger rivals, because they are closer to the trades they represent.

The unions had played a huge role in providing much of the organisational support for the rebirth of the Labour Party, but somehow risked overlooking their own requirements.

And yet all of this was happening at a time when unions were desperately needed. Wages were stagnant and in some places decreasing. The new world of work was often temporary, or home based, or required great mobility and dexterity.

It was a difficult environment in which to organise. Even the *Daily Mail* or *Daily Telegraph* would have been hard put to find many readers prepared to blame union bosses for the fact that Britain was for the most part a low-paid, low-skill economy; one where workers worked long hours, with old machinery, for companies that often failed to invest in new equipment or their workforces. What was left of the welfare system was for the most part based around subsidising astonishingly low wages. Rodney Bickerstaffe's fear that the minimum wage could one day become the maximum wage appeared to be coming true. As a consequence, the British economy was still marked by poorer rates of productivity than most of its competitors, a still shrinking manufacturing base and a dependence on services and financial services in particular. Nothing had been learned from the great Anglo-American banking crash, not a single banker had faced charges, let alone imprisonment. Britain had largely become a rentier economy. Its public services were pared to the bone. In the aftermath of the appalling and completely avoidable Grenfell Tower fire in 2017, it became apparent that the fire services were simply not fully equipped to tackle such blazes. Had there been a similar fire outside of London, the lack of resources would have made for even worse scenarios. The austerity policies put in place by David Cameron and his Chancellor George Osborne gutted the fire service, as it did many others. Between 2010 and 2018, 12,000 firefighters lost their jobs.

Decades of laissez-faire economic policies had encouraged a stripping out of much of the best of the skilled, productive base, and its takeover by larger, usually foreign, corporations. The country's public assets had been largely looted and sold off. Contracts for running trains in Britain's privatised railway industries often went to state-owned operators from countries like France and Germany, with China waiting in the wings to build the new trains for the high-speed HS2 network.

The vultures atop this steaming heap of ordure, the rotting remains of what used to be a fairly efficient and well-run mixed economy, kept stuffing their pockets, buying new Gulfstream aircraft and digging out mega-million-pound basements in west London. These people would have been unsurprised at being joined at the trough by some of the nomenklatura from the New Labour years, including the now immensely rich Tony Blair and his former 'Mini-Me', Peter Mandelson. Britain was by far the most unequal country in Europe, and the Blair–Brown years had done little to alleviate this shocking indictment of Britain's ruling classes. This was a country of food banks, overcrowded hospitals, collapsed mental health services and prisons running to rot and potential riot. Forty years of neoliberalism had more or less destroyed forty years of post-war civilised progress towards a healthier, happier and more equal country.

In this festering environment, now presided over by a teetering Tory administration apparently determined to deliver Brexit while not believing in it, sat a massively grown Labour Party. It had got so far, but what next?

Britain today has more or less the same political parties as it did in the 1920s. A number have come and gone, of course – the Independent Labour Party, the Commonwealth Party, the SDP and more recently UKIP (although we think it may soon be back). For a while, it looked as though support was slipping away from the two major parties, yet recent elections have shown a return to a two-party system.

Much of this may well be due to Britain's traditional first-past-the-post system for electing MPs to Westminster. Had there been proportional representation, would so much youthful support have flocked towards Labour? Would it have done so if there had been a credible new Green/Red party? (It does not take away from the case for a proportional representation that is fair and which maintains a link between the MP and his or her constituency.)

We do not know. What we do know is that it was Labour's good fortune that it became the beneficiary of this new lifeblood. This was hardly the curse that Labour's Blairite right wing believed it to be. In fact it is quite the reverse and something to be hugely celebrated.

Corbyn himself seems transformed. Walking the streets with him, you feel he is simply an average, friendly human being, connecting easily and happily with others. But around him, his entourage frets and worries and tries to make sure no one gets to know him. The office's strategy is unchanged.

In June 2018, Corbyn went to Brighton to address two trade union conferences taking place in the town at the time, those of the GMB and the FBU.

He had five or six 'minders' in tow, the chief of whom seemed to be David Prescott, son of the former deputy Prime Minister John Prescott. Prescott came from a six-year stint with a big communications consultancy to be Corbyn's strategic communications consultant. He told the trade magazine *PR Week*, 'I want to see a much sharper operation in Corbyn's office and an increased level of professionalism in being a leader inside and outside the Commons.' Even Prescott's famous father would have struggled to construct a sentence so devoid of meaning.

Prescott strode about with a mobile phone more or less permanently in use, and did not speak to any of the union people present, except to bark at one of them when he wanted something. He also frequently barked instructions to Corbyn, to stand in a specific place or appear to be talking to a particular person, and Corbyn would obey, though it was perfectly obvious that he could not see the point of the instruction, any more than anyone else could. He even made sardonic comments about it to the person standing nearest to him, who happened to be one of the authors of this book, Francis Beckett.

The FBU had arranged that after Corbyn spoke at the conference, he would record a television interview with one of their officials to be uploaded to YouTube. The union had told journalists covering the conference they could be present in the room during the recording. The questions had been agreed with Corbyn's office in advance, and covered the same ground as his speech. Nonetheless, Prescott bustled into the room and rudely evicted the journalists, saying this was a 'private interview'.

Francis Beckett took the opportunity to ask Corbyn about our six-month-old request for an interview for this book. 'You're working with Mark on it?' Corbyn responded. He was clearly surprised that he had been told nothing about an interview request from two left-wing writers he knows fairly well.

He liked the book's title a great deal. 'Of course I'll talk to you and Mark,' he said. Unfortunately, Prescott caught him at it, and brusquely hustled him away to stand somewhere else for the cameras, though there were no cameras present at the time. Despite several more desultory conversations with Corbyn's office, our interview with him never took place. Just as Charles Clarke and Peter Mandelson did with Neil Kinnock, some of Corbyn's people have taken someone who possesses a natural talent for connecting with people and stopped him from doing it.

We, like everyone else, have no idea what will happen next. Brexit has intruded as the overarching issue, crowding out almost everything else. It has paralysed government and prevented the opposition focusing on the changes to our society that it really cares about.

Corbyn, McDonnell and the Labour leadership have tried to negotiate their way through a minefield. Although Labour Party members on the whole voted for Remain, at least a third of Labour voters voted to leave, especially in the most deprived parts of the country. Two-thirds of Labour MPs represent Leave constituencies. These voters are reminded frequently by Remainers that they made a terrible mistake, for the most part because they didn't really understand what they were doing, and that they will suffer the most from Brexit.

It is entirely possible that this prediction will come true, but the logic of telling voters they are a bit dim and got it wrong is to urge them now to get it right by having a second referendum. This idea is not going down well in parts of the Midlands, the north and Wales. People are suspicious of the sudden concern being shown on their behalf by political leaders who either took their votes for granted (New Labour) or dumped on them from a great height, repeatedly (the Tories and the Tories aided by Nick Clegg's Liberal Democrats). Brexit is a serious dilemma for Corbyn, as it would be for any Labour leader.

Barely a year since Labour's revival was confirmed at the general election, a perennial leadership hopeful, Chuka Umunna, is preening his feathers in preparation for launching a breakaway party.

He is amassing a personal war chest. The magazine *Total Politics* reported that last year Umunna was given £25,000 by Victor Blank, the former chairman of Lloyds TSB, and £15,000 by property tycoon Sir David Garrard, both previously Labour Party donors; Umunna also took £5,000 from Paul Myners, the former chairman of Marks & Spencer and Guardian Media Group who was City minister during Gordon Brown's premiership.

If it happens, Umunna's new entity will probably gain a vast amount of media coverage for an equal amount of hot air from Chuka and friends. It will also do enough damage to rob some Labour MPs of their seats and to make it much more difficult for Labour to win a general election.

And then there is the former Prime Minister, still feted by the media, yet largely derided by the voters. Tony Blair never loses an opportunity to attack the new direction Labour is heading in. By contrast, Gordon Brown, despite some of his obvious misgivings, is helping the party in Scotland and in England, behind the scenes. He has been advising the new Scottish Labour leadership and has offered policy advice to Labour's shadow International Development minister, Kate Osamor.

Labour's burgeoning grassroots are demanding and getting the ability to make policy again. Political debate, once discouraged at a local level, is happening again. The top-down model favoured by New Labour is being replaced by a bottom-up democracy.

For the most part, the grassroots and the leadership are marching in step, although on some issues, Brexit in particular, the demands from below may become increasingly uncomfortable for the party leadership. On others such as Trident, the membership is much more in step with the leadership than with the parliamentary party.

There is less time now for seeking consensus between the two main parties; indeed, the divide between them grows ever deeper, mirroring what is happening across the Atlantic. There is no doubt, for instance, that a Corbyn-led Labour government would restore many of the powers taken away from trade unions, and would take some key public services back into public control. It seems doubtful that a Chancellor McDonnell would continue to allow the Bank of England the power to set interest rates without taking into consideration a raft of other economic and social determinants.

A Labour government would inherit public services that have been cut to the bone and which in some areas now barely function. Expectations will be very high, since it will have been the votes of the dispossessed and angry that will have put the party into power. This could be happening during a period of massive economic difficulty in the post-Brexit era.

The closest comparison could be with New Zealand, whose

mainly agricultural economy had been largely geared to export-
ing to Britain – until the latter joined the common market in
1973. Overnight, traditional ties of trade were completely disrupted as preferential trade deals were ripped up. New Zealand,
a small country, was left to stand alone and completely refashion
its economy, looking towards east Asia rather than to Britain.

Britain is, of course, a rather different proposition, but the
massive disruption and change likely to be experienced in a new
post-Brexit world is going to present a very special challenge
to an incoming Labour government. Tony Blair will remain
the only new Labour Prime Minister ever to inherit a strong
economy.

Presenting a new, positive progressive of a future European
family of nations – a real federal model, where power is redistributed to Parliaments and people – that Britain could happily
sign up to would restore the confidence of many left-inclined
voters who have been deeply perturbed by the circumstances of
Britain's departure from the EU.

Tariq Ali recently recalled in the *London Review of Books* a
meeting in the early 1970s of supporters of the radical and revolutionary *Black Dwarf* magazine. During the meeting, a young,
upper-middle-class convert to the cause recounted in hushed
tones what she had heard at a lunch she attended, whose other
guests included the Duke of Edinburgh, the Queen and the
former Conservative Prime Minister Harold Macmillan. One
vexed topic, she told Tariq and his revolutionary friends, had
been about the actions of Arthur Scargill and the Yorkshire
miners at Saltley Gate. Prince Philip, unsurprisingly, had called
for the toughest measures possible to be deployed, but somewhat
surprisingly the Queen had also weighed in heavily, attacking
Scargill and the miners for 'holding the country to ransom'.

It was Macmillan who had said that neither the Queen nor

Philip should worry too much, as the pendulum could swing the other way and quite quickly. He was right – by 1979, Margaret Thatcher was in Downing Street.

She had been carried there, not so much as a result of the industrial unrest that marked that period, but because of far deeper and broader global disruption – caused primarily by the OPEC oil embargo that followed the Yom Kippur War and the price hikes that followed in its wake which caused a massive spike in inflation. The unions in Britain – and in particular the powerful NUM – were reacting to the effect that inflation was having on the pockets of their members, although the Tories and much of the press successfully turned the story around to blame the unions.

The point is that global economic and political instability is likely to have a profound effect on the British body politic. What seems permanent at the moment could easily be swept away in a remarkably short period.

In America and much of the rest of Europe, populist, nationalist parties are on the rise. In some European countries they are even in government. Right across Europe, parties that once described themselves as being on the left are in sharp retreat. This is not the case in Britain. Brexit may have marked something of a high-water mark. Certainly, UKIP has been in sharp retreat ever since a majority of British voters decided to give the political establishment the biggest kicking it had had in living memory. But complacency is a dangerous drug. Social media has given a massive platform to extremism of all kinds. All kinds of bigotry are on vitriolic display, as a variety of damaged individuals suddenly discover that there are others out there like them. Fads grow and multiply. The opportunity for a charismatic and fascist movement grows ever stronger.

We have seen how Labour went in the 1970s from being an

essentially grassroots movement, rooted more in Methodism than Marxism, to being a reinvented New Labour, top-down, command-and-control political vehicle with a membership that virtually vanished. Today, a more recognisable Labour Party has re-emerged.

It is something that neither of us had thought would ever be possible a few years ago. It has the potential to create a new Labour England. But the rebirth has, on occasion, been very painful. All of the multifarious efforts of its enemies, both inside and out, to ensure that it was either stillborn or strangled at birth have so far failed dismally.

The people are different, too. Labour's newest MPs, so far largely unnoticed by the media, contain some remarkable figures very much in a new mould. Mike Amesbury is a former UNISON official being tipped for early promotion. There is Dan Carden, the young Liverpool Walton MP – he previously worked for Len McCluskey and his father was a prominent dockers' leader in the city – who has recently been promoted to shadow spokesman on International Development. Then there is single mum and former nurse Laura Smith, who scraped in with a forty-vote majority in Crewe, and Laura Pidcock, a feisty platform performer who is currently shadow Minister for Labour. Other MPs to watch include the new Birmingham Edgbaston MP and shadow International Development minister Preet Gill; Paul Sweeney, a former army reservist with an extensive background in the Scottish engineering and shipbuilding industries; the new MP for Leigh and parliamentary private secretary to Angela Rayner, Jo Platt; and the nimble Lloyd Russell-Moyle (who has a striking resemblance to a young Jeremy Corbyn and who represents Brighton Kemptown).

The strange rebirth of Labour has changed the political discourse and it is changing attitudes and policies.

This is a big movement again and one that is by right and necessity a broad church. It will need to find new ways of accommodating a whole range of views and encouraging them. A thousand flowers must begin to bloom if Labour is to catch the zeitgeist in time for the next general election. That will not happen if there is near-permanent trench war, or if members and supporters are intolerant of others.

Nor will it happen if the Labour MPs who may effectively have deprived Labour of victory in the last general election continue to snipe at every opportunity or try and set up a new party with the support of many of Labour's opponents.

Dark forces will once again be lined up in order to try to frustrate and prevent a Labour government from being elected, and, if elected, from implementing its policies. Motivation is not a complex beast. Many of the most powerful and wealthy in the land are absolutely terrified of a Corbyn-led Labour government, because they believe – quite rightly – that they will have to pay higher taxes.

We got a rare glimpse of what is going on at the 2018 Westminster correspondents' annual dinner. There was a really creepy moment when the devil's pact between the Conservative government and the media was suddenly laid bare for all in the room to see. Though the room was full of journalists, no one has ever reported it.

After the lobby chair and the Prime Minister finished their witty, light-hearted speeches, the serious business of the evening was conducted by the political editor of *The Sun*, Tom Newton-Dunn.

He thanked the Prime Minister for 'upholding press freedom', which was code for saying that she had just stifled Leveson Two, the second stage of the Leveson Inquiry into the media. Newton-Dunn's employer Rupert Murdoch had vigorously urged the government to do just that. There had been quite enough media wrongdoing uncovered by the first inquiry. Murdoch wanted very much to avoid a second one.

Newton-Dunn then promised Theresa May the Murdoch empire's support for 'the difficult decisions you have to make in the next six months'. She sat in front of him and simpered.

The terms of trade were disgustingly clear. In return for stifling the second Leveson Inquiry, the newspaper proprietors are going to bolster May's tottering government for a few more months at least.

The grubby little deal inspired former TUC official Bert Clough to begin to compose a poem, with apologies to John Betjeman:

> Mr Tom Newton-Dunn, Mr Tom Newton-Dunn,
> Burnished and tarnished by Murdoch's dark Sun…

The more enlightened sections of the establishment are probably aware that the grotesque levels of inequality and poverty, personified most visibly in the mushrooming food banks, are not only intolerable, but risk spilling over into increased social disorder and surging crime. The social fabric of the country may not have been under such strain since the 1920s and 1930s. Public services in many areas are either at breaking point or are in the process of breaking up after years of austerity and the starvation of the public purse through gross tax avoidance by many of the best-known company names and years of cuts.

Members and supporters are any organisation's lifeblood. Before Labour became a mass party more than half a million strong it was on life support. It is now alive, enthusiastic, determined to make Britain a decent, more equal place, which cares for its people from cradle to grave.

These activists are not just the people who will help elect a Labour government, they are also the people who will create a new and different Labour England. The nation has changed and now votes in fundamentally different ways, and the class analysis upon which the Attlee settlement was built no longer applies, or at least no longer applies in the same way.

That was suddenly very clear in the 2018 local elections. At first glance, the results seem to indicate little major change – a slight shift to Labour from the general election, but nothing spectacular. However, if you study them closely, an odd and entirely new pattern emerges. Labour is losing votes in certain white working-class neighbourhoods – but making spectacular gains in some of the most affluent areas, which remained Tory strongholds even during the Blair years.

The investigative journalist David Hencke, analysing the results, reported that in Tory Westminster, Labour did amazingly well, gaining four new council seats and far more votes than it has had in living memory. It even, for the first time, gained a seat in the ward containing the superrich areas of Mayfair, Soho and Fitzrovia.

Hencke writes, 'Oxford Circus, Park Lane, Bond Street, Grosvenor Square, the Dorchester hotel, Savile Row, Regent Street and the editorial offices of *Private Eye* are now represented by a Labour councillor. Since the ward was created in 1978 Labour has never been in sniffing distance.' We only want to point out, with a discreet cough, that the ward also includes the currently shuttered Gay Hussar, in which this book was born.

In Harrow, north London, Labour increased its majority to seven over the Tories, and took affluent Harrow on the Hill, including Harrow School, which boasts Winston Churchill among its alumni. Outside London, Labour did well in the affluent seaside town of Worthing, of all places. Labour managed to win a seat in a by-election in the centre of the town in 2017 – the first to be won in the area since Harold Wilson's second general election victory in 1966. In 2018, Labour won another four council seats and came close to winning in a number of others.

Yet in the traditionally Labour town of Nuneaton, Labour lost eight seats – some by big margins. Nuneaton, writes David Hencke, 'is 88.9 per cent white British with a large proportion of pensioners. Immigration hardly exists – the biggest group are Poles – but it had strong support for UKIP, which has transferred to the Tories'.

Local Labour activist Dr Malcolm Clarke tells us that in the Manchester mayoral election,

> Andy Burnham's spectacular result on a day when Labour didn't do well elsewhere didn't get the analysis it deserved. To win in all except six of the near 300 wards across Greater Manchester and in all of the boroughs, by a margin of forty percentage points – including the Tory flagship of Trafford, where his opponent was leader of the council – was quite extraordinary.

Burnham won 63 per cent of the vote in an eight-candidate election, with the Tory candidate and leader of Trafford Council, Sean Anstee, trailing in second with just 23 per cent. Burnham even managed to win 56 per cent of the vote in Trafford, Anstee's home territory. There are 287 wards in Greater Manchester. Labour won 281 of them with the Tories winning the other six.

Labour is gaining votes in areas that Tony Blair could never have even dreamed of winning, but losing votes in traditional English working-class areas. The class nature of Labour England is crumbling. The new Labour England is already shaping up to look very different from the old.

AFTERWORD

The Labour England of the future isn't waiting for a Labour government to come along and create it. It's already growing, in places where governments can't reach.

The job of a Labour government will be to encourage it to grow; not to channel it and canalise it and corral it, but to create the conditions where it can grow into whatever shape it will. It will grow stronger, as the old Labour England grew stronger, under a government that welcomes it, instead of a government that fears and loathes it.

The new Labour England will be fundamentally different from the old one, the Labour England we described in the introduction – the Labour England that Clem Attlee knew and loved and helped to enable, that Margaret Thatcher knew and hated and tried to destroy, and for which Tony Blair felt a mixture of fear and patrician contempt; a Labour England that flourished from Attlee's time to Thatcher's, and one that Jeremy Corbyn and the authors of this book grew up in.

The next Labour government will not shape it. It will be enough that it enables a new Labour England to evolve. Labour England's near-death experience gives it a chance to get rid of the things that did not work well before. And there were many of them.

Perhaps we were too tied to a political ideology, too prone to debate how many angels could sit upon a socialist pinhead. The bitter ideological disputes of the '70s and '80s have bequeathed us the present set of Labour MPs, so bitterly divided that one feels that some of them would rather never see a left-wing government again than envision one led by a sect that is not their own.

This has not just happened. It is, as we've tried to show in this book, the product of years of sectarian politics, and few people in the Labour Party or the trade unions are free of blame. From Tony Blair to Tony Benn, they have all stridently asserted that they nurtured the only correct flame of faith.

Perhaps our trade unions developed a rigid outlook that inhibited their effectiveness and made them easy prey for Thatcherism. Certainly they developed into huge organisations with their own internal dynamic, and they may have begun to take themselves too seriously as political players. They became institutions, with their own set ways of doing things, top-heavy and extremely vulnerable to a hostile government.

Now, with the creative encouragement of the first woman to lead the TUC, Frances O'Grady, they are starting to develop ways of dealing with the new world of work – but there are decades of assumptions to be jettisoned along the way.

As the Labour left invented litmus tests for the purity of belief, and scorned those who failed to pass them, the right watched, wondered – and learned. Now the right are setting the same tests for the left.

Perhaps, too, Labour England really was, as its enemies always claimed, inclined to imagine that one size fitted all.

The new Labour England will be a community, not a collection of warring factions and interests and ethnic groups. It will value leisure, and it will despise deference. In the 1980s, foolish commentators spoke of the 'death of deference' but the balance of power between employer and employee was shifting fast in favour of the employer, and that brought deference with it; there is nothing that makes a person so deferential as fear of unemployment. This is a far more deferential society than the one we had in the '70s. It is also one that crushes creativity, artistic licence, confidence and the desire to do things differently.

It will want to move, however gradually, towards reducing the gap between the very rich and the very poor, a gap which in Britain, for the past four decades, has been steadily widening.

Education will be central to the new Labour England. The truly shocking idea that your life chances should depend on how good an education your parents can afford to give you will be banished – this time for good. The equally shocking idea that a child is mainly educated to be useful to his or her future employer must also be consigned to the scrapheap.

Labour England will have schools for all – not fee-charging schools for our future corporate bosses, grammar schools and well-funded academies for future middle managers, and utilitarian concrete jungles for the proletariat.

And there will be second-chance education – the chance to study later in life, especially if, for any reason, you were not afforded the opportunity to learn early in life.

Most of all, a new Labour England will loathe food banks and all other forms of charitable assistance to the poor. Charity is not part of the solution, but part of the problem. In a book called *The Social Worker*, published in 1920, a quarter of a century before its author became Prime Minister, Clement Attlee wrote, 'A right established by law, such as that to an old age pension, is better than an allowance made by a rich man to a poor one, dependent on his view of the recipient's character, and terminable at his caprice.' He recalled the charitable clergyman he had met, who ensured that the poor in workhouses were given breakfast – but that the porridge should always be slightly burned, to avoid giving the poor an incentive to come to the workhouse for their food.

The trouble with charity, Attlee wrote, 'is that it tends to make the charitable think that he has done his duty by giving away some trifling sum, his conscience is put to sleep and he takes no trouble to consider the social problem any further'.

Attlee quoted Robert Louis Stevenson, 'Gratitude without familiarity … is a thing so near to hatred that I do not care to split the difference.' Charity 'is always apt to be accompanied by a certain complacency and condescension on the part of the ben-efactor; and by an expectation of gratitude from the recipient, which cuts at the root of all true friendliness'. The rich, Steven-son had written, should instead 'subscribe to pay the taxes. These were the true charity, impartial and impersonal, cumbering none with obligation, helping all.'

Attlee described the alternatives with his characteristic terseness:

> In a civilised community, there will be some persons who will be unable at some period of their lives to look after themselves. The question of what is to happen to them may be solved in three ways. One, neglect them. Two, leave them to the goodwill of others. Three, care for them as of right by the organised commu-nity. I advocate number three.

Today this is far more urgent and obvious than it was in 1920, yet almost no one questions charity, which is simply assumed to be a universal good. It has even, in recent years, awarded itself the pompous and self-aggrandising title of 'the voluntary sector'. There are two sectors of the mixed economy: the public sector and the private sector. Status-hungry charities may like to think that they form a third sector, but they do not. You might as well talk of the trainspotters' sector.

Charities have been so successful that huge sums of public money, raised by taxation, instead of being spent by people we elect, are now syphoned off into grossly inflated 'charities', which bid for it just like a commercial organisation, often bidding against each other, spending public money to get more public money. They have become part of the privatisation racket.

A high street full of charity shops is an unmistakable sign of a community in near-terminal decline. And these shops are not only signalling decline, they are helping cause it too. Well-meaning volunteers replace the people who used to earn a living working in those premises. By agreeing to work for free, the volunteers are unintentionally swelling the ranks of the unemployed, and the higher the unemployment locally, the faster traditional shops will shut, replaced by charity shops in a vicious cycle.

Those in the community who can still afford to buy new clothes are forced to go to out-of-town shopping centres, which are rapidly replacing high street stores, thus further impoverishing communities. When they do go to the high street it is with bags of old clothes, which they give to the charity shops. The charity shops then sell the clothes to the poor and unemployed, who cannot afford to travel to out-of-town shopping centres. And a proportion of the money the poor spend buying these items in charity shops will be fed back to other poor people elsewhere in the country, unless it goes to alleviate poverty elsewhere in the world, or helps to find a cure for cancer, or whatever else.

The state, ultimately responsible to the people for what it does with their money, could do a better job of deciding priorities than the charities who often decide them now. The electorate may not be perfect, but it's a better arbiter of social priorities than the market.

Being able to give money is power, for it enables you to decide who should benefit and who should not. That is why the rich and powerful are keen to advocate charity, but less keen to pay their taxes. They are more inclined to be generous than to grant social justice. As long ago as 1932, the notion of charity was already under fire; American theology professor Reinhold Niebuhr wrote in his book *Moral Man and Immoral Society* that a powerful person's donation to charity was a display of his power as well as an expression of his pity. Niebuhr added, 'His generous impulse freezes within him if his power is challenged or his generosities are accepted without suitable humility.'

Charity absorbs the efforts and energies of well-intentioned people, who might otherwise pressurise governments to bring about needed change. And governments might be more likely to focus on dealing with poverty if they weren't being helped by charities.

Large-scale philanthropic activity changes the balance of funding from the public to the private sector, thereby exposing those most in need to the vicissitudes of the market. Charitable giving can even worsen social inequalities, for charitable tax breaks reduce the revenue that the state has available for social projects. And this is especially true in Britain, where our charity laws are in such a mess that Eton College, which educates the sons of the very rich, is a registered charity and is permitted the same tax breaks as any other charity.

Wealthy donors are not shy of using their power. Religious donors have been known to withdraw their money from a charity which gives out free condoms. The late Sir Roy Shaw, former director general of the Arts Council, pointed out that charitable funding of the arts was a means by which companies could censor political plays of which they disapproved. In his 1993 book, *The Spread of Sponsorship in the Arts, Sport, Education, the Health Service and Broadcasting*, he wrote, 'The excellent Theatre Royal at Stratford

East was refused sponsorship by a bank on the grounds that it had put on a play satirising Mrs Thatcher and her government.'

The new Labour England has already started to develop, often as a response to austerity. All over the city of Leeds, you will find strategically placed book cabinets in the streets, each cabinet capable of holding maybe a dozen books. This is the Leeds Little Library. You come along and deposit books, or you take books away to read them. The city's library service was once a key element of Labour England. It's now being slashed to pieces – but when Labour England is rebuilt, Leeds will have a tradition upon which to build a new one.

All over the country you will find the University of the Third Age (U3A) – there are more than 1,000 U3As in Britain now – providing education for its own sake, to retired people, at minimal cost, in subjects which have nothing at all to do with the world of work. The U3A has grown every year since it was founded in 1983. Legally, it is a charity – this is just one example of the wretchedly confused state of British charity law. Though resolutely non-political, we see it as one of the building blocks of the future Labour England, which is ironic because new Labour England will be built upon the young, and the anger of the young, who rightly feel they have been betrayed by the old. Ben Judah described this sentiment in the *Financial Times*:

> This is my generation. The furious tweeters. The self-taught YouTube Marxists. The failed hipsters and freelancers. The last protesters trying to stop the cuts who stayed up all night cursing corporate tax avoidance and the Cayman Islands ... 'The trouble with our generation', my then housemate James Schneider emailed me in October 2015 when he co-founded Momentum, 'is we don't have any power.' Now, though, that power is building, and its spearhead is social media.

How committed are all of these new members to Labour itself? The answer, we suspect, is that it is Labour's ideas and principles that engage them, less the structures or the party. Labour's grassroots are fully revived; they are active, engaged and full of fizzing ideas, but new members are not necessarily turning up to branch committee meetings or writing the minutes. This is just the way it is. Labour will have to adapt.

The new members are, however, committed to Jeremy Corbyn. Can he bear the weight of that responsibility? Being a party leader in the British system is lonely and a little frightening, and it is not surprising that inexperienced Labour leaders have hastened to surround themselves with people who make them feel secure.

Neil Kinnock, we believe, would have become Prime Minister in 1992 if he had had a better office – or the confidence to ignore the office that he had. But, as we have seen, he was surrounded by people who thought they were cleverer than him. In a small, secret place in his heart, Kinnock may have shared their incorrect estimate of their, and his, abilities.

Corbyn's office, peopled like Kinnock's, with folk who think they are much cleverer than their boss, is more dysfunctional than Kinnock's, and does Corbyn considerable harm.

It also distances him from the young, who are his natural friends and supporters. This leader, loved (with good reason) by the angry and idealistic young, has hugged close to him the old, crabbed, bitter, sectarian left, in the human form of some of his closest advisers.

Saddled with a large number of Labour MPs who give the impression that they would far rather see May's government totter on for ever than have a Labour government led by Corbyn, his position is difficult. Labour's rebirth could yet falter, especially if the attrition of its enemies, inside and out, forces its leaders to firefight constantly as every passing squall is blown out of all proportion and fastened onto by rent-a-quote MPs.

It is not hopeless; we could yet see a Corbyn-led Labour government, and Corbyn in 10 Downing Street would at least show that there is an alternative. It would shout 'yes we can' across the land.

An election, under the Fixed-terms Parliaments Act, is in theory some time away, in 2022. But, as the snap election of 2017 proved, elections can happen much sooner if MPs of all parties feel that the time is right.

Jeremy Corbyn may lead Labour into the next election. Shadow Foreign Secretary Emily Thornberry told us she thinks he will, and that the election will happen before 2022. She believes that a government as obviously incompetent and catastrophically split as Theresa May's cannot last the course. Something has to give, though Thornberry is at a loss to say precisely what.

There would be no shortage of credible candidates to succeed Corbyn. From his closest political stable, John McDonnell has surprised even some of his sternest critics by proving to be a weighty shadow Chancellor. He suffered a heart attack a few years ago, and he told the Fire Brigades Union's 2018 conference, 'I thought, well, I'd retire and I'd watch from the back and say, they should have listened to me. And now suddenly I've got the chance to do something about it.'

Emily Thornberry has been impressive. Outshining the now ex-Foreign Secretary Boris Johnson, a buffoon and embarrassment who only kept his job (until he finally quit over Brexit) because the Prime Minister was too afraid of hard-line Brexiteers to fire him, was a low bar to jump. But Thornberry jumped it so easily that one feels the bar could be raised a bit.

Shadow Education Secretary Angela Rayner is tipped for high office by the political cognoscenti. Brought up on a council estate, she left her local comprehensive at sixteen, pregnant and without qualifications. Getting her into 10 Downing Street would give Labour England a lot of satisfaction.

Shadow Business Secretary Rebecca Long-Bailey is spoken of with enthusiasm. So is the fiercely clever former Director of Public Prosecutions and current shadow Brexit Secretary, Keir Starmer, whose handling of the conflicting currents of opinion has earned him praise.

Whoever it is, what will he or she need to do in government to help Labour England recreate itself?

Government provides the context. Government can provide a few necessary things. A strong, confident public sector – we used to have one of those, but it was vandalised in the Thatcher and Blair years. Some local autonomy, so that communities can to some extent decide their own priorities and their own destinies – we used to have that, too, but it was punished for not doing things the way government ministers thought they ought to be done, and it isn't there anymore.

If Labour is elected, there will be huge expectations that could be difficult to meet, not least when it comes to the fractured public services and the partly outsourced National Health Service. But Labour England's strange rebirth came about because enough people came to believe that Labour was at long last serious about the redistribution of power and wealth.

It is also serious about the generation of new wealth – and this is not going to come from a country that has turned its back on productive manufacturing industries, that uses clapped-out machinery or pays its workers peanuts.

Labour, when last in power, talked about a high-wage, high-skills economy. But it did little to tackle the rentier economy, and nor was there much evidence of the high wages even if there were substantial technical advances. Instead, governments fell back on the financial services sector, seeing it as the panacea. A future Labour government would likely model its interventionism on the sensible German economic model that Britain had a key role in creating at the end of the Second World War but then forgot about. It could, as the French government did after the upheavals of 1968, substantially increase wages, and in turn demand.

There would be an effective national investment bank, regional investment banks and an industrial policy worth its name. There would also be a serious bid to harness artificial intelligence for the benefit of all, and a serious bid to resurrect the sort of inter-European trade deals that industry wants.

John McDonnell recently told the BBC's Iain Watson – a journalist who does understand how the Labour Party works – that even if he and Jeremy Corbyn were to depart the scene, Labour would remain an anti-austerity party – and 'there will be no triangulation', where the main parties compete on similar territory. 'That has gone now,' McDonnell said.

Jon Lansman, also speaking to Iain Watson, said that there would be no going back to the politics of the Blair–Brown era. 'The party has fundamentally changed,' Lansman said. 'We're not going to go back to neoliberalism; we're not going back to privatising the health service. That's decided for ever. Well, for a generation or two.'

He subsequently mused that an incoming Labour government could face a 'run on the pound'. This somewhat alarmist talk is what many in the media are confidently predicting and hoping will happen. But if business and financial leaders had any real knowledge of economics and really mean what they say about desiring 'stability' above all else, they would know that an incoming Labour government promising to boost economic growth, spending and public services is precisely the sort of government not to run away from.

Today we have a Labour leader, elected by a landslide and then re-elected because, like Bernie Sanders in America, his political platform represented a break with austerity. He has a majority on the party's ruling National Executive Committee and a shadow Cabinet made up largely of those willing to support him.

Corbyn's agenda, described by pollster and journalist Peter Kellner prior to the general election as 'hard left', is, of course, nothing of the sort. It more resembles a mild form of social democracy – which has had its echoes in the sort of *Guardian* editorials we have been reading for almost as long as we can remember. The fact that it can be described as hard left shows how far to the right Britain has allowed itself to be marched.

But it would be social democracy fashioned for its time. Britain is a very different place from what it was when Tony Blair and New Labour won in 1997. Measures such as more public ownership, a state investment bank and more co-operatives are things any European would recognise as fairly straightforward social democratic policies. Quite why they seem to frighten the centrist carthorse is anyone's guess. But the centrists don't appear to have anything else to offer.

This would be a government that took its international treaty obligations seriously. It would be a fully paid-up and supportive member of the United Nations, pushing for the urgent reform that the organisation needs, while at the same time committing some serious manpower to UN peacekeeping and other operations where the skill of the British military – about the only substantial national capacity kept 'in house' – can be put to good use.

This government would be doubly attractive to many people because it would likely re-evaluate Britain's hugely costly and frankly unnecessary commitment to having nuclear weapons, which are claimed to be independent, even while most people are well aware that they are nothing of the sort. Nor do they provide any realistic defence unless mutually assured destruction is a desirable outcome from a nuclear war.

On climate change to plastic pollution, to recognition and support for an independent Palestine as part of a two-state solution, the policy changes will be obvious and some of them immediate.

The early years of the Thatcher government were taken up by slow, almost incremental change. That process stepped up apace as confidence grew and as the trade unions and the big Labour-controlled metropolitan authorities were challenged and rolled back. It is possible that a similar pattern might develop with a Labour government that challenged the big banks and unaccountable corporations, a government that had a very clear idea about what it was there to do, but which understood that really big change can take time.

This will be largely a new generation in power. Many people now in their thirties or early forties are unfamiliar with the postwar Labour governments of Attlee, Wilson, or Callaghan. They will be more reflective of modern Britain; there will be many more women and ethnic minorities, and, hopefully, they will be more diverse, worldly wise and, above all, tolerant.

Can Corbyn, or a successor, win the next general election whenever it comes? With likely parliamentary boundary reorganisations that will hit Labour and the still low base for the party in Scotland, it would be extremely hard for any Labour leader to win, but it has to be worth a try – whoever it is.

Just getting rid of the present crassly incompetent and self-absorbed Conservative government would be some kind of victory. And if it meant, say, a coalition or a parliamentary deal with the Scottish National Party, would that really be so much of a disaster as senior Labour folk, from all factions, seem to think? Of course it seems so to Labour's older sectarian warriors, but Labour's new supporters care nothing for their long-festering resentments.

Whoever leads the campaign will have to broaden Labour's appeal, not by the triangulations of yesteryear, but by acknowledging that political gravity is shifting away from what has gone on for the past forty years. If Labour's strange rebirth is going to produce long-lived progeny, it had better start listening a lot more closely to many of the party's traditional supporters in the sort of blue-collar areas that produced UKIP in England and Donald Trump in the United States.

Corbyn may lead the party to victory and become Prime Minister, which before the 2017 election looked impossible. But whether he or someone else leads Labour into the next election, he has dramatically changed the left, and the genie cannot be put back in the bottle.

The Blairite hegemony is over. Labour England, as Neil Kinnock insists he didn't say, has got its party back. Labour believes in something again, and the once high-flying heirs to Blair – the likes of Chuka Umunna and Angela Eagle – will not return, whatever happens to Corbyn.

And if, by some means, Labour's old right were to arrest and reverse what has happened under Corbyn – if they were not to claim just Corbyn's head, but also destroy the better future he seems to represent – we do not like to contemplate what would happen. Where would the anger and the desperation for a better world go to, if Britain no longer had a party of the left that was willing to fight for it? Where did it go in the US?

Labour will never again be led by someone who, faced with the choice between supporting the poor and supporting the rich, will instinctively choose the rich. If Corbyn were to go tomorrow, we can be sure that the next leader will believe in something, and that something will have to do with righting the balance between the rich and the poor, between the powerful and the powerless. That is Corbyn's legacy, his achievement. If he does nothing else, that's a pretty good epitaph for a Labour leader.

INDEX

INDEX